DISENCHANTED WANDERER

A VOLUME IN THE NIU SERIES IN

Slavic, East European, and Eurasian Studies
Edited by Christine D. Worobec

For a list of books in the series, visit our website at cornellpress.cornell.edu.

DISENCHANTED WANDERER

THE APOCALYPTIC VISION
OF KONSTANTIN LEONTIEV

GLENN CRONIN

NORTHERN ILLINOIS UNIVERSITY PRESS
AN IMPRINT OF CORNELL UNIVERSITY PRESS
Ithaca and London

First published 2021 by Cornell University Press

Library of Congress Cataloging-in-Publication Data

Names: Cronin, Glenn, 1950– author.
Title: Disenchanted wanderer : the apocalyptic vision of Konstantin Leontiev / Glenn Cronin.
Description: Ithaca [New York] : Northern Illinois University Press, an imprint of Cornell University Press, 2021. | Series: NIU series in Slavic, East European, and Eurasian studies | Includes bibliographical references and index.
Identifiers: LCCN 2020056453 (print) | LCCN 2020056454 (ebook) | ISBN 9781501760181 (hardcover) | ISBN 9781501760198 (ebook) | ISBN 9781501760204 (pdf)
Subjects: LCSH: Leontév, Konstantin, 1831–1891. | Leontév, Konstantin, 1831–1891—Criticism and interpretation. | Leontév, Konstantin, 1831–1891—Political and social views.
Classification: LCC B4249.L44 C76 2021 (print) | LCC B4249.L44 (ebook) | DDC 197 [B]—dc23
LC record available at https://lccn.loc.gov/2020056453
LC ebook record available at https://lccn.loc.gov/2020056454

For Peggy Darran (1937–2019)
An installment on a debt that cannot be computed, much less repaid.

To the memory of a man who tried his hand at everything and brought no benefit to anyone, aside from three or four people.
　—Konstantin Leontiev on himself in a letter to
　　Anatoly Aleksandrov from the monastery of
　　Optina Pustyn, 19 November 1889

Contents

ACKNOWLEDGMENTS

My special thanks go to Bob Owens, professor emeritus of English Literature at the Open University, and to his wife Patti, who badgered me mercilessly to commence this work and saw me through to completion. To my friends Alison and Rob Chaplin, Lesley and Tony O'Shaughnessy, and Denise Merry, who stood by me in my darkest moments and whose love and support never wavered (however sorely they were tried). And to Donald Rayfield, professor emeritus of Russian at Queen Mary University of London, without whose guidance Konstantin Leontiev would have remained to me, as to many another, "a riddle, wrapped in a mystery, inside an enigma."

My grateful thanks also go to Amy Farranto, Senior Acquisitions Editor at the Northern Illinois University Press, and to Kate Gibson, Production Editor at Westchester Publishing Services, for their invaluable help and advice in the preparation of this volume.

ENGLISH NAMES OF NEWSPAPERS AND JOURNALS

Bogoslovskii Vestnik	The Theological Herald
Den'	The Day
Golos	The Voice
Grazhdanin	The Citizen
Otechestvennye Zapiski	Notes of the Fatherland
Russkaia Mysl'	Russian Thought
Russkoe Obozrenie	The Russian Review
Russkii Invalid	The Russian Veteran
Russkii Vestnik	The Russian Herald
Sankt-Peterburgskie Vedomosti	The St Petersburg News
Sovremennik	The Contemporary
Svet	Light
Varshavskii Dnevnik	The Warsaw Diary
Vostok	The East
Vremia	Time
Zaria	The Dawn

Note on Translation, Transliteration, and Dates

Where primary source citations in the text are from the Russian or German languages, the translations and transliterations are my own. The Library of Congress transliteration system is generally used, I have however kept some authors' names in the form more familiar to the English-speaking reader: for example, Leontiev, rather than Leont'ev. The use of italics for emphasis, to which Leontiev was much addicted, is in every case his own unless otherwise indicated. Dates are Old Style unless otherwise indicated.

DISENCHANTED WANDERER

Introduction

In July 1871 the forty-year old Russian consul in Salonika lay in bed dying, as he thought, of cholera. Now sweating, now shivering, alone and terrified, Konstantin Nikolayevich Leontiev—scion of minor gentry from the Kaluga Province of Russia, social commentator, literary critic and aspiring novelist, formerly a doctor in the Army of the Crimea, now attached to the Russian diplomatic mission in Constantinople—took stock of the course of his life with the urgency of a man facing the prospect of imminent annihilation.

"I looked on the icon of the Virgin," he wrote to his friend and disciple Vasily Rozanov shortly before his death in November 1891:

> And although I am not usually a cowardly person, I was seized by such horror at the thought of my *physical demise* that I suddenly found myself, in an instant, believing in the reality and power of that very Mother of God. I believed in her as strongly and intensely as if there was before me an *actual living woman*, a woman well known to me, kindly and all-powerful, and I cried out to her: "Mother of God, *I'm not ready*, I'm not ready to die yet, I've still done nothing worthy of my capabilities and I have led in the highest degree a life of dissolution and refined sinfulness. Raise me from this bed of death!"[1]

Leontiev vowed to the Virgin that if he recovered he would go to the nearby holy mountain of Athos to repent his past life and, if necessary, to receive ordination as a monk. The illness was not cholera however but a severe bout of malaria, the onset of the chronic malady that was to beset him on and off for the rest of his life. When the attack subsided his sense of relief was palpable: "In two hours I was on my feet. The attack passed even before the doctor arrived. Three days later I was on Athos."[2]

Leontiev's appeal to the Virgin seemed to have been answered, and the consequences were momentous. He remained on Athos until the middle of August when he returned to Salonika ostensibly to look for a document of importance to the monastery. Instead, he gathered all his manuscripts for a monumental series of novels from Russian life, with the collective title *The River of Time*, and threw them into a blazing fireplace, thus severing, as he thought, all connection with his past life.[3] Following this brief return to Salonika, where the inhabitants concluded he had gone mad, Leontiev abandoned his duties, took extended sick leave, and went back to the Holy Mountain in September, staying there until August 1872.

This crisis of 1871 is usually regarded as the great watershed in Leontiev's life, the moment at which the pagan aesthete and anti-moralist of his youth and early manhood disappeared to be replaced by the gloomy pessimist and God-seeker of his maturity and premature old age. But Leontiev's conversion was by no means the clear cut Damascene experience that his letter to Rozanov might suggest. On the contrary, Leontiev's entire life was spent in a continuous, and only partially successful, struggle to achieve a resolution of the competing impulses within his soul, a struggle which repeatedly gave rise to conflicts of one kind or another, conflict within himself but equally conflict with his contemporaries.

A particularly striking example occurred in January 1880, two weeks before Leontiev's fiftieth birthday, when he wrote the following words for the Russian language newspaper *Varshavskii Dnevnik* (*Warsaw Diary*), of which he was then deputy editor: "For one who does not regard felicity and universal justice as mankind's destiny there is nothing objectionable in the thought that millions of Russians were compelled to endure whole centuries under the yoke of the three estates, the bureaucracy, the landowners and the Church, just so that Pushkin could write Onegin and Godunov, the Kremlin and its cathedrals be built, Suvorov and Kutuzov attain their patriotic victories."[4]

It is difficult to overstate how out of season these sentiments were in the Russia of the time. In June of the same year Fyodor Dostoevsky would deliver to general acclaim his famous speech at the Pushkin festival, which among other things urged his hearers to "imagine that you yourself are building a palace of human destiny with the final goal of making all men happy and giving them peace and rest at last. And imagine too that for that purpose it is necessary and inevitable to torture to death one single human being . . . Would you consent to be the architect on this condition? Can you for one moment believe that those for whom the building had been built would agree to receive happiness from you if its source was such suffering?"[5]

For Dostoevsky then the suffering of one man was too high a price to pay for the happiness of millions; for Leontiev, the suffering of millions was an acceptable foundation for the outward symbols of Russian cultural and patriotic achievements. Thus the greatest literary figure of his day delivered himself of a sentiment so diametrically opposed to that espoused by Leontiev just five months earlier that one wonders if it was not composed with him in mind. Yet the curious thing is that Leontiev knew perfectly well the kind of reception his views were likely to receive, for he acknowledged in an article in February of the same year that "the stomachs of the majority of people are not yet prepared for the nourishment of this kind."[6]

It is possible that this may have included the paper's financial backers, for despite the success of Leontiev's trenchant editorials and other articles in raising the paper's circulation from a hundred to over a thousand copies, it closed in July 1880, leaving him with an "irreparable wound" he said was "consuming him."[7] He had pinned great hopes on this editorship which, although it was only of a provincial newspaper, gave him for the first and ultimately only time the freedom to express his ideas in print. He attributed the paper's failure to lack of financial support from the very circles of Russian conservatism whose spokesman he believed himself to be, and he blamed this, as he styled it, typical "weakness and treachery" for the "month of moral and intellectual Nirvana" which he underwent as a result.[8]

Of course the proprietors of the *Warsaw Diary* may have simply intended to cut their losses and close the paper down for financial reasons. At the same time however, in a Russia that had for decades been suffering from what has been called a "chronic ethical itch,"[9] and where the supreme duty of the writer was seen to lie in "unmasking" the injustices and hypocrisies of contemporary society, it stretches credulity that the almost fifty-year-old Leontiev could have expected the sentiments expressed above to be received with anything other than outrage and condemnation. Yet he had no hesitation in expressing them in the most definitive terms, and this in circumstances where his well-being and that of his family was most intimately connected with the success or failure of the newspaper.

Was this merely recklessness on his part, or was he driven to seek and welcome opprobrium by the same kind of deep and overriding conviction that has led martyrs to the stake over the centuries? A study of Leontiev's life certainly inclines one to the latter view, for the episode of the *Warsaw Diary* was by no means the first time that he had put his fortunes to the hazard when he found himself swimming against a strongly flowing tide of opinion with which he was profoundly at odds.

The first occasion came in the field of literature. Leontiev had studied medicine at Moscow University and saw war service as a doctor in the army in the Crimea, after which he spent two years as family physician on the estate of Baroness Marya Fyodorovna Rozen in Nizhny Novgorod Province. These were life-changing experiences that sharpened his sense of the dichotomy between health and vigor and sickness and debility and contributed to the development of a world-view based predominantly on aesthetic criteria. Then in the winter of 1860 he precipitately abandoned medicine and moved to Petersburg to try to live by his pen as novelist and literary critic.

The timing of this move could hardly have been worse. While Leontiev was serving in the Crimea and studying natural sciences on the Rozen estate, the 1850s had seen the rise to a position of dominance in Russian letters of a highly moralizing attitude which became indissolubly linked to the names of its chief protagonists, Nikolai Chernyshevsky and Nikolai Dobrolyubov, as well as to the vehicle for their ideas, the journal *Sovremennik*. This outlook subordinated all other considerations to the overriding imperative that the artist must further the social good as this was conceived by its leading ideologues, and it was an orientation to which Leontiev's aestheticism could not accommodate itself. His war experiences, exacerbated by a certain personal fragility of health, had generated an intense and lifelong dislike for what he regarded as the pathological aspect of Russian literature, a tendency he described as the "Gogolian caricature," and in his novels of the period and his literary criticism he clashed head-on with *Sovremennik* in a doomed attempt to reassert the primacy of the aesthetic in artistic production. His efforts were met by incomprehension and silence in the Saint Petersburg literary world of the 1860s and, faced with penury, he joined the Russian Foreign Service and subsequently served for ten years in the Russian diplomatic corps in various parts of European Turkey.

This period sowed the seeds of the second major conflict in Leontiev's life, which hinged on one of the greatest controversies to engage the Russian intelligentsia in the nineteenth century. In the preceding age the reforms of Peter the Great, continued under Catherine II, had aimed at shifting the center of gravity of Russia decisively toward Western Europe and away from the Muscovy of the Boyars and of the Byzantine inheritance. The limited success that this change in emphasis had enjoyed was brought into sharp focus in the 1820s by the Philosophical Letters of Peter Chaadayev (1794–1856), who extolled what he regarded as the progressive spirit and scientific leadership of

Europe and berated the continuing backwardness of Russia in comparison with the West. Chaadayev's thesis found an echo among many in the Russian intelligentsia, among others the influential literary critic Vissarion Belinsky and, most notably of all, the voice of the Russian conscience in exile Alexander Herzen.

This "westernizing" camp brought forth a reaction among those who feared that it might entail the loss of the traditional Russian values of autocracy, Orthodoxy, and the peasant commune. Among them were the moderate "Pochvenniki," prominent among them Dostoevsky and the poet Apollon Grigoriev, who wished to see a synthesis of the native Russian virtues with best that progressive Europe had to offer. But there were also more radical devotees of Slav separateness such as Alexei Khomyakov (1804–60) and Ivan Kireyevsky (1806–56), who advocated a complete rejection of Western values with the aim of developing a truly Russian culture to set against the encroachment of European utilitarian ideology. Thus was ignited the polarization between Westernizers and Slavophiles which was a defining feature of nineteenth-century Russian thought and in many ways has continued until the present day.

Under Grigoriev's influence Leontiev had a brief period of attachment to the Pochvenniki, but he soon eschewed all sympathy with contemporary Europe and came to regard himself as the standard-bearer of the Slavophilism of Khomyakov, Kireyevsky and above all Nikolai Danilevsky (1822–85), the man whose theory of the rise and fall of historical cultural types was said to have brought science to Slavophilism. Unfortunately, Leontiev's experiences in the Ottoman domains had imbued him with a suspicion of the western liberal inclinations of the Southern Slav intelligentsia which led him to reject the core element of Slavophile philosophy, the primacy of the Slav racial type, and to propose instead the development of an anti-Western culture based on an ideal community of faith, which he styled "Byzantinism," open to all those prepared to embrace Orthodoxy, including non-Slavs and even peoples from deepest Asia. This led to the second debacle in Leontiev's life, when in 1874 he was anathematized by the leading Pan-Slavist Ivan Aksakov and effectively ejected from the ranks of the Slavophiles.

The third great conflict in Leontiev's life was religious. At university and in the Ottoman domains Leontiev sought to put his aesthetic ideals into practice in his mode of living, something that itself brought him into conflict with many of his contemporaries since he had strongly sensuous and bisexual tastes which he appears to have made little attempt to curb or even disguise. The attempt to live by the standard of aesthetics also created serious internal conflicts in his psyche, which came to a head in July 1871 in his existential crisis in Salonika.

After Salonika Leontiev's thought became profoundly religious in character, based on a rigorous adherence to a severe and uncompromising Orthodox asceticism, which he viewed as the only antidote to man's fallen nature and accordingly as the only sure route to the salvation of his immortal soul. It was a pessimistic concept of religion founded on existential dread as the natural response of the human creature faced with the incommensurable power of the divinity, the power of life and death as experienced by Leontiev on his sickbed in Salonika. As such it eventually came into bitter conflict with the foremost, and generally more optimistic, religious thinkers of the Russia of his day, including Dostoevsky, Leo Tolstoy, and the philosopher and theologian Vladimir Solovyev. At the same time however it also gave rise to some of the most striking and thought-provoking ideas of Leontiev's later period.

Leontiev's life spanned the so-called golden age of Russian literature which, if we accept that it was ushered in by the publication of Gogol's *Evenings on a Farm near Dikanka* and Pushkin's *Tales of Belkin*, commenced in the very year that he was born, 1831. Yet he plotted a lonely course and found few disciples in his day, at least few prepared openly to acknowledge their indebtedness. A bare quarter of a century after his death came the catastrophe of war and revolution and with his contemporaries, supporters and adversaries alike, scattered to the four winds, or dead, what stuttering interest there remained in Leontiev's life and works existed in the minds of specialist researchers within and, more visibly, outside of Russia. To the general public, whether in Russia or abroad, he had either ceased to exist or was regarded as a curiosity from a vanished era.

This is certainly no longer the case in Leontiev's homeland, where attitudes toward him have changed dramatically in the decades since perestroika. A trickle of renewed interest in him emerged in Russia in the early 1980s; with the advent of glasnost this trickle became a flood, and since the fall of the Soviet Union in 1991 a considerable scholarship about him has appeared in Russian, including a new twelve-volume edition of his collected works which includes previously unpublished works and much archive material.[10] Indeed, Leontiev has been described by a contemporary Russian academic as "the most popular representative today of Russian socio-political thought in the nineteenth century."[11]

So why should someone who exercised so little influence over the great men of his own day have come alive a century later to influence the course of contemporary Russian politics? No doubt this renaissance is partly to do with the glamour associated with gaining free access to a controversial author simplistically anathematized by the old regime as a czarist reactionary. But there is more to it than that. No less a figure than Vladimir Putin has championed

Leontiev as a prophet of the true Russian culture. In his *Inside the Mind of Vladimir Putin*, Michel Eltchaninoff quotes from a 2013 speech by the Russian president: "Russia—as the philosopher Konstantin Leontiev vividly put it—has always evolved in 'blossoming complexity' as a state civilization, reinforced by the Russian people, Russian language, Russian culture, the Russian Orthodox Church and the country's other traditional religions."[12]

Eltchaninoff also quotes the conservative Russian political scientist Boris Mezhuev on what the latter calls the "fathers of Putinian conservatism." "We can count Leontiev alongside Nikolai Danilevsky and Konstantin Pobedonostsev as the 'triad' of the most outstanding representatives of conservative thought in nineteenth-century Russia," declares Mezhuev. "From the new start of the 1980s and 1990s began Leontiev's true 'renaissance' . . . Interest in his work has not diminished since . . . The relevance of his ideas to current events simply must be stated."[13]

As post-communist Russia seeks to find its place in a rapidly changing world, and as the now centuries-old dichotomy between Westernizers and Slavophiles makes itself felt once more in new forms, it is not surprising that a figure like Leontiev, who had so much to say, and that so trenchantly, on the possible courses of his country's future development, should find himself very much back in vogue. Eltchaninoff himself finds Leontiev's Byzantinism, based as it is on the twin pillars of autocracy and Orthodox Christianity, at the very heart of the resurgence of messianic Russian nationalism under Putin.[14]

One does not need to be a Kremlin watcher or Putinologist, however, to appreciate the instinctive attraction that the author of *The East, Russia and Slavdom* must exert on any Russian concerned with the present course and future destiny of his native land. At a simplistic level, the Russian nationalist, dismayed by the reaction of the West to Russian interventions in the Crimea, Ukraine, and Syria, will find a ready ally in Leontiev the critic of European cosmopolitan liberalism. Typical of this mindset is the view that: "Reading, studying and digesting Konstantin Nikolaevich Leontiev will make the Russian understand that he is the representative of a great people and, waking from the narcotic of half-baked democratization surrounding him on all sides, he will comprehend the full emptiness of contemporary bourgeois 'civilization' and be strengthened in his awareness that Russians are a great people, great in culture, great in statecraft, great in history."[15]

This assessment is more than a little ironic, given that Leontiev was a lifelong adversary of racial nationalism, describing it as "one of the strangest self-delusions of the nineteenth century."[16] But anxiety about the direction of travel of their societies under the impact of globalization is by no means confined to ultra-nationalists in Russia or elsewhere. It has been observed that

Leontiev's vividly titled essay "The Average European as the Ideal and Weapon of Universal Destruction" was ahead of its time and that only now, under the impact of worldwide neo-liberalism, are we seeing the emergence of the truly "average individual" of Leontiev's nightmare on a global scale.[17] Against this background Leontiev's contention that Russia has its roots in the spirit of Byzantium and can only achieve her cultural flowering if she remains true to the Byzantine legacy must appeal strongly to any Russian concerned that the tendency of the modern world in the post–communist era is to sever his homeland from her natural and historical roots.

Then there is Leontiev's "Turanianism," his view that Russia has benefited culturally from its contacts with the peoples of Asia and that the Asiatic component of the Russian psyche can act as a prophylactic against contamination by Western liberalism; this also has resonance among Russian cultural nationalists. On this aspect of Leontiev's thought, the historian Aleksandr Repnikov quotes the philosopher V. V. Zenkovsky: "Leontiev's conceptions about the special path of Russia come alive and find development above all in Eurasianism. It is not Danilevsky, with his belief in the racial Slav type, who comes closest to Eurasianism, but precisely Leontiev, with his skeptical stance toward Slavism."[18]

This view was confirmed by Lev Gumilev, historian and ethnologist and leading exponent of neo-Eurasianism. Asked in 1990 which philosopher he felt himself closest to, Gumilev replied: "Konstantin Leontiev. I am attracted by the truth of his utterances on the subject of historical processes . . . Leontiev was the first to work out the natural lifespan of a people's development, although naturally he didn't have a full understanding of the matter. I tested his theory and it turned out to be correct. Leontiev left out of account only the incubation period and the memorial phase. This is easily explained: he was a political scientist and I am an ethnologist."[19]

If however Leontiev's intellectual rehabilitation in Russia seems now to be an established fact, there has yet been no comparable revival of interest in him in the West. Indeed one of the few recent English-language studies, by Ethan Alexander-Davey in the 2018 compilation *Aristocratic Souls in Democratic Times*, concluded by asserting that "it is difficult to see, at first glance, how the aristocratic political thought of Konstantin Leontiev could have any application in the modern era . . . Most of Leontiev's prescriptions would not be appealing to a mass, bourgeois public, much less to any central government in the West."[20]

Beside Alexander-Davey's essay, the small number of studies of Leontiev that have appeared in English since perestroika include Mondry and Thompson's *Examination of His Major Fiction* in 1993, brief appraisals in Richard Pipes'

Russian Conservatism and Its Critics of 2005 and Paul Robinson's *Russian Conservatism* of 2019, the introduction by K. Benois to his 2020 translation of Leontiev's *Byzantinism and Slavdom*, and a handful of specialist articles in the journals *Studies in East European Thought* and *Russian Studies in Philosophy*.[21]

Does this relative paucity of literature on Leontiev in English mean that Alexander-Davey is right in his estimation that Leontiev remains an interesting historical curiosity but that his political thought has little to say to us in the West? If one takes a narrowly utilitarian view of Leontiev's ideas as a blueprint for the Western polity in the twenty-first century, then perhaps. But there is much more to the man than this. If Russia is no longer quite the "riddle wrapped in a mystery inside an enigma" of Winston Churchill's vision, Russia under Putin still gives the West much to puzzle over, and Leontiev's social, political, and religious insights furnish us with as good a compass as any, and better than most, for navigating the subtleties of the Russian psyche, the shoals and quicksands of what is to many still what it was when Gogol wrote of the Russian Troika, an elemental force leading to an unknown destination.

Neither does the value to a Westerner of an acquaintance with Leontiev stop at Russia's borders. As we have observed, Leontiev had definite views on the effects, in his eyes mostly deleterious, of a process which, although in his day it was not called such, was the forerunner of what we now know as globalization.[22] And in his polemical interactions with the Russian moralists, from Chernyshevsky in the 1860s to Tolstoy in the 1880s, and in his stalwart defense of aesthetics as the primary driver of human creativity, Leontiev has much to say about the obsession with ethics as the solution to all social and political questions which was so prevalent among the Russian intelligentsia of his day and which has become such a cardinal feature of our own times.

It is not surprising then that Leontiev has been called the "Russian Nietzsche." His writings on the importance of beauty as a counterweight to utilitarian ethics in human affairs and on the nature of good and evil and the relationship of man to God address timeless questions about human existence and prefigure not only the anti-moral pathos of the German philosopher himself (whose own writings they predated by some twenty years) but also Dostoevsky's attempts to comprehend the problem of evil, and Søren Kierkegaard and the philosophy of existentialism which played such a significant role in the development of the twentieth-century thought.

In a personal sense Leontiev's lifelong efforts to get his message across to a wider public availed him little. He died largely unrecognized at the age of sixty following many years of chronic illness, and after his death, with the

FIGURE 1.   Konstantin Leontiev aged thirty-two in 1863, the year he joined the Russian diplomatic service.

exception of a small band of loyal disciples, he was over the course of a century reviled, ridiculed, and largely forgotten. With the radical change of atmosphere in Russia following the fall of communism, and in light of global developments in the twenty-first century, it seems that a thorough re-evaluation for the English speaking reader of his place in the Russian pantheon is long overdue.

CHAPTER 1

The Divided Self

The seeds of future conflict were already present when Leontiev entered Moscow University in the winter of 1849 to study medicine. At this time he claims to have "paid his dues to European liberalism," reading in his spare time the works of Belinsky, Herzen, and George Sand.[1] "With a sharp and frightful stab of youthful disillusion," he reminisced, "I came close to tears over Nekrasov's "Troika" and the verses of Ogarev."[2] He soon came under the influence of Ivan Turgenev, whose 1850 novella *Diary of a Superfluous Man* seemed to speak directly to his heart, as it did to many another young Russian. "I had no time for happy and cheerful things," he recalled. "Only Byronesque pieces spoke to me, touched my very soul. When Turgenev wrote of the *Superfluous Man* it seemed to me that he had found *me* out, even though he'd never set eyes on me."[3]

The refined and urbane Turgenev exercised something of a fascination over the young Leontiev. "I wanted a mentor," he wrote in his memoir *My Literary Destiny*, "*a gentleman*, one of the nobility, with a soul just as suffering as my own, but with gravitas, and not knowing Turgenev personally I dreamed about him." When he met Turgenev in the flesh, he was not disappointed: "I liked him enormously, everything in him and about him seemed writ large. I never envied him, but I always admired him."[4] The admiration was not to last. Although Turgenev exercised considerable influence over Leontiev's early development as a writer (he styled himself the younger man's "literary midwife"),[5]

Leontiev appears to have arrived at the conclusion that Turgenev's influence had done him more harm than good, and their relations were certainly much cooler after he left the university. By the end of the 1860s he was ready to openly deprecate Turgenev's talents. "Turgenev lost his way *spiritually* after *Fathers and Sons*," he declared. "The novel *Smoke* showed that spiritually he was as *ashes*."[6] The view stayed with him: fourteen years later he told the critic V. G. Avseyenko that in his view Turgenev's literary reputation was "undeserved."[7]

Leontiev did not especially enjoy his time at university. For one thing he had coughed blood shortly after coming to Moscow and feared he was developing consumption, the first recorded instance of the chronic health problems that were to plague him throughout his life. Added to this was uncertainty over his sexual orientation, which made him covert enemies. During his time in Moscow he carried on a relationship with one Zinaida Kononova (who subsequently married another), which he describes as "veering between friendship and the most burning and reciprocal passion, but undefined, hazy, unstable and bringing more pain than pleasure."[8] He later recalled that "my first two years as a student in Moscow were cruel. I was mercilessly afflicted by the incomprehension of others, by external circumstances, by the first unexpected onset of physical infirmity, and by the wild maelstrom of my thoughts which were then seriously *consolidating* for the first time. What a cruel, what a bitter process was this first mental upheaval!"[9]

This youthful *weltschmerz*, which he was later to describe as a "bloody conflict of ideals in one's own heart, between the ideal of duty and the ideal of poetry,"[10] found artistic expression in one of Leontiev's earliest works of fiction, the story "The Germans," written in 1851–52.[11] Reflecting the conflicted personality of its author, "The Germans" has dual protagonists. One is the honorable, yet pedantic and slightly absurd, schoolteacher, Fyodor Fyodorovich Angst, an "honest toiler" and seeker after truth in a provincial Russian grammar school. Angst falls in love with Dorotea, the daughter of a corrupt local official. On his deathbed her father extracts from Dorotea a promise that she will marry the unprepossessing Angst, for whom she feels nothing but disgust. They wed, but their unhappy marriage is interrupted by the arrival of a romantic Baltic German, one Lilienfeld, who soon manages not only to cuckold the hapless and aptly named Angst but to supplant him in his job. Angst returns from a fishing trip to find that his wife has flown with his rival, whereupon he collapses into madness and dies.

Beneath the Gogolian grotesquerie of "The Germans" one can see the moral dilemma that haunted the young Leontiev, the clash of duty and desire, as Dorotea's promise to her father leads one way, her inclinations another.

This pattern is also visible in Leontiev's other works of this earliest period, the play *A Love Match* and the story fragment "The Bulavin Sugar Factory," both written circa 1850–51; and the story "Summer on the Farm," written between 1852 and 1854 but published only in 1855. (The text of the first two of these works has been lost, but an outline of their plots can be reconstructed from Leontiev's memoirs and letters.) They are slight pieces, essentially juvenilia, but they show the direction in which Leontiev's thoughts were moving. Each of them is to a great extent autobiographical, the plot turns on the resolution of a central and rather knotty ethical problem, and there are two opposing protagonists, seemingly reflecting the duality and conflict in the author's mind, which he seeks to resolve in the denouement along with the pivotal issues of the narrative.

Turgenev was encouraging of these early efforts. Leontiev recalls him saying that *A Love Match* was "morbid but very good. Especially for someone of your age. You don't imitate others, your writing is your own."[12] And Leontiev's friend and disciple Iosif Fudel' recalled that Turgenev, as promised, sent *A Love Match* to Andrei Krayevsky, the editor of *Otechestvennye Zapiski* with a recommendation that he publish it.[13] On "The Bulavin Sugar Factory" Turgenev spoke even more warmly. "You have considerable talent," he told Leontiev, "Rudnev [the hero, a young doctor] is an original figure . . . an entirely new character. And your descriptions are very nicely drawn."[14]

Problems in the real world were not amenable to the clear-cut resolution of literature however, and the student Leontiev continued to suffer emotionally. Eventually though external circumstances intervened to provide him with an escape route. In 1853 war had broken out between Russia and an alliance headed by England and France in defense of the Ottoman Empire. And in August 1854, just as the Allies were about to land on the Crimean Peninsula, the youthful Leontiev cut the Gordian knot and escaped both his unsatisfying university existence and his problematic relationship with Kononova by enlisting, taking advantage of the war-regulation which allowed student doctors willing to serve in the army to dispense with their final year of study.

The decision was fully justified by the outcome. As Leontiev recalled in his memoirs: "I recovered my health in this period, my freshness, my vigor, I became happier, steadier, more relaxed, ready for anything, even my whole series of complete literary failures over the last seven years failed to shake my self-assurance, my almost mystical belief in *my particular and exceptional star*."[15] Tellingly, the moral qualms he admits to having felt about the possible damage his inexperience might do to his patients are suppressed through an aesthetic comparison: "To kill a man in a duel or battle, that's strength. Kill him in bed, that's ignorance, clumsiness, i.e. weakness. It's not only inhumane, it's

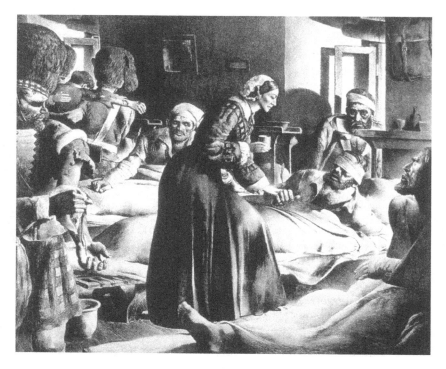

FIGURE 2. Florence Nightingale at Scutari during the Crimean War. Leontiev was serving at the same time and under similar conditions in the Russian field hospitals.

worse than that, it's dishonorable . . . Know how to succeed, gain your autonomy, and all will be forgiven. And if at first a few people suffer from my ignorance, well, it can't be helped, that's their destiny!"[16]

These fears were to prove groundless. In his first winter in the Crimea Leontiev carried out seven amputations, of which four survived, seemingly an acceptable rate of attrition for the time and conditions. The experience of war did not entirely live up to his expectations however. He suffered boredom verging on despair in the stifling atmosphere of the military hospitals of Yenikale, Simferopol, and Feodosia, where he spent much of his time, and he narrowly escaped a court-martial for leaving the latter without permission to visit his future bride, Liza Pavlovna Politova, a local girl of Greek extraction. But an interlude on the steppe with a regiment of Don Cossacks proved an exhilarating escape and appeared to give that sense of moral certainty for which he had been searching. He looked back on the experience in later years: "Killing and being killed is real," he wrote, "much more real than doctoring and healing. In battle there are no illusions. The more brave warriors we possess, the more we will slaughter and repel the foreign foe. But medicine? I did my duty in hospital as best I could but I *didn't really believe* in the positive effects of our treatments in those days."[17] Compared to dealing with endemic disease war seemed a marvelously uncomplicated business: "Bullets and grenades, they are *noble*. But frostbite, coughing, consumptive gasping, that's just a tedious repetition of the familiar *urban* prose."[18]

Leontiev's letters from the Crimea to his mother, the somewhat imperious, if impecunious, Feodosia Petrovna, speak eloquently of his youthful inner conflicts. These letters, a burning mixture of bitter reproaches, usually over money, passionate endearments, love and spite in quick succession, are in general much more suggestive of a lover writing to his mistress than a son to his mother. "How strong was my love," he recalled much later in his memoirs, "toward my mother, so graceful and refined, but not the least bit tender, on the contrary severe and wrathful."[19] In a letter of August 1856 he states without circumlocution: "You accepted long ago that your relations toward me are not the same as those toward your other children . . . I love you not only as a mother but as a woman."[20] And a letter of May 1857 gives us the key to the fundamental *casus belli* between the two: "Cut-price pleasures are not my thing," he says. "You are painstaking and penny-pinching, I am careless in my expenditure. You are puritanical in your outlook, my morality is more *à la Béranger*."[21]

It seems clear from these exchanges that Feodosia Petrovna had imbued her son, the youngest of seven siblings, with aristocratic tastes and propensities for which their small estate, Kudinovo in Kaluga Province some 150 miles southwest of Moscow, could never provide, thereby unconsciously preparing the ground for his varied, adventurous, and often uncomfortable afterlife. Leontiev was deeply attached to Kudinovo and believed he was the only one among his siblings fitted to appreciate it. "In my Kudinovo," he wrote, *"mine spiritually if not de jure,* should exist only those things *in which I find poetry."*[22] He persuaded his mother to leave the property to him jointly with his niece Marya Vladimirovna and did eventually inherit it in 1874. In 1882 though he was forced to sell again due to the financial difficulties that plagued him for most of his life.[23]

In addition it is probable that Leontiev was a love-child, with all the feelings of exclusiveness, on both sides, that such a relationship would imply; in his *Chronology of My Life* of 1883 he states explicitly that his father was his mother's friend Vasily Dmitrievich Durnovo and not Feodosia Petrovna's husband Nikolai Borisovich Leontiev, "whose name I bear."[24] For her part Feodosia Petrovna may well have observed early on signs of volatility and headstrongness in her son, which led to difficulties, especially when it became evident that his literary ambitions were serious. "I know," he wrote to her in

October 1855, "that I am speaking of something to which you are hostile. But I expect that you have reconciled yourself to it seeing how little it interferes with my medical work, and that you won't now be condemning my egoistical chatter even to yourself."[25]

Feodosia Petrovna may or may not have been reassured by comments of this kind. She was as keen as possible to see her son established in a conventional profession, preferably as a doctor in Moscow but also afterward when she urged him to stay in the army in the Crimea to obtain a higher position. On both occasions her son was deaf to her entreaties. "Rank?" he wrote to her, "with regard to medicine it's much like mustard to a beefsteak: if it's there, fine, but if not to the devil with it, you'll still be full up! God knows, I've better things in mind than becoming a collegiate assessor."[26] And in the winter of 1856 Leontiev left the army, ostensibly on six months leave, though he did not return, going instead to stay with a friend, Iosif Nikolaevich Shatilov, at Tamak, the latter's estate on the Crimean steppe. He was well aware that his decision to throw over his university studies and join the army in the Crimea had taken place "against the wishes of my mother and my whole family,"[27] and also that she now wanted him to stay on and gain rank. Yet he went his own way on each occasion, thereby incidentally adding to an impressive store of filial guilt, which almost certainly contributed to his spiritual crisis of 1871.

During his stay at Tamak Leontiev began to develop what would later become the cornerstone of his socio-political philosophy, the naturalistic principle of "unity in variety," though at this period he was more concerned with art than politics. "Staying with Shatilov I read Cuvier and Humboldt," he recalled, "and I believe I got the idea of introducing into art some *new forms* based on the *natural sciences* . . . Zoology, comparative anatomy, botany, when you get beneath the surface they are full of poetry: a multitude of forms subject to common laws."[28]

Also at Tamak Leontiev paid unsuccessful court to a local heiress, Masha Kushnikova, then returned briefly to Moscow where, somewhat surprisingly and doubtless to the dismay of his mother, he turned down a flattering offer from one of the university doctors to make a medical career under his patronage and instead accepted the post of family physician to Baroness Rozen on her estate in Nizhny Novgorod Province. He spent two years with the Rozens, from the spring of 1858, and the first literary fruit was the short story "Second Marriage," published in 1860, a well-observed account of the flowering of love between a young official of German extraction and a young widow. In essence the story is a study of mood and motivation as the hero finds his initial purely financial interest in the widow give way to genuine affection, while she, in turn, tries to take a rational view and avoid the mistakes of her first, unhappy marriage. In the end love just about triumphs for them both. The moral of the story is the capacity of love to transfigure ordinary lives and surmount even base motives, or as Leontiev puts it: "Love and happiness can make even humdrum people shine with beauty."[29]

Unfortunately there could hardly have been a worse moment for an aspiring author to publish a love story, as this was the heyday of the journal *Sovremennik* and the Russian ethical school of literature. One has only to recall its editor Chernyshevsky's strictures on the writing of romance to see the inevitability of the critical failure of "Second Marriage." "We pass over the fact that loving couples, suffering or triumphant, imbue thousands of works with stultifying monotony," Chernyshevsky declared, "we will not mention that romantic adventures and depictions of beauty marginalize real life . . . The habit of portraying love, love and nothing but love makes writers forget that life has other sides to it, aspects in general much more relevant to humanity."[30] This was a climate in which love stories by unknown writers were most unlikely to flourish, and "Second Marriage" sank without trace.

A similar fate awaited Leontiev's first novel, *Podlipki*, published in 1861. It depicts a series of incidents in the life of its well-intentioned youthful protagonist, Vladimir Ladnev, an introspective but basically optimistic young man clearly modeled on his author, in and around the country estate of the title, again modeled on Leontiev's Kudinovo. The story is elegiac in tone, seeming at times to hark back to Ivan Goncharov's *Oblomov*, published two years before, and at others to look ahead to themes of selfishness and despoliation in Chekhov. It is told in flashback and whenever the action returns to the present from the idealized past, a Chekhovian sense emerges that something indefinable but precious is being lost as the old patriarchal way of life is supplanted by a new individualism. Published in the year in which serfdom was effectively abolished by the reforms of what has come to be known as the Russian Emancipation, the novel was out of tune with its times, and despite some passages of descriptive power and flashes of genuine psychological insight, it was a critical failure.[31]

To be fair to the critics though, it would be hard to maintain that *Podlipki*, overlong and overstuffed with confusing secondary characters and situations, is a lost masterpiece. As a novelist Leontiev could never quite shake off a tendency to over-elaborate. As one contemporary critic observed: "From this habit flows that mass of introductory episodes, interesting in themselves but continually interrupting the wholeness of the action and the continuity of the plot."[32] As unsatisfactory as it may be as a whole, it is worth spending a few moments on the novel, as it contains, in embryo, one or two themes that have significance in Leontiev's later writing.

One is Leontiev's growing conviction that aesthetic distaste provides a firmer ground for moral action than ethical stricture, an outlook he often subsumes under the Latin tag *Quod licet Jovi non licet bovi* (what is permissible for Jupiter is not so for an ox). Ladnev has an impecunious cousin, Modest, who is unprepossessing both physically and mentally and deserts a serf-girl, Katya, shortly after the birth of their child. When Ladnev is himself attracted to another servant girl, Pasha, whom he attempts to seduce on a visit to an old barn after dark, the vision of Modest and Katya floats before his mind's eye, and he realizes with horror that his life after the seduction will be a doomed attempt to do the right thing by Pasha, an attempt that will end miserably in "awkwardness, misunderstanding, lying words as love cools." He blushes at the probable verdict of others: *"He thought he was in love, but he loved his fantasy, not her."*[33] Pasha's virtue is salvaged, and Ladnev's aesthetic revulsion is confirmed when five years later he meets Katya and Modest again. She is now consumptive, while Modest has married a wealthy woman and become the quintessence of bourgeois vulgarity. Ladnev recoils at this image of the man he might have become. "I am grateful to him for the example," he reflects, "sentimentality alone would not have saved Pasha."[34]

Much later, in his novel *The Egyptian Dove* of 1881, Leontiev expanded on the "aesthetic morality" that guided his youthful actions. "My ethical outlook at that time was informed neither by the teachings of Orthodoxy nor the commandments of God," he confessed, "but by the codex of my personal conceit, a system of arbitrary morality which could sometimes be magnanimous but was often in fact in the highest degree immoral. If I say that I not only thought, but often said aloud, that the best criterion for action was 'if the hat fits, wear it,' then I think I've said it all."[35]

Later in the novel Ladnev rediscovers an old schoolfriend, one Yuriev, who is working as a tutor in Moscow. Yuriev is an embittered individual with piercing intelligence and cutting humor who, in effect, reeducates the naively optimistic Ladnev by initiating him into the subtle duality that lies at the heart of all created things. The line between good and evil, which for Ladnev had been absolute, now begins to waver. "Up to now," Ladnev reflects, "science had only made the world friendlier for me . . . But when Yuriev was speaking science acquired such a corrosive and toxic quality that sometimes during our evening and after-dinner talks I found myself running hot and cold by turns . . . *Everything*, he insisted, *was relative*; envy, greed, vanity, he told me, were innate to all persons; in every one of us, he said, lurked everything that was in everybody else."[36]

Under Yuriev's tutelage Ladnev gradually comes to see the possibility of rebuilding his worldview on more durable foundations by curbing his natural optimism and accepting that the darker side is concomitant to all human activity, thereby affirming life in all its manifestations. He even begins to understand that the relationship between Modest and Katya, plagued as it is by dissension and recriminations, is not wholly negative: "And it suddenly seemed to me that I was the one at fault, that I was asking too much, that they were happy, and that their quarrels, like pepper and salt in cooking, only served to enhance the flavor."[37]

The implications of his hero's change of heart, the possibilities inherent in a dualist and relativist worldview, which were of great significance for Leontiev, are not explored further in *Podlipki*. A period of gestation was needed before they would find full expression in his major novel *A Place of One's Own* of 1864, in which his efforts to achieve a synthesis of the warring impulses of aesthetics and ethics in his soul were to produce some of his most striking, and controversial, ideas.

dualism

That lay some way into the future when in the spring of 1860 Leontiev left the Rozens and spent much of the year on the family estate at Kudinovo. Then, six months after the appearance of "Second Marriage," he made the radical decision to abandon his medical career and move to Saint Petersburg to try his luck as a professional man of letters. Given the lukewarm, or rather nonexistent, critical response to his earlier stories this was a courageous, one might even say reckless, move and it brought fateful consequences in its wake. For, as we have just seen, the atmosphere in literary Petersburg in the 1860s could hardly have been less propitious for the attempt.

Leontiev's departure for the capital was sandwiched between the appearance, in the journal *Otechestvennye Zapiski*, of two critical essays: "A Letter from a Provincial to Turgenev," which appeared in May 1860, and "Regarding the Stories of Marko Vovchok," in March 1861.[38] Possibly tiring of the lack of recognition his stories were receiving, Leontiev had followed advice given him by Turgenev to try his hand at literary criticism, for which the latter was "sure he had the gifts."[39] It must be doubtful whether Turgenev remotely envisaged what the result would be however, since Leontiev came to this new branch of letters "possessed of an urge to distinguish the moral side from the aesthetic."[40] In other words, he had decided to reverse the prevailing tendency of literary criticism in Russia, which under the leadership of Chernyshevsky and *Sovremennik* was to downplay aesthetic considerations and concentrate attention on the overriding goal of furthering social justice.

Curiously, both Leontiev and Chernyshevky could claim that their views on art were descended from the aesthetics of Vissarion Belinsky (1811–48), regarded as the father of literary criticism in Russia and author of the famous letter to Gogol denouncing the latter's supposed conversion to reactionary views.[41] In both cases the claim is dubious and based on partisan interpretation. Belinsky had certainly stressed the social role of the Russian artist, but he had also emphasized that the primary duty of any artist is to create a work of art. "It is beyond doubt," he wrote, "that art has to be first and foremost art and only after that can it be the expression of the soul and direction of society at a given time. However filled with splendid ideas, however driven by contemporary concerns, if a poem lacks poetry, it can express neither splendid ideas nor contemporary concerns, and the most that can be said of it is that it is a good intention badly executed."[42]

Leontiev and Chernyshevsky both cherry-picked from this thesis. Leontiev seized on Belinsky's defense of artistic integrity and simply ignored his requirement that art should further the social good. Chernyshevsky, conversely, discarded the aesthetic imperative and laid his whole emphasis on the social role of the artist. In his *The Aesthetic Relationship of Art to Reality* of 1855 Chernyshevsky consigned to oblivion all products of art that appeared to him to lack relevance to contemporary social questions. Shakespeare, to take just one example, he dismissed as "rhetorical and precious, the artistic construction of his plays would be fine if they could be revised a bit."[43] Gogol's best works, by contrast, "delight the reader through their artistic quality and, more importantly, through the candor and power of their noble indignation."[44] For Chernyshevsky it was axiomatic that legitimacy in art depended on its compliance with the moral imperative to unmask the shortcomings of society. "Belinsky demonstrates historically," he declared, "the necessity of the current direction of literature, aesthetically its absolute legitimacy, ethically, in view of the demands of our society, its indispensability."

Leontiev's first two attempts at literary criticism departed radically from this manifesto. The first essay, "A Letter from a Provincial," was a response to the appearance in the magazine *Nashe Vremya* in March 1860 of an article by the literary critic Mikhail Ivanovich Daragan titled "On the Eve (a Story by Ivan Turgenev)."[45] Daragan had attacked a supposed moral failing in the story's heroine Yelena in abandoning her parents and her country to follow the Bulgarian adventurer Insarov. Leontiev fastened on this to attack the prevailing confusion, as he saw it, of aesthetic and ethical criteria in art. "I don't know why," he wrote, "but Daragan is unable clearly to delineate the moral side from the aesthetic. Although both sides usually find themselves organically linked both in life and in art, it is not difficult to distinguish between them, especially when, as in "On the Eve," the *unconscious* element is sacrificed to the *conscious*."[46]

The last part of this quotation is a direct reference to the aesthetic doctrine of the idealist philosopher F. W. J. Schelling, who had argued, in his *System des transzendenten Idealismus* of 1800, that existence had arisen as the result of a

primal splitting of the original principle into the duality of spirit and nature, mind and body, universal and particular, and so forth. For Schelling reconciliation of this phenomenal disharmony occurred in the natural world as the result of organic activity, which was unconscious but had the appearance of conscious purpose, but for consciousness it was only possible through art, which combined the dual principles of conscious intent and unconscious inspiration. In Schelling's system accordingly, art alone reflects the identity of conscious and unconscious activity.[47]

This was a typically bold stroke on Leontiev's part. In the eyes of Chernyshevsky and the adherents of *Sovremennik* Schelling was the epitome of romantic obscurantism and a leading exponent of the school of "art for art's sake," which they despised. So to begin a piece of literary criticism in the Russia of 1860 with a quotation from Schelling was a gesture that defined one's position with unusual candor and indeed invited anathema as it could not but be seen as a frontal attack on the prevailing orthodoxy. The head of the criticism section of *Otechestvennye Zapiski*, S. S. Dudyshkin, evidently felt uncomfortable with the tone of Leontiev's article, for he took the unusual step of publishing it side by side with another article about "On the Eve," by one P. E. Basistov which, he said in an editorial, "would act as a counterweight to the strident and one-sided aesthetic demands of the *Provincial*."[48]

All true art, Leontiev continued, depended (and this is a characteristically idealist formulation) on nature having passed through and been transformed by the mind of the artist, "the abstract subject matter of life reworked by human reflection."[49] The sacrifice of art to the "ethical itch" of the age, Leontiev argued, in Platonic vein, explained why with "On the Eve" Turgenev "failed to cross *that boundary beyond which lives beauty*, the existential ideal for which the world of appearances serves only as a blurred symbol. And what value has a work of art which does not transcend this magic frontier?"[50] Put simply, Leontiev concluded, the ascendancy of the moral and social imperative in "On the Eve" had led to a corresponding fall in its artistic quality, to an "artistic self-abnegation fatal to poetic effect."[51]

The "Letter of a Provincial to Turgenev" did not set the literary world of Petersburg by the ears. It was met largely, as might have been expected, with mystified silence, receiving only one review, a relatively positive but brief note by Dostoevsky in his journal *Vremya*. Undaunted however, Leontiev returned to the theme of the relationship of ethics to aesthetics in art some ten months later, in March 1861, in his next piece, "Regarding the Stories of Marko Vovchok."

The early stories of Marko Vovchok, otherwise the Ukrainian woman writer of stories from peasant life M. A. Markovich (née Vilinskaya), were translated from the Ukrainian by Turgenev and received considerable acclaim. Later she wrote in Russian and for a time was a great favorite of Leontiev's. Even though he felt her later work had been "spoiled by the nihilists encouraging her to develop an *orientation*," he declared he would still have liked to see the erection of a monument to "the elevated, classically graceful *austerity* and tender harmony" of her stories.[52]

Leontiev's second essay was quite openly a polemic against Chernyshevsky's collaborator on *Sovremennik*, Dobrolyubov, whose own article on Marko Vovchok had appeared in the September 1860 issue of the journal under the title "Character Traits of the Common People of Russia."[53] Dobrolyubov's views on the role of aesthetics in the art of his day were nothing if not trenchant; one of his better-known sayings was: "Aesthetic criticism has become the preserve of sentimental young ladies."[54] Accordingly, the question for him was not whether Marko Vovchok's tales met some hazy and irrelevant standard of pure art, but whether they gave an accurate rendering of (which meant condemned) the social reality of Russia. If they did, then "the goal of our literary criticism will have been achieved without the help of those aesthetic contortions which are always stale and unfruitful."[55]

Dobrolyubov claimed to have sensed a change in emphasis in Marko Vovchok's most recent work, a shift away from outright condemnation of serfdom and its brutalizing effects on both landowner and peasant toward a gentler, more indulgent attitude. In characteristic fashion he attempted to trace this perceived change back to a social cause. In Dobrolyubov's view Marko Vovchok had been the first to sense intuitively that on the eve of the emancipation it was no longer necessary to expose the evil nature of a doomed social order. This objective had long since been achieved, and it was now the task of the writer to expose the "typical situation of the peasant whose landlord does *not* seek to abuse his rights, in short to describe to us, without anger or tears, how lamentable and cheerless is that situation."[56]

This analysis ushered in a polemic between Dobrolyubov and Dostoevsky, who called it an example of how "tendentiousness destroys art."[57] Leontiev then entered the fray on Dostoevsky's side, on this occasion throwing down the gauntlet even more vigorously than before by prefacing his own article with the same extrapolation from Schelling we met with above, this time in the more striking form of an epithet: "The creations of nature are unconscious creations, but similar to the aesthetic creation of the artist, which is a conscious creation similar to an unconscious one; the opinion of Schelling in Schwegler's *History of Philosophy*."[58]

In passing we may note that it was in accordance with Leontiev's attitude toward philosophy, and to study in general, that he should quote Schelling at

second hand. He was envious of those who could "spin unbroken dialectical threads out of themselves as a spider does its web,"[59] and he later admitted in a letter to Anatoly Aleksandrov that "I cannot call myself strong in metaphysics, all this stuff just keeps slipping through your fingers."[60] Nonetheless he followed up this quotation from Schelling with a defiant gesture, a long quotation from, or paraphrase of, Belinsky on the absolute necessity for art to be primarily the product of creative inspiration: "If a work of art is lacking in living, historically conditioned subject matter, if art for art's sake was the goal of the artist, it can still achieve a relative, if restricted, merit; but if it does not bear the stamp of creative genius and free inspiration then however much it is inspired by questions of contemporary life it can possess no value in any respect."[61]

Ultimately, Leontiev suggested (and for us today the point has a striking resonance), the ethical school of literary criticism failed because it sat in judgement on an author's intentions, whereas criticism really only had competence to judge the results of his labors, the completed work of art. In an earlier article Dobrolyubov had suggested that, unlike Marko Vovchok, writers of the "educated class" like Apollon Grigoriev, Turgenev, and Alexei Pisemsky had looked on the folk as "curious playthings" and not taken them seriously. Leontiev reacted violently to this suggestion. "Who can know," he asked, "who would dare to guess, what techniques an author uses for observation? Criticism is not competent to answer this, it deals only with the end result. If an author is not taking his work seriously, his depictions will not ring true."[62]

Predictably, Leontiev's essay on Marko Vovchok received not a single review. Reading both these articles today it is difficult to say whether one is struck more by the extraordinary chutzpah which allowed Leontiev the fledgling littérateur to point out to his face alleged defects in the work of his mentor Turgenev, already firmly established as one of the most revered figures in Russian letters, or by the self-confident naivety with which he expresses opinions which, regardless of their merits, were in the prevailing atmosphere almost certain to attract either condemnation or, as it turned out, cold indifference.

Turgenev himself may have been somewhat less than amused by Leontiev's trenchant criticisms of "On the Eve," for his attitude toward Leontiev's talents underwent a revision after this time. A coolness is discernible in his letters to Leontiev of 1860–61, especially the letters of 16 February 1860, in which he describes "Second Marriage" as "cold, bloodless and pallid" and questions whether its author is suited to writing; of 22 April 1860, where he admits to his self-esteem having been stung by Leontiev's criticisms; and 21 September 1860, where he turns back on Leontiev the latter's suggestion that he had spoiled "On the Eve" by allowing his conscious intentions to intrude too visibly on his art, telling him, with reference to "Second Marriage" and *Podlipki*, the latter being then a work in progress, that "a poet must be a psychologist, but beneath the surface."[63]

Leontiev was never to recover Turgenev's good graces. The latter's subsequent letter to P. V. Annenkov of 9 February 1869 contains slighting comments about Leontiev, while his letter to Leontiev himself dated 4 May 1876 is vituperative, suggesting that he should have stuck to writing ethnographic and historical articles since his fictional characters were "lifeless" and "it seems to me that so-called belles-lettres is not your true calling."[64] Turgenev's sincerity from the beginning in regard to Leontiev's abilities is questionable though. In a letter to the critic I. I. Panayev of 10 July 1855, five years before the appearance of "A Letter from a Provincial," he agreed "precisely" with the latter's assessment that the author of "Summer on the Farm," Leontiev, was a "very poor" [writer].[65]

At face value then, it seems as if the full ramifications of the radical change of climate in Russian literary circles between the 1840s and 1860s had passed Leontiev by. Otherwise how can one explain the appearance of articles as out of tune with their times as his "Letter of a Provincial to Turgenev" and "Marko Vovchok"? As late as 1857, while staying with Shatilov in the Crimea, he had read Chernyshevsky's *Outline of the Gogolian Period in Russian Literature* and seemingly failed to detect which way the wind was blowing, seeing in him only "a young *aesthete of the Forties* and a very good writer." Indeed, Chernyshevsky's assertion that "there will be more accomplished writers than Gogol" seems to have played its part in inspiring Leontiev's decision to abandon medicine for literature.[66] However that may have been, Leontiev appears to have arrived in the capital still imbued with the ideals of the 1840s, of the *Fathers*, apparently without realizing that for the *Sons*, the disillusioned men of the 1860s, these ideals had now become anathema.

But did Leontiev really fail to appreciate the true nature of the milieu into which he was about to step? Since 1854 he had been successively in war-torn Crimea, in the remote depths of Nizhny Novgorod Province, and on the family estate at Kudinovo, making it tempting to explain his ignorance by his relative isolation from literary circles in the capitals. But he still had access to books and periodicals and it is hard to believe that he should have arrived in Petersburg viewing Chernyshevsky primarily as an aesthete of the old school and Dobrolyubov as a kind of evil genius who was perverting Belinsky's teachings and setting Russian letters on the road to ruin.[67] It may be that in the late 1850s, as Leontiev claims in his memoirs, Chernyshevsky had not yet "unfurled his banner of revolution and negation,"[68] but he had been editor of *Sovremennik* since 1853 and his *Aesthetic Relationship of Art to Reality*, with its assault on the very ideals Leontiev was to defend in his "Letter from a Provincial" and "Marko

Vovchok," had been widely available since 1855. Far from the capital or not, could Leontiev really have been unaware that Dobrolyubov now represented the mainstream of literary criticism in Russia and that the idealist aesthetics represented by Schelling were so comprehensively out of season that anyone using them as the basis of literary criticism would appear hopelessly anachronistic if not simply deluded?

It is not impossible, for Leontiev seems to have had a considerable blind spot on occasion and it would not be the last time in which he gravely misconstrued a situation. On the other hand, as we have seen with reference to his editorials for the *Warsaw Diary*, when Leontiev had something to say he generally said it, without paying overmuch regard to the consequences. And regarding the state of Russian literature, and particularly the subordination of artistic merit to moral indignation, Leontiev had something very definite to say. "We need to discover," he wrote in his third and for the time being last essay in literary criticism, "Our Society and Our Belles Lettres," published in the journal *Golos* in March 1863, "whether life as depicted in our literature approximates to our life as it really is, is on a par with it, or is beneath it. It seems to me that it is altogether beneath!"[69]

This is an early instance of a theme, one might almost say fixation, which was to remain with Leontiev through all his mental and moral upheavals, the conviction that Russian writers, under the baneful but unshakeable influence of Gogol, consistently depicted Russian society as considerably lower, uglier, more humdrum, and more morally reprehensible than it was in reality; in other words, that the "realist" school of Russian writing was anything but realistic in its portrayal of Russian life. In this third essay Leontiev attempted to show that "in the life of our society there is incomparably more that is tragic, that is appealing, that is good, than in our writing."[70] This need not, in Leontiev's view, lead to a Panglossian refusal to see the darker sides of life, depict those by all means, he argued, but depict them in the round, do not make them a vehicle for ethical, political or religious tendencies, the outcome of which is to serve up "a false picture of the worst of the worst!"[71] As one of the characters in Leontiev's novel fragment *From Autumn to Autumn*, circa 1865–67, declares: "The sort of revolution we need in Russia is an aesthetic one!"[72]

This advice naturally went unheeded in the ethically charged atmosphere of Saint Petersburg in the early 1860s. Leontiev has found support among later commentators however. For example, in his *Pioneers in Russian Thought* Richard Hare criticizes "the idée fixe that a literary work is valuable solely for the social utility of the message which it propagates." And in his discussion of Chernyshevsky's *Outlines of the Gogolian Period* Hare comes close to paraphrasing Leontiev. "By overstating the case for Gogol and pouring cold water on

Pushkin," Hare writes, "these essays may be held partly responsible for pushing so many younger Russian writers under the crushing influence of Gogol in his most perverse and gloomy style, obsessed with morbid self-analysis and piling up repulsive detail from the ugliest underworld of Russian life."[73]

In his own day nonetheless Leontiev's first forays into literary criticism found as little resonance as had his first attempts at fiction. Should we assume then that this brief crusade, this attempt to rescue the aesthetic in art from the overweening dominance of the "ethical itch" to dragoon literature as a vehicle for social improvement, was simply a Quixotic gesture that was bound to end in failure? In the short term perhaps it was, for it did indeed fail. But things look differently if we take a longer perspective. At the beginning of the twentieth century Vasily Rozanov observed that the fin de siècle "aesthetic" movement in Russian art, comprising the "decadents," the "symbolists," and others, had emerged almost contemporaneously with Leontiev's death and that, without their knowing anything about him, his doctrine that what is beautiful in art must first be beautiful in life "could have been written on their banner."[74] The aesthetic movement has been defined as "a late nineteenth-century movement that championed pure beauty and 'art for art's sake' emphasising the visual and sensual qualities of art and design over practical, moral or narrative considerations."[75] There could be no better summary of the stance taken by Leontiev in his disputes with the "denunciatory" school in Russian letters. As with much else in his life, Leontiev was vindicated by events, even if he did not live to see his vindication.

"Our Society and Our Belles Lettres" marked the end of Leontiev's attempt to live exclusively by his pen. Naively self-confident he may have been on his arrival in Petersburg, but two difficult years of "poverty, misery and despair," as his *Chronology of My Life* eloquently describes them, living mostly with his brother's family in the unappealing capital, the daily grind alleviated only by his growing friendship with his niece Marya Vladimirovna, soon convinced him that he needed to look elsewhere for sustenance.[76] In 1863, following a lightning trip to the Crimea where on 19 July 1861 he married Liza Politovna, a sojourn with his mother in Kudinovo, and a failed attempt to enlist as foreign correspondent for the Slavophile Ivan Aksakov's newspaper *Den'*, he turned his back on the capital and joined the Asiatic Department of the Russian diplomatic corps.

CHAPTER 2

The Best of All Possible Worlds

Entry into government service and subsequent departure for the Ottoman domains did not mean that Leontiev had abandoned Russian literature. In 1864 he fired off a stinging Parthian shot at the Saint Petersburg ethicists with his second novel, *A Place of One's Own*.[1] The novel is essentially a *roman à thèse*, a psychological and philosophical study and clash of ideologies representing the opposite sides of its author's divided self. The dialectical progression in *A Place of One's Own* is more complete than in the earlier works and marks both a high-water mark in Leontiev's crusade to defend the aesthetic principle in art and a conscious attempt on his part to promote devotion to beauty as a template for the productive and worthwhile life. The novel thus encapsulates the feelings of its author during what was a critical moment in his intellectual development. It also stands as one of the most remarkable and neglected works of nineteenth-century Russian literature.

Leontiev set out the framework of *A Place of One's Own* in a letter of May 1863 to the publisher Nikolai Strakhov. His ideas were that the beautiful is more important than the useful; breadth of development is more important than happiness; only from the soil of evil springs good (and great individuals); war, political superstitions, and valiant prejudices are better than universal blandness; in Russia especially, national characteristics are more important than philanthropy.[2]

It is difficult to imagine a manifesto that differed more radically from the ethicist view of the purpose of art as a vehicle for social reform. Indeed *A Place of One's Own* has been regarded as a conscious polemic against Chernyshevsky, whose influential novel *What is to be Done*, which called on the Russian intelligentsia to devote their lives to the welfare of the common people, was published virtually contemporaneously with Leontiev's letter.[3] What Strakhov made of Leontiev's abstract is not recorded, though his fellow publisher Andrei Krayevsky must have been sufficiently impressed since he agreed to serialize the novel in *Otechestvennye Zapiski*.

A Place of One's Own sees the return of the idealist young doctor Rudnev from "The Bulavin Sugar Factory." As in the former story, Rudnev shares many of his creator's traits: he is a conscientious doctor, somewhat antisocial and preferring the certainties of science to the vagaries of social intercourse. "Happy the zoologist and the botanist," he reflects, "they collect plants and dissect animals without running the risk of squandering the detachment of science in the whirlwind of accursed feelings you experience as a member of society!"[4]

A devotee of Jean-Jacques Rousseau, Rudnev sees his ideal in the honest toil of a country doctor in his own corner of the earth, where he belongs, "in a place of his own." But he does not necessarily expect happiness. "Live alone," Rudnev tells himself, "what are people to you? They won't love you, and maybe you won't love them either, just coldly and silently pity them and dress their wounds, helping them steadily, without passion, without words. Don't tire of silence, and if you feel something stirring and burning in the depths of your soul, keep it to yourself for special days. A feeling is like a fragrance; it flies away as soon as it is exposed to the air!"[5]

This rather dour outlook reflects the desire for escape from stifling convention that drove Leontiev to the Crimea and to Nizhny Novgorod Province and would soon drive him to the outposts of the Ottoman Empire. Yet by the time of *A Place of One's Own* Rudnev's uneasy mix of escapist fantasy and utilitarian humanism was already something of an anachronism, representing feelings that Leontiev himself harbored in the early 1850s but which were now turned pathological, the antithesis of the life-affirming philosophy he was attempting to espouse.

Rudnev's philosophy of renunciation of the world's pleasures in the name of science, an austere ethicism he regards as "voluntary self-castration for the general good," is rudely challenged when he meets the alternate hero of the story, Vasily Nikolaevich Milkeyev.[6] Like Rudnev, Milkeyev is a graduate of Moscow University and is now a tutor on a nearby estate. His watchword is "Beauty is unity in variety," and he holds radical views on the relationship of ethics to aesthetics which could not be more different from Rudnev's.[7] "Don't you agree, doctor," he asks in a disparaging reference to Rudnev's Rousseauism, "that morality is a niche component of the beautiful, one of its aspects? The chief measure of things is beauty. Otherwise, what do we do about Alcibiades, or diamonds, or the tiger?"[8]

This view of morality as a subordinate category of aesthetics is not entirely a new departure for Leontiev—we saw it in embryo in his letters from the Crimea—but it is a step beyond the conclusion of *Podlipki* that "evil may salt the good." And in fact Milkeyev rejects any idea of autonomous morality as a "last resort for mediocre souls."[9] He expands on this idea after the local Marshal of Nobility declares that all morality is relative and is asked by Milkeyev's patroness, Katerina Novosilskaya, if that view would therefore justify even violence. Milkeyev seizes the moment. "Justify it with beauty," he declares, "that's the only reliable yardstick because it's an end in itself. Every struggle involves dangers, hardships, and pain, but man is higher than other creatures precisely because he finds pleasure in the struggle, in overcoming hardships. Xenophon's march was a thing of beauty, despite achieving no practical end!"[10]

This definition of beauty as universally valid, as an "end in itself" may be another instance of Leontiev's youthful debt to Schelling's demand for autonomy in art, and it echoes Immanuel Kant's view that beauty must be "purposeful without an end." It was no passing phase however; the primacy of the aesthetic viewpoint is a notion which stuck with Leontiev throughout his life. Twenty-seven years after the publication of *A Place of One's Own*, just three months before his death, he reiterated to Vasily Rozanov that "aesthetics is the best yardstick to judge history and life, for it is applicable to all times and to all places."[11]

Not content with asserting the primacy of the aesthetic view, Milkeyev goes on to mount a frontal assault on the moral categories. "Why fear struggle and evil?" he asks his somewhat bemused hearers. "That nation is great in which good and evil flourish . . . The main thing is to foster the production of the good. So don't for God's sake be afraid of evil, don't you see, evil given its head will generate good! . . . If for the existence of Cordelia at one pole, a Lady Macbeth is unavoidable at the other, then bring her on! But preserve us from debility, slumber, indifference, turpitude and mercantile caution."[12]

This would be heady stuff at any time or place. It seems to anticipate the notorious analogy propounded by Harry Lime in Carol Reed's 1949 film *The Third Man*: "You know what the fellow said—in Italy, for thirty years under the Borgias they had warfare, terror, murder and bloodshed, but they produced Michelangelo, Leonardo da Vinci and the Renaissance. In Switzerland, they had brotherly love, they had five hundred years of democracy and peace—and what did that produce? The cuckoo clock."

Could Lime's unidentified "fellow" have been Leontiev? In Milkeyev's follow up remark, the similarity is even more striking: "Give us real people and there will be real achievements! What should we prefer, the bloody but spiritually opulent age of the Renaissance, or something in the way of modern Denmark, Holland or Switzerland, moderate, peaceful and dull? Beauty—that's the goal of life, and morality and self-sacrifice have value only as one of the offshoots of the beautiful, the freedom to choose what is good."[13]

The inspiration for Lime's cuckoo clock analogy has never been entirely cleared up. The commonly accepted derivation is James McNeill Whistler's 1885 public lecture "Ten O'Clock," in which he speaks of the Swiss as having produced nothing more original than the cuckoo clock. However according to the author Graham Greene, who wrote the script, Orson Welles added the lines himself during shooting, saying that he thought they came from "an old Hungarian play."[14] Whatever the derivation, for us perhaps the key virtue of the comparison lies in highlighting the moral gulf that separates Lime's immoral aestheticism, the use of beauty to justify evil, from Leontiev's aesthetic morality, the "freedom to choose the good" conferred on mankind by the contemplation of the beautiful and the concomitant acceptance of the necessity—not the desirability—of evil.

Certainly the idea of Switzerland as the embodiment of bourgeois mediocrity remained with Leontiev until the end of his life. Twenty-four years after *A Place of One's Own* he wrote to his friend Iosif Fudel': "Let us now imagine modern Switzerland and a contemporary Russian province . . . In Russia it is still possible in our time to envisage Father Ambrose of Optina Pustyn, a splendid warrior such as Skobelev, a novelist like Leo Tolstoy, and there will be many vices and passions at all levels of society. In Switzerland, with approximately the same population, the average level of morality is greater, but neither Father Ambrose, nor Skobelev, nor Tolstoy would be thinkable."[15]

Milkeyev's views were too rich for the blood of the arbiters of literary excellence in Moscow and Petersburg however, and like Leontiev's other works of fiction up to that time *A Place of One's Own* sank without a trace. Or almost. Mikhail Saltykov-Shchedrin gave it a negative, not to say nasty, review in *Sovremennik*, dismissing it as merely derivative, "hardly a novel, more a montage," cobbled together from odd bits of Tolstoy, Turgenev, Pisemsky, and Apollon Grigoriev.[16] Such tunnel vision suggests that Leontiev had a point in his belief that their frenetic search for the "social good" had rendered Russian critics of the time incapable of judgement, either of art or ideas. *A Place of One's Own* has its defects and its derivative moments, but few novels are blameless in that respect, and in any case such borrowing as there is only affects the framework of the story. Like them or loathe them, the ideas in it are highly original and certainly Leontiev's own.

Some four years after the publication of *A Place of One's Own*, a similarly discouraging critical reception awaited a novel by one of Leontiev's contemporaries containing an idealization of beauty akin to Milkeyev's. That novel was *The Idiot*, the writer Dostoevsky, and the sentiment Prince Myshkin's famous aphorism that "beauty will save the world." Despite acknowledged structural issues, *The Idiot* is now widely accepted as one of the four canonical masterpieces created by Dostoevsky following his return from Siberia. At the time of publication, however, the response among critics in Russia was largely negative, partly because of what they considered a pointless eccentricity of characterization,[17] but also (as with Leontiev) in response to Dostoevsky's perceived conservative orientation. Prominent among the latter group was, once again, Saltykov-Shchedrin, who accused Dostoevsky of making cheap jibes at "so-called nihilism" and disparaging "those people whose efforts are wholly directed to the objective which is on the face of it his dearest goal."[18]

It may be argued that the gulf in character and outlook between Myshkin and Milkeyev is too great to allow for any real overlap of their attitudes toward the role of beauty in the universe. But only two years after *The Idiot* Dostoevsky returned to the theme in a novel containing characters every bit as radical in their different ways as Milkeyev. In *The Devils*, of 1871, Dostoevsky gives the idealist Stepan Trofimovich Verkhovensky a speech that echoes Milkeyev's views on the paramount importance of beauty to mankind's well-being. After declaring that in Shakespeare and Raphael "the ideal of beauty has been achieved," and that he personally would not consent to live in a world without beauty in it, Verkhovensky asserts that "mankind could get along without Englishmen, without Germany, definitely without Russians, without science, without bread, but beauty is the one thing it could not do without, because without it there would be no point in living. That's the whole secret of things, the lesson of history!"[19] Milkeyev would surely have recognized in Verkhovensky a soulmate and a kindred spirit.

Where did Milkeyev's provocative ideas come from? Impressions gained in Leontiev's early medical studies may have played a part. "The occupation of medicine," he wrote, "the study of physiology and anatomy of themselves dispose a thinking young man to cherish health, strength and beauty and often to despise the pitiful physical manifestations of urban civilization."[20] The single most important formative influence though was probably the poet Apollon Grigoriev, who became something of an icon for Leontiev after they met in the spring of 1863, just over a year before the poet's death. Leontiev recalls

Grigoriev telling him that "what is beautiful in a book will be beautiful in life, it may be uncomfortable, but that's another matter. People should not live for comfort alone, but for the beautiful."[21]

More generally, Milkeyev's outbursts can be seen as the logical conclusion of Leontiev's rejection of the excessively moralizing tendencies in Russian literature and social thought at the time. Milkeyev's views are often extreme, and it is difficult not to see them in part as deliberate barbs aimed at Leontiev's metropolitan persecutors (at one point Milkeyev describes Petersburg as a "place fit for woodlice to crawl in").[22] As we will see when we consider his later political writings, Leontiev believed that these tendencies would culminate in a leveling simplification of society, in the triumph of the universal "average man," and in the destruction of beauty and the negation of everything that made life worth living. In addition, he was sufficiently persuaded from his own inner experience that truly moral action required a more reliable stimulus and guide than a series of dry ethical propositions which in his eyes took too little account of the complex inner workings of the human soul. As he had Milkeyev declare, for him beauty was the only reliable yardstick.

In seeking the beautiful, Leontiev argues, man will produce the greatest good. Inevitably, there will be casualties, pain, and suffering along the way, but taken in the round humanity will profit as men will be able to fulfill their potential and achieve the greatness of the kind epitomized by the European Renaissance. The alternative, in Leontiev's eyes, was a gradual decline into mediocrity as the creative impulse found itself bound, Gulliver-like, in the chains wrought by one-sided ethicism and a doomed attempt to bring about universal welfare. His solution was for ethics to become a sub-category of aesthetics. Men would then remain free to choose the good precisely because they were free to choose the bad, and in choosing the good they would thereby make the highest moral choice; whereas a strict utilitarian ethicism would end by denying them the opportunity to choose the bad and thereby rob them of the virtue of choosing the good. For Leontiev this would be the death-knell for people as moral agents: "Removing from *a man* the possibility of personal moral conflict would mean removing morality from *mankind*, removing the ethical element of life."[23] In simple terms: "For the Samaritan to have someone to pity and wounds to bind, there had to be robbers first."[24]

Perhaps the most radical aspect of this "aesthetic morality," and for many the most difficult to digest, is that it implies an acceptance of existence as it is and a rejection of any attempt to "improve" society through the application of ethical strictures. We might term this outlook "radical quietism." Yet despite the predominance of social improvers among the intelligentsia of the day such acceptance was by no means unprecedented among Russian thinkers in the early nineteenth century; characters as different as the critic Belinsky and the anarchist Mikhail Bakunin had fallen under the spell of Hegel's famous dictum that "what is rational is real and what is real is rational" and had at least temporarily followed his precept that "to recognize reason as the rose in the cross of the actual and thus to rejoice in it, this rational insight is reconciliation with reality."[25]

Leontiev has Milkeyev in *A Place of One's Own* take the concept of reconciliation with reality to another plane. He had, we are told, "studied Hegel and Leibniz and did not hesitate to declare in front of an innocent young girl that all that is real is rational and that suffering is a necessary element of the beautiful."[26] Milkeyev's views clearly echo Hegel's, yet the philosophical system from whom Leontiev seems to have taken most in the construction of the novel, and in support of the outlook that underpins it, belongs to the second member of this duo, Hegel's predecessor Gottfried Wilhelm Leibniz and especially to his *System of Pre-Established Harmony*.

According to this system, since all events occur in accordance with God's predetermined plan, and since God is perfectly good, the world as constituted is famously the "best of all possible worlds" and the attempt to alter one part through what might be termed "radical interventionism," for example by seeking to eradicate or reduce evil through ethical stricture, runs the risk of reducing the perfection of the whole. This is precisely Milkeyev's view, although he puts it more vividly: by getting rid of Lady Macbeth you risk losing Cordelia as well.[27] It is also worth noting that Leibniz's conception of universal harmony is essentially an *aesthetic* idea, his "monads" being conceived as the means of achieving the greatest possible variety within the greatest possible order, which coincides neatly with Milkeyev's (and his creator's) dictum that "beauty is unity in variety."[28]

Expounding further on his aesthetic quietism, Milkeyev gives Katerina Nikolayevna another instance of the practical effects of his philosophy after she complains about the many trials she has undergone at the hands of her immoral rake of a husband. She should be grateful to him, Milkeyev tells her: "What a full and vibrant life you have, all thanks to him, how much good he has done you, this man! Oh I understand the Hindus, that they dedicate temples to evil!"[29] When Katerina Nikolayevna responds by asking if his outlook would sanction even the spilling of blood, Milkeyev oversteps the bounds of the permissible in polite society: "Blood?" Milkeyev asked, and again his eyes shone, not with malice but with energy and inspiration. "Blood?" he repeated. "Blood does not disturb divine composure . . . This one-dimensional humanitarianism makes me want to weep. What is our physical existence anyway, by itself? It's not worth sixpence! One majestic, centuries-old tree is worth a score of mediocre people and I wouldn't cut it down to buy cholera medicine for the peasants!"[30]

It is a matter for conjecture whether the expression of sentiments such as these in the editorial columns of the *Warsaw Diary* may not have contributed to the untimely demise of that newspaper. Leontiev, however, was not one to allow fear of the public reaction to cloud the rigor of his analysis. In this context it is interesting to reflect that Leibniz, despite ostensibly regarding evil as a negative quality, a privation, nonetheless seems to have been uncomfortably aware (as evinced by his constant attempts to refute the notion) that the view of evil as a positive, creative principle was a natural corollary of his system. Leibniz lays the blame for the existence of evil now on cosmic necessity and the distinction between evil in the metaphysical and moral senses, now on the original limitation of the created being and his consequent unreceptiveness to the good. What he cannot help admitting though is that "a little evil renders the good more discernible, that is to say, greater." His alternative formulation that "evil often serves to make us savour the good the more" recalls strongly Ladnev's conclusion in *Podlipki* that "quarrels, like pepper and salt in cooking, only served to enhance the flavour."[31]

Typically, Leontiev is prepared to go where Leibniz feared to tread and is unafraid to regard evil as a constructive agent in the world, necessary for the fulfillment of God's plan. This is a view of evil that he never relinquished. In the second of his *Four Letters from Athos*, written in 1872 after his religious conversion, he still speaks of the "Godhead . . . who created man and gave him reason and will for the fight against the evil principle *inherent in the creation of the world*."[32] Not only did the evil principle form part of the act of creation, for Leontiev it will persist as long as the earth continues, whatever humanity may do to eradicate it, for in his eyes this world is irredeemable. Thus Leontiev regards true religion as exhorting us to conserve our good qualities in order to counterbalance the bad that will exist forever. The universe is, in short, essentially "a harmonious law of compensation, and nothing more . . . a poetical, living arrangement of bright flowers and dark, and nothing more . . . A fully worked out, half-tragic, half-comic opera in which frightening and melancholy notes swap places with tender and touching ones, and nothing more."[33] Man's sole duty lies in worshipping God and reconciling himself to the reality of existence: "Life itself in its totality, with that equilibrium of evil and good in it which is intelligible to the sagacious mind."[34]

There is a strikingly dualist cosmology in these statements, the last of which was written only a year before Leontiev's death. It seems that even after his conversion Leontiev never fully internalized the Christian doctrine that evil exists as a result of man's choosing it in defiance of God and continued to adhere to the dualistic notion that the evil principle was generated by the deity as a counterweight to the good in order that creativity should flourish and banality be avoided. The most famous proponent of religious dualism was of course the ancient Iranian prophet Zoroaster, and there is indeed evidence that Leontiev was acquainted with his teachings. There is, for example, mention of the opposing poles of the Zoroastrian faith in Leontiev's novel *Odysseus Polichroniades*, written largely in 1873: "Alas! Greece and Russia have now become fire and water in our soul, darkness and light, Ahriman and Ormuzd."[35]

Certainly Leontiev took an interest in the ancient empires of the East which was unusual for his time, and it is not difficult to see why a man of his temperament might be attracted to Zoroastrian dualism (an attraction that endured and for which, toward the end of his life, he was severely criticized by the theologian Vladimir Solovyev). Leontiev repeatedly warned that the exclusively ethical strivings of the nineteenth-century social reformers would end in the destruction of beauty and the negation of the human spirit. It is natural then that he should have been attracted by what he understood to be the resolution of the problem of evil proposed by Zoroaster. An article Leontiev wrote for the *Warsaw Diary* in 1880 provides a good example of this and a direct reference to the ancient faith. "There is no way," he insisted, "that we are going to remove all the burdens of humanity. Manifold and unexpected problems lie concealed even behind the discoveries of science, just as much as in ignorance, behind all discoveries, all inventions, behind every kind of new institution and reform . . . so we're never going to overcome this horrid Ahriman, and neither are the Ahura Mazdas of Paris and Petersburg, for all their pince-nez and abominable dress-coats."[36] For Leontiev it was a conundrum to which the liberals in Russia and elsewhere refused to face up: "How to reconcile the indestructible, ever present *Ahriman*, that is to say, evil, with their hopes for the reign of universal welfare."[37]

These extracts notwithstanding it is probable that Leontiev's acquaintance with Zoroastrian theology was relatively superficial and its significance to his thought need not be exaggerated. He appears to underestimate (though possibly deliberately) the moral duty Zoroaster places on his disciples to combat the evil principle, Ahriman. His use of Zoroastrian motifs is an interesting extension of his attraction to Hegelian and Leibnizian quietism but at the same time another instance of his method, which we will find later on to have been a consistent trait, of "flitting" through philosophies and theologies to find support for his social theories. As with his interpretation of the *System of Pre-Established Harmony*, and with much else in his writing, it is likely that his discovery of the dualistic faith simply provided a framework for ideas which had already been forming in his mind, in this case a possible solution of the problem of how to comprehend the evil in the world without reducing human existence to blandness and banality.

Indeed to understand Leontiev's thinking it is necessary to bear in mind that his ideas were overwhelmingly his own and that his sources—Schelling, Hegel, Leibniz, or Zoroaster—served mainly to provide a theoretical underpinning for these ideas. It is clear that he early on formed the conviction that the eradication of evil, if it were ever to be achieved, would defeat God's plan and render human life meaningless and insipid, and he held to this view until the end of his life. He even went so far as to contend that the existence of evil was necessary to the apocalyptic struggle for supremacy of the true Orthodox Church. In a letter written in the year of his death he cites the example of the Byzantine empress Irene, who was canonized by the Church notwithstanding she had her own son blinded for iconoclasm. Irene's action was barbarous and cruel, he admits, but: "It was thanks to the overthrow and blinding of the iconoclast Emperor Constantine that the seventh Ecumenical Council was able to raise the veneration of icons to dogma. Where would we be now without icons and without all that 'outward' ceremony which is the most refined incarnation of the dogma of the Eastern Church and the whole history of Orthodoxy from Adam to our own time!"[38] For Leontiev God needs more than the meek and humble to work his ends in a world given over to sin and unbelief; he needs the likes of St. Irene, St. Cyril, and Constantine the Great, who wrought the establishment of His Church despite their personal cruelty and ruthlessness. "Let God judge their vices as He sees fit," he wrote, "their vast and enduring merit lives on in us, for it is thanks to them that we are what we are now, disciples of Orthodoxy who believe in the Trinity, in the God-manhood of Christ and the holiness of icons."[39]

Leontiev's fearless eulogizing of the positive role of evil in the world may appear extreme, but beneath the admittedly somewhat tactless outbursts of his hero Milkeyev there resides an inconvenient truth. As historian Christopher Dawson has pointed out in his discussion of Karl Marx, in any social theory which proceeds in a dialectical manner it is the "bad" side of the equation, the evil, which produces the forward movement by precipitating the struggle to overcome it. Leontiev's unique insight is that the eradication of evil, in Marxian terms through the overthrow of the bourgeoisie and the establishment of the dictatorship of the proletariat, will necessarily result in the end of history, as the dynamic element, the "evil," will have disappeared along with the conflict which it fostered and which is the motive force of historical development. It is this elimination of the creative moment, in Dawson's words "the victory of the Marxian apocalyptic over the Marxian philosophy," which Leontiev identifies as the ultimate negation of cultural aspiration.[40]

The sentiments discussed in this chapter have led to Leontiev being condemned as an amoral thinker, his aestheticism sometimes even dismissed as a smokescreen for personal vices.[41] Yet the briefest acquaintance with his works shows that he was far too concerned with the problem of good and evil to be considered an amoralist, even if his conclusions are for many, perhaps for most people, not easy to digest.[42] In this Leontiev has frequently been compared to Friedrich Nietzsche. For example, his disciple Rozanov regarded him as "plus Nietzsche que Nietzsche même" (more Nietzsche than Nietzsche himself) and "more powerful and more original than Nietzsche."[43] Yet although much has been written on the subject, it is perhaps best to look at the similarities between the two men as an example of what might in a different context be regarded as "convergent evolution."[44] There is no evidence that either was even aware of the other's existence, and if Leontiev's spokesman Milkeyev's rejection of traditional norms of morality seems to anticipate Nietzsche's anti-morality, this is explicable in terms of the common enemy against which they both rebelled, which was the seemingly unstoppable spread of nineteenth-century utilitarian ethics, with all that it implied for the reduction of humanity to the common denominator of the "average man," flourishing in what Milkeyev's alter ego Rudnev envisages as his earthly paradise: "Peace and the calculated welfare of millions in flourishing settlements with an equitable division of toil."[45]

In *A Place of One's Own* Milkeyev exposes the vulnerability of the utilitarian position in pitiless fashion:

> The more a man develops, the more he believes in the beautiful and the less he believes in the useful. The underdeveloped man everywhere believes firmly in utility, but the greater our understanding of life the more difficult it is to decide what is truly useful for others, for the *race*. Saving you I may possibly be oppressing or even ruining a dozen others; ruining them I may indirectly be saving a hundred . . . But beauty never dies. It may disappear there, but it will arise here. Armed with beauty we comprehend and love our history; with only utility, probity and philanthropy to help us we see in the life of peoples only tears, blood, and hopes confounded.[46]

Compare Nietzsche:

> "Alas! The time is coming when Mankind will no longer give birth to stars. Alas! The time of the most despicable man is upon us, the man who can no longer despise himself."
> "'What is love? What is creation? What is longing? What is a star?' The last man asks thus, blinking."

"Thus is the earth grown small, and the last man, who makes everything small, hops on to her. His race is ineradicable, like the flea; the last man lives longest."

"'We have invented happiness'—say the last men, blinking."

"Everyone wants the same thing, everyone is the same: whoever thinks differently volunteers for the madhouse."

For Leontiev the goal of history is the exact opposite of this fearsome vision of mankind's descent into mediocrity. As he has Milkeyev put it: "We should be guided by nature, which worships luxuriousness of forms . . . The chief constituent of diversity is the individual who stands above his creations. More than anything else the goal of history is to develop the manifold potency of the individual and drive his fearless determination to achieve his goals."[47] And this "aesthetic morality," this comparison of the "developed and underdeveloped man," really does seem to anticipate the appearance of the "Übermensch." Again, compare Nietzsche:

"Behold, I commend to you the Higher Man! The Higher Man is the meaning of the world. Let your volition assent: the Higher Man shall be the meaning of the world!"

"What is the greatest thing on earth? It is the hour of the great revulsion. The moment in which your happiness begins to sicken you, as does your reason and your virtue."

The above quotations are all from one of Nietzsche's best-known works, *Thus Spake Zarathustra* of 1885, which *A Place of One's Own* preceded by some twenty years.[48] It is perhaps no coincidence that both Nietzsche and Leontiev should both have developed a fascination with the ancient Iranian prophet. For Nietzsche, Zarathustra, or as he is generally known in the English-speaking world, Zoroaster, is the father of monotheistic morality and in *Thus Spake Zarathustra* he makes the prophet reverse the burden of his thinking to produce a kind of anti-morality in favor of the "Higher Man." Leontiev is more attracted to the inherent dualism in the Zoroastrian faith, seeing the eternal combat between the good and evil principles, between Ahura Mazda and Ahriman, as the great source of creativity and beauty in the world. For both men, though, the goal was a common one: to strive to ensure that mankind could continue to "give birth to stars," to preserve richness and diversity in a world that appeared to them to be rapidly sinking into uniformity and banality.

One could go on for a long time selecting passages where the thoughts of Leontiev and Nietzsche on the defects of utilitarian morality and its deleterious effects on the fate of mankind seem to coincide. To reiterate: if the conditions are right similar trees bear similar fruit. In the last analysis, what the two men most had in common was an unusual talent for introspection and the ability to penetrate beneath the surface of ideas and beliefs to the psychological truths that lay concealed, deliberately or otherwise, below. That, and the boldness of spirit to reveal what they found there, whatever the cost.

If the cost to Leontiev would turn out to be great, it was a price he was willing to pay. "The aim of our life cannot be contentment," Milkeyev insists, echoing Apollon Grigoriev, "for those who want to leave something behind them contentment is only good as a stopover. Our goal should be a richness of ideas that will remain in the world like a shadow when we are gone. If a man has managed to live a full life then his personality is safe from destruction. His body will decay but his individuality will have completed its cycle."[49]

Commentators have seen in Milkeyev's ideas a foretaste of the outlook which later became known as existentialism.[50] Certainly, if perhaps superficially, Leontiev's formula that "the fear of God is the beginning of wisdom," which was to become the basis of his religious thinking after his spiritual crisis of 1871, would seem to echo Kierkegaard's concept of dread as the natural relation of man to the deity. More significantly perhaps in this context, Nietzsche too is widely regarded as a forerunner of existentialism, notably in the concepts that in modern times man alone is called upon to give meaning both to his own existence and to the existence of the world and that men in society are divided and ordered according to their willingness and capacity to participate in a life of spiritual and cultural transformation. It follows that a failure to live, to take risks, is a failure to realize human potential.

This is a view of the human condition with which Milkeyev, and his creator, would have agreed wholeheartedly.

CHAPTER 3

The Gathering Storm

Leontiev had taken a big gamble in rejecting the comfortable life of a Moscow society doctor in favor of the precarious existence of an aspiring novelist in Petersburg. Yet if that venture had been a failure in material terms, it did inspire a creative outpouring which has left to posterity a remarkable essay in radical ideas, however much those ideas may have been ignored and reviled by his contemporaries.

The ending of *A Place of One's Own* represents the most comprehensive synthesis of opposites to be found anywhere in Leontiev's works. Milkeyev disappears, his work done, and the young doctor Rudnev, whom we saw at the beginning of the story seeking to ameliorate life for others while refusing to embrace it himself, is now reconciled to the coexistence of light and darkness in God's plan. "If we are to believe in the highest, universal reason," he reflects, "which pervades the whole of nature just as our spirit pervades the whole of our bodies, then we won't wonder that the cruel raptor devours the gentle hare."[1] And this adoption by Rudnev of Milkeyev's values has led at least one critic to suggest that the pair correspond very well to the division of Russian fictional heroes into "predatory" and "passive" types proposed by the poet Apollon Grigoriev, whom Leontiev greatly admired, and that the synthesis of the two may have been Leontiev's attempt to create a new holistic Russian hero.[2]

A Place of One's Own accordingly ends on a note of optimism and "reconciliation with reality": in the last sentence two of the minor characters are described as "happy to be what they are," an attitude redolent of Nietzsche's
Amor Fati, of acceptance of the parameters of existence, which sums up the
thrust of the novel as a whole.[3] This optimism is understandable enough, for
by the time the novel was published in 1864 Leontiev had left his literary mis-
fortunes behind him and was a serving diplomat attached to the Russian Embassy to the Sublime Porte in Constantinople. The life was hugely more to
his liking than his impecunious and dismal sojourn in Petersburg, and one can
easily imagine the sense of relief he must have felt when he entered the service in February 1863 and not long afterward found himself en route for Crete.

The sights and sounds of this new world stimulated Leontiev's aesthetic
sensibilities to an extraordinary degree. He later recalled "the heartfelt relief
which I experienced initially on the island of Siros, where for the first time after
Petersburg, Vienna and humdrum Trieste I at last saw crowds on the streets
who were not Western in appearance but for me something new and capti-
vating. I saw for the first time on Siros that it's not always only the theatre that
is similar to life, but that there are places where life itself resembles an opera
or a graceful ballet . . . What joy I felt, leaving behind all that nineteenth-
century formality."[4]

Leontiev later looked back warmly at his time on Crete, his first posting.
He apparently had few official duties to perform and described his stay on the
island as "a kind of enchanting honeymoon in my time in the service."[5] More
than this though the experience was instrumental in crystallizing his political
outlook, as he compared the traditional life in Cretan society with the scenes
of proletarian degradation he had witnessed in Petersburg. "I spent seven
months in Halepa [a suburb of Chania]," he recalled, "and never witnessed
drunkenness, nor loutish behavior, nor brawling . . . Here you don't see men
chasing disheveled women through the streets with whips and sticks, you don't
see bloody faces or drunken girls . . . It's a picturesque place, a clean village
with spotless houses, cheerful faces, bright children, handsome girls and still
handsomer boys, courage, dignity, hospitality, piety, patriotic fervor, political
awareness."[6]

During this period of service in the Christian provinces of Turkey Leontiev's ideal of the aesthetic life at last became a daily reality, "a kind of exhilarating whirlpool of good and evil, poetry and prose, European politesse and
Tatar abandon."[7] One product of this time was his long novel *Odysseus Polichroniades*, which contains an idealized self-portrait of the author in the heroic figure of Blagov, the Russian consul in Epirus.

FIGURE 3. Russia's window on Europe. An early nineteenth-century view of the old St. Petersburg Stock Exchange and Rostral Columns.

In the eyes of the eponymous Greek youth Odysseus, Blagov appears as "a bronze effigy of a haughty and ineffable deity," comparable to the ancient Athenian general who was one of the key symbols of Leontiev's aesthetic morality.[8] "This greatest hero of my youth," muses Odysseus, "sometimes I wanted to compare him to Alcibiades, if only Alcibiades had not often been too shameless in his vainglory, in his power and luster."[9] (Alcibiades was also openly and notoriously bisexual, which has some significance for Leontiev's sexual preferences.) And the warrior-aesthete in Blagov indeed favors the Turkish aristocracy over the Christian mercantile population he is supposed to be protecting. "You are a Turkish Bey," he tells a local Muslim dignitary, "I am a Muscovite Bey, and you are more to my taste than all these shopkeepers."[10]

Leontiev himself enjoyed the cut and thrust of his diplomatic activities, which form the backdrop to his later novel *The Egyptian Dove*, but like Blagov he had little time for the Christian trading class who formed his main clientele in his dealings with the Porte. "I got lost," he lamented, "in the dark wood of this tiresome, cunning and obtuse Westernized bourgeoisie who are hostile to us anyway."[11] The chief thing he derived from his posting in the East was pleasure in the aesthetic spectacle of Ottoman life. In the novel *Two Chosen Women* Leontiev's hero, Colonel Matveyev, dreams of being "an Orthodox

FIGURE 4.   Escape to the East. A nineteenth-century view of Constantinople, capital of the Ottoman Empire, where Leontiev was attached to the Russian Embassy to the Sublime Porte.

at least as much intrinsic interest to a Greek or Southern Slav ethno-historian as to a student of Russian letters.[32]

The tragic denouement of "Hamid and Manoli" suggests that by the late 1860s clouds had begun to veil the sun of Leontiev's aesthetic Eden. It is also suggestive that beneath the outward assurance of the letter of February 1868 from Adrianople, there also lies a hint of darkness. It was written a little over two years before the crisis of Salonika, and already the cracks in the facade of Leontiev's aestheticism were beginning to show, leading him to confess to his colleague that: "Alongside these things I have other memories of Adrianople on which I prefer not to dwell. I pray nothing of the kind befalls you."[33]

This sense of gathering darkness beneath the bright surface of life in the East is also apparent in Leontiev's novel *A Husband's Confession*, first drafted, under the title *Ay-Burun*, in Constantinople in 1864 but only published, with revisions, in 1867. Once again, the background to the story is the flight of the hero, known only as "K," from refined society to the depths of the country-side, this time a picturesque estate, "Ay-Burun," near Alupka on the southern shore of the Crimea (as if giving him the initial "K," and his wife the name of Leontiev's wife Liza, were not enough to identify the protagonist with the au-thor, we find him confessing to a youthful love for one "Zinaida K" who can hardly be anyone else than the Zinaida Kononova of Leontiev's Moscow University days). The story of K's attempt, in his rural seclusion, to rebuild his life on the basis of aesthetic morality, and of the ultimate failure of this attempt, encapsulates neatly the divided mind of his creator, veering between optimism and deepest pessimism, as his life moved inexorably toward its confrontation with eternity.[34]

K claims to be happy in his isolation, a state he calls "living oblivion," in which he has "ceased to struggle."[35] However, he cannot escape a gnawing sense of emptiness despite the beauty of his surroundings and his hospitable Tatar neighbors. "Yes, it's so lovely here," he muses, "but yet I miss that music made up of tears and sighs which drifts quietly across our desolate Russian fields . . . Yesterday I lay face down in the grass and wept, today I smashed my stout walking stick against a tree, broke it into tiny pieces."[36] Ceasing to struggle is strongly indicative of K's depressed mental state, as the need to "struggle" was always a key concept for Leontiev. "We will struggle on" were among his last words on his deathbed, alternating with "No, we must submit."[37]

K is possessed of a distinct moral relativism. He notes that the world outside looks different, brighter or gloomier, when he views it through the different colored panes in the stained glass in his windows: "In the yellow glass everything's more cheerful, as if bathed in sunlight, in the red it's menacing and resplendent, like the afterglow of a conflagration or the beginning of the end of the world, while as for the blue and lilac I don't know which of the two gives a greater impression of horror and death." Reflecting on this, K questions why we assume we get the true picture through the clear glass when perception is just a matter of atoms conveyed through nerve cells. Developing the metaphor, he continues: "On this subject, why are we so confident about the moral categories? Why does man have to live in society? Why does common sense have to be right, and not a catastrophic error?"[38]

In this questioning of moral norms and "common sense" may be discerned the influence of George Sand, whom Leontiev much admired in his younger days and who was frequently recommended by him as an antidote to what he regarded as the excessively crude realism of the post-Gogolian school in Russia. Indeed the plot of *A Husband's Confession* is a reworking of Sand's 1833 novel *Jacques*, in which the eponymous hero kills himself to avoid getting in the way of his wife's finding happiness with a younger man. K's skepticism about common sense is given an ironic point by the fact that he has on his bookshelves the works of the French philosopher-statesman Royer-Collard (1763–1845), whose system was based on the "philosophy of common sense" of the Scot Thomas Reid (1710–96). K's use of colored glass to question the

CHAPTER 4

Desperate Times

By the late 1860s the evidence suggests that the attempt to live by aesthetic values alone was foundering and that Leontiev had come to feel the need for a moral framework capable of comprehending the disillusionment that lurks behind any cult of beauty and strength in a capricious and uncertain world. His chosen escape would eventually be the adoption of a severe and uncompromising version of Orthodox Christianity. Before that, however, he would make one last and desperate attempt to achieve a synthesis of the aesthetic and the ethical, of duty and desire, which might provide some firm footing in the treacherous morass that his existence had become.

Leontiev's "honeymoon" on Crete came to a sudden end in the summer of 1864 following an incident where he whipped the French consul in his own office on account of slighting remarks the latter had made about Russia. Leontiev was recalled to Constantinople but appears to have suffered no adverse career consequences and indeed to have had his reputation enhanced by his action. He spent the next two years as consular secretary in Adrianople, part of the time as acting consul, and was then appointed successively vice-consul at Tulcea on the Danube in 1867, consul in Ioannina in Epirus in 1869, and temporary consul in Salonika in 1871.

During his time in the East Leontiev kept up a regular correspondence with his friend and colleague Gubastov. We have noted already a hint of darkness beneath the bright facade of Leontiev's advice to his friend, in February 1868, on how to get the most from life in Adrianople. It is from about this time, in Tulcea, that his letters begin to complain of two things that were to darken his remaining years: the onset of mental illness in his wife and his ever growing debts. He describes Adrianople, for all its subtle delights, as "noisome."[1] The Europeanized bourgeoisie with whom he had to deal there in the course of his official duties he called "a kind of revolting combination of Sobakievich and Gambetta" (referring to Gogol's mercantile character in *Dead Souls* and Léon Gambetta (1838–82), the French Republican statesman who was prominent during and after the Franco-Prussian War).[2] To his horror, he found Ioannina even worse, especially after enjoying his time in Tulcea, which he liked best of all his postings.

Leontiev's letters of this period chart the decline in his mental and emotional condition. In the summer of 1867, he enthuses over his "nest in Tulcea . . . here you have bustle and you have peace, East and West and North and South, constant arrivals on the Danube steamers, here there is Russia and Moldavia, Turkey and Austria, you have the expanse of the countryside and at the same time you are in the middle of Europe. It's splendid."[3] Tulcea also conformed to Leontiev's growing political convictions, based on the aesthetic concept of "unity in variety," as he recounts in his memoirs: "Reflecting on this living ethnographical museum that surrounded me I thought it ought to be studied by a serious Russian academic . . . these various religious and national entities all come together on the great river delta, under the same heaven, in the same climate, on the same soil, under one and the same Turkish authority . . . yes, one and the same authority, that's the key thing in our days of destructive and sentimental tendencies."[4]

A letter from Ioannina of October 1869 paints a different picture. "I most definitely don't want to carry on serving in provincial Turkey," he tells Gubastov, "except maybe on the Danube or, if possible, in Constantinople . . . It's unbearable here! I'm not a young man anymore . . . But the worst thing is such a cheerlessness in my heart I never felt before, a kind of *leaden lethargy* . . . Believe me when I tell you all this is unbearably painful. I don't even believe that Ioannina itself is the main reason. The main reason is my inner life. To my horror I see that for the first time in my life *I am starting not to desire anything except material comforts.*"[5]

Shortly after this letter was written, an already difficult situation was exacerbated by the onset of a series of further physical and emotional crises. In particular, in late 1869 in Ioannina Leontiev contracted a malarial fever that lasted intermittently throughout the next two years and was at times so intense that a single spoonful of cream in his morning coffee could bring on a

Despite herself Sonya is impressed by Matveyev's physical beauty and the strength of his convictions. Paraphrasing the poet Mikhail Lermontov, she calls him fondly "a hero *not of our time*" and styles his military outlook "Pechorinism" (referring to the melancholy and Byronic hero of Lermontov's story).[32] She gradually falls under his spell and begins to lose faith in her progressive ideology, coming to view it as a poor substitute for the simpler certainties of her youth and innocence, indeed as possibly the cause of her losing them. "There are moments when I feel like ditching all these things," she reflects, "why did they have to take from me my former beliefs? I used to pray, now I don't, I used to love, not anymore, I used to be alive, now I'm not living."[33] She begins to feel that it is not, after all, a crime to admire qualities in a man—"stylish manners, fragrant sideburns, elegant hands, a fine figure on a horse,"—which are not to be gleaned from books and philosophies, and that neither is religious faith necessarily inferior to nihilist ethicism.[34] In short, she is falling in love.

Sonya's conversion is only part of the story however. The other "chosen woman" is Matveyev's wife, Lina. The story of this marriage provides a fascinating insight into Leontiev's psychological condition at this time, for although Lina appears to have been based on a real person, there is every reason to believe that her relationship with Matveyev in the story is nothing less than a thinly disguised retelling of Leontiev's own marital relationship.

Like Leontiev, Matveyev saw service in the Crimea. Captured by the French at Sevastopol, he is taken to Constantinople and later to the fortress of Metz. While on parole in Constantinople he meets his future wife Lina, a Romanian girl who, of all things, is working as a prostitute in one of the city's brothels. Matveyev insists that the immediate attraction he felt for Lina had no sexual motivation. Rather, he was captivated by a certain indefinable air of total innocence and lack of guile in this "half-wild child," by her adherence to her faith that prevented her from escaping prostitution by marrying a Jew, by the ingenuousness that makes her ask for ice cream immediately on waking. Matveyev, we are told, "was utterly captivated by her simplicity and naturalness, by her sudden caprices, her momentary anger. He loved everything about her, but most of all he loved her truly fathomless ignorance."[35]

The story of Lina's provenance may have been based on real events. A series of letters from Gubastov to Leontiev between August and September 1867 describes an apparently failed attempt to buy a girl named Lina out of a brothel in Constantinople and have her sent to Tulcea on the Danube where Leontiev was Russian consul at the time.[36] Leontiev appears to have encountered this Lina en route via Constantinople to take up this appointment. Despite the failure of the first attempt at rescue, it would appear that Lina herself did eventually arrive in Tulcea later the same year.[37]

Exactly why this ignorance and simplicity should have affected him so deeply is something Matveyev cannot fathom, even after twelve years: "Fair enough, I always found simple folk congenial, but no, that's not it . . . I almost immediately loved Lina, like a mother loves her daughter, and from that time I came to regard her happiness, or at least some amelioration of her condition, as my dearest wish and even as my duty!"[38] Continuing to reflect on his attraction to Lina, Matveyev comes to see that what he found lacking in his relationship with the society lady was any element of compassion: "That abiding sense of pity, mounting at times to torment, overpowering, irresistible, but at the same time sweet, that noble compassion which a strong, experienced and decent man will often look for in his relations with a woman who is poor and abandoned, or ignorant and simple-minded, or with a simple, inexperienced and trusting girl."[39]

Leontiev must have been aware of the negative interpretations that might be put on this statement, not least by those who already harbored reservations about his sexual orientation (though, as noted above, the extent to which Leontiev himself was aware of those reservations is unclear), for he makes Matveyev attempt to forestall them: "Matveyev hastened to explain to Sonya *what exactly* Lina had been in Constantinople before they met, and how wrong people would be who thought that in this affair he was a common seducer of a poor and simple girl."[40]

The device of making Lina a prostitute "saved" by Mateyev may go some way to exonerate the colonel from a charge of depravity. But what of his creator? The need to have someone for whom he could feel the kind of "compassionate" affection described by Matveyev seems to have been with Leontiev for a long time. The protagonist of the unfinished novel *The Egyptian Dove*, a thinly disguised proxy for his creator, referring to blemishes in a woman's beauty, declares that: "From a young age I loved to *pity* . . . Taking pity was for me a source of pleasure in those days."[41] And in his memoirs Leontiev recalls how as long ago as 1850 or 1851, some five or six years before he met Liza Pavlovna, he had the Rudnev of "The Bulavin Sugar Factory" acquire a seventeen-year-old peasant girl as a mistress, confessing that it was a piece of wish fulfillment: "I wished for a young, a very young, sweetheart, a Russian Gretchen, someone simple, gentle and biddable, who wouldn't keep demanding ever greater things from me, but would ask only for goodness."[42]

Then in 1861 Leontiev actually married a "simple, inexperienced and trusting girl," Liza Pavlovna, the merchant's daughter of Greek extraction he had met during his service in the Crimea. And there is evidence, circumstantial but compelling, that Liza Pavlovna's lack of sophistication, and possibly her inability to surmount the conventional morality of her ethnic background (as exemplified by the Greek Mavrogeni in *A Husband's Confession*), rendered her unqualified to deal with her husband's "unendurably manifold demands." During the early years of their marriage she developed serious mental health issues, seemingly of a bipolar nature, which by the time of Leontiev's consulship in Ioannina in 1868 had reached such a pitch that he asked Marya Vladimirovna to come and stay with them for an extended period as housekeeper and, probably, peacemaker. As Leontiev acknowledges in a letter to Gubastov of April 1868, Liza Pavlovna's problems were widely thought to stem from jealousy over her husband's unfaithfulness, though he denied this: "Arrival of Liza. Petty worries; added to which she is seriously ill, and if it is not dealt with thoroughly it could end in insanity . . . Here they put her illness down to jealousy, but that's not right, she was ill when she arrived from Petersburg."[43] When, however, one considers that his letter to Gubastov detailing how to extract maximum pleasure, including sexual pleasure, from life in the East was written just two months earlier, it seems that Liza Pavlovna may indeed have had some cause for concern.

Without straying too far into the labyrinth of psychoanalysis, it is difficult not to see Leontiev's need for a simple and compliant girl on whom he could exercise "compassion" as rooted in his attitude to his mother. We have already noted Leontiev's attitude toward Feodosia Petrovna as being more akin to that of a lover to his capricious mistress than a son to his mother. In the light of this unusual and somewhat fraught relationship Leontiev's comment in his memoirs that a young and naive girl "wouldn't keep demanding ever greater things from me" is suggestive. It may be that what attracted Leontiev to Liza Pavlovna was the fact that she was the exact opposite of his beloved but overdemanding mother, that she would not judge him, would not in her simplicity and lack of education be *able* to judge him, and above all would not "demand ever greater things."[44]

In *The Egyptian Dove*, written in 1881 but set during his time in Adrianople, Leontiev has the "now deceased" Consul Ladnev reflect on his feelings toward women, whether a fifteen-year-old Bulgarian girl whom he briefly considers seducing, or the society woman Masha Antoniadi, wife of a local Greek merchant, with whom he is conducting an arms' length affair which is doomed to remain unconsummated. In both cases Ladnev insists that his motivation was not carnal desire but the need to possess them in his particular way: "How possess? Above all she should be *mine*, as my soulmate, the companion of my heart, whose pride would be my pride, whose success would be my success, and whose failure would be my failure, a sister, friend, daughter, mother, wife, mistress, a Russian helpmate in a foreign land. In a word - *mine*."[45]

If we accept that the stimulus was not primarily carnal, it is a reason for giving Leontiev the benefit of the doubt and taking Matveyev at his word (on his own behalf and that of his creator) when he maintains that he is no common seducer. Leontiev's novels all contain strong elements of autobiography and wish-fulfillment. For example, when Matveyev volunteers for the Crimea, his mother pales slightly but accepts his decision: "Go! Go, my dear one! We live in difficult times! I understand what you're feeling and I won't stand in the way of your desires"—the opposite of Leontiev's mother's reaction to his decision to join up.[46] And one interpretation of the framework of *Two Chosen Women* is that Leontiev was trying to reconcile his manifold sexual desires with a love for his wife which was emotionally authentic but which tended toward the platonic. The novel is set against the background of his four months leave in Petersburg in the autumn of 1868, during which time, as he told Gubastov: "There were matters of the heart, and how!"[47]

Matveyev returns to Russia after the war but is unable to rid himself of the image of Lina enslaved in a Constantinople brothel and four years later he returns impulsively and marries her, just as Leontiev had returned to the Crimea four years after the war to marry Liza Pavlovna. It was not conscience, Matveyev insists, that drove him to this act, but compassion for the girl's unfortunate position and in any case the marriage was intended (by him) to be a relatively open one in which he would retain the discretion to seek pleasure and more refined company elsewhere—"the freedom to break his vow to her *a bit*"—thus reconciling his "duty of responsibility and thirst for life and freedom."[48] He does not regard adultery under these conditions as a sin, the only sin for him would be to "cause pain to his kind and tender, loving and simple wife . . . the beloved sister of his soul in all eternity."[49] As to the possibility of divorcing Lina to regain his freedom, Matveyev discounts the idea absolutely. "Freedom?" he asks. "What was that kind of freedom to me. I considered myself free already."[50]

Matveyev leaves Lina in comfort and security on his Crimean estate and returns to Petersburg, where he meets the other "chosen woman," Sonya, whom he not only finds physically attractive but whom he has marked out as his ideal helper in his project to found a new anti-European and Slavophile political movement. Here again Matveyev is confronted with a difficult ethical problem. On the one hand, he sees the opportunity to make of Sonya "an entirely new woman, not just a simple and good-hearted patriot who spends her day sewing bandages in wartime . . . but not a dry civic matron either, one who reckons it the highest duty to work in a telegraph office or sit a doctor's exams."[51] On the other he has the demands of the flesh to consider: "He asked himself if he had the right to make Sonya his mistress. And his conscience responded severely that *of all women* he had the *least* right to do so with her."[52]

Here the first part of *Two Chosen Women* breaks off. The second and third parts were never published, although the text of the second part was preserved, whether in whole or part is not certain, in Marya Vladimirovna's papers. It is largely concerned with Matveyev's efforts to deal with the double dilemma of reconciling the two chosen women with each other and coming to terms with his feelings for Sonya. "The thing is," he muses, "how can I have Sonya fully without damaging her, or her grandmother, or Lina? . . . I must think how to prepare the soil so that the flowers which are to bloom on it are only fragrant and not poisonous, not harmful to anyone."[53]

Matveyev eventually resolves his dilemma with the help of what he calls his "mysticism," that is by convincing Sonya that she should become a sister to Lina and to that end vowing to forego carnal knowledge of her. Sonya agrees to accompany Matveyev on these terms and writes the letter to Lina with which the second part of the novel closes: "Neither you nor I alone can make your husband's life complete—his needs are too complex . . . together we can create for him a happiness such as people have never seen nor experienced. I will be like a sister to you, but if you find it too difficult I will leave and put the blame on fate . . . above all we must never blame each other for anything."[54]

Leontiev always found it easier to envisage a moral dilemma than to resolve it, and the second part of *Two Chosen Women* is a disappointment after the first, being overly didactic and psychologically unconvincing. To paraphrase Turgenev, the psychologist in Leontiev is too much in the foreground for the dramatic structure to bear, and what might have been a dynamic synergy between two strong and very different characters instead falls flat, and indeed seems occasionally to stray into the realm of light opera, as when Matveyev asks Sonya whether "*carnal* possession should be dearer to us than the exalted union of our souls?"[55] These defects notwithstanding, Matveyev's vacillations between desire and duty, and his tender regard for his "simple" wife Lina, do serve to illuminate Leontiev's predicament in the late 1860s with regard to the increasingly difficult Liza Pavlovna. It is surely the authentic voice of Leontiev himself speaking when Matveyev tells a rather bemused Sonya: "Perhaps I have never loved anyone as tenderly as I love her, and I confess I am unlikely ever to love anyone else as tenderly and indulgently."[56]

Despite the inherent improbability of Matveyev's resolution of his moral dilemma, we can be fairly certain that when his physical attractions overcome Sonya's nihilist ethics we are witnessing the last flaring of an aesthetic in his creator which was on the verge of annihilation. A further decisive blow was the death in February 1871 of Feodosia Petrovna. Apart from a brief visit to Kudinovo during his four months leave in Russia two years before Leontiev had not seen his mother for over six years, and one can imagine his crushing sense of guilt that she should have died alone without him.[57] His filial guilt comes across strongly in his memoirs, where he recalls his mother, "abandoned by me," bitterly crying when she had the main house at Kudinovo demolished for timber to raise the money for Leontiev to buy his brothers out of the inheritance. One wonders in this context whether Colonel Matveyev's statement in *Two Chosen Women* is not psychologically suggestive: "That's the terrible thing about life. It wasn't the death of my mother that distressed me, but my indifference to it."[58]

Shortly afterward, in April 1871, Leontiev was transferred to Salonika, partly on health grounds, partly as a prelude to his obtaining a general consulship in Bohemia. Salonika was the nearest station to the large Orthodox monastic community of Athos and Leontiev, as consul, became responsible for the offerings sent annually from Russia in support of the Russian monastery of Saint Panteleimon. This duty brought him into close contact with the monks of Athos, especially the Archimandrite Makary and the renowned ascetic Ieronim.[59]

It is possible that this contact may have crystalized an idea that had been growing in Leontiev's mind for many years as an alternative means of escape from the moral dilemmas which had been gnawing at him since his youth, a path more reliable perhaps than the "aesthetic morality" on which he had pinned so many hopes. "Dear Lord," had prayed the hero of *Podlipki*, Vladimir Ladnev, ten years before with reference to his own emotional difficulties, "wouldn't it be better to be an ascetic or a monk, but a staunch and luminous one who knows what the soul desires, free and clear like a crisp autumn day?"[60] Six years later the hero of *A Husband's Confession*, K, had considered resigning himself to a remote monastery in the Crimean mountains to clear the way for the flowering of love between his young wife Liza and the Greek youth Mavrogeni.[61] And when Leontiev's niece returned from her sojourn with him in Ioannina in 1870, she told his mother that her son: "Despite his recent career successes, had begun seriously to pine and to think about finishing his life in a monastery."[62]

It is worth noting in this context that Leontiev had acquired an enduring love of the rites and rituals of the Orthodox faith almost, one might say, with his mother's milk. During the same conversation, Feodosia Petrovna told Marya Vladimirovna of an incident that occurred when she took her son as a small boy to the nearby monastery of Optina Pustyn. The young Leontiev was apparently so entranced by the place that he told her "not to bring him there again or he would stay forever."[63]

Then came the crisis of 1871. At the end of his life Leontiev told Rozanov that this event was ushered in by, among much else, "a sudden and unexpected series of the *most devastating* shocks to my heart—you've heard the French expression, *cherchez la femme*."[64] As to the identity of this enigmatic "femme," one possibility is that may have been Feodosia Petrovna, who died six months before the crisis in Salonika.[65] Or she may have been Marya Vladimirovna. An intriguing alternative theory for Leontiev's religious crisis and conversion maintains that the forty-year-old consul had contracted a "forbidden love" for his twenty-two-year-old niece and had attempted unsuccessfully to arrange a ménage in Ioannina in 1869 between himself, her, and his wife Liza Pavlovna along the lines envisaged by Matveyev in *Two Chosen Women*.[66]

Marya Vladimirovna visited Leontiev three times between 1869 and 1871, the first two times in Ioannina and then once in Salonika, the chief reason being ostensibly to help her uncle cope with his increasingly unstable wife. In Ioannina Marya Vadimirovna stayed with her uncle and his wife and appears at first to have been enchanted by the sights and sounds of the East, although her recollection hints at a darkness beneath the bright surface. "Everything in our home was young, fresh, pleasant, graceful and colorful," she wrote. "That was the external framework of Konstantin Nikolaevich's family life. All he wanted from his family were fresh and fragrant flowers."

It is possible that Marya Vladimirovna is consciously alluding here to the fragility of her uncle's aesthetic morality. "He wasn't thinking then about the foundation that every family needs," she continues, "that the strength of a family lies not in the flowers but in the roots. The flowers in his family were luxuriant, but the roots were weak. And after only a few months the flowers faded. Konstantin Nikolaevich remained in his charming house but his wife became seriously ill. And I went back to Russia, where my loving father was waiting for me."[67] Elsewhere in this reminiscence she concedes that amid the beauty of her surroundings: "We each of us, my uncle, his wife and I myself, had our dark clouds in our hearts."[68]

In Salonika Marya Vladimirovna stayed in the same house as her uncle throughout the period of his religious crisis and left her own detailed account of the events surrounding it.[69] She confirms the details of the crisis set out in Leontiev's letter to Rozanov cited in the introduction to this volume and states enigmatically that her uncle's illness was "not cholera, it was a sign from on high."[70] It is unclear whether this sign refers to improper advances made toward Marya Vladimirovna by her uncle, or to his moral condition more generally, or to something else. In his letter to Rozanov Leontiev refers to having led a life of "dissolution and refined sinfulness," which would more than justify a "sign from on high" that things needed to change if he were to save his soul. It is possible that in Marya Vladimrovna's eyes the "sign" was intended for them both.[71]

It is certainly the case that Leontiev and his niece were close. The literary historian Sergei Nikolaevich Durylin recounts that Leontiev said many times that only two people really knew him properly: his friend and diplomatic colleague Gubastov and Marya Vladimirovna.[72] In 1925, toward the end of her life, Marya Vladimirovna met and conversed with Durylin, who wrote afterward: "If the day ever comes when Russian literature will beg forgiveness of Konstantin Leontiev's memory and acknowledge the greatness of his thought and his abilities, on that day we must also remember that Russian woman who gave him all that a Russian woman has to give: undying love, total comprehension, steadfast and incomparable devotion to the man and his works, in love, in toil, in prayer, from her earliest youth until deepest old age."[73] In later life Marya Vladimirovna became her uncle's literary heiress and, after his death, the guardian of his mentally unstable wife, Liza Pavlovna, until the latter's death. As Durylin says: "All the most significant events in Leontiev's inner and outer life, his fiction and his philosophical speculations, all are inextricably tied up with Marya Vladimirovna Leontieva."[74]

The onset of closeness between Leontiev and Marya Vladimirovna dates to 1860–61 when Leontiev was living in Petersburg with his brother Vladimir, Marya's father, and began, at the latter's request, to give lessons to his then adolescent niece.[75] For her this was the "dawn of a new life"[76] and Leontiev was later to describe her as "a clever and very well educated Russian woman,"[77] which is not surprising if we are to credit the statement of his biographer Konoplyantsev that these lessons were "almost at university level."[78] Then in 1865 Leontiev persuaded his mother to leave the family estate of Kudinovo jointly to himself and to Marya Vladimirovna, and she was overwhelmed with gratitude. "You know what it means to me to have property and independence," she wrote. "You're giving me the one and the other. I will read and work and of course the happiest day of my life will be when I see that you've written: 'Well done Mashka!'"[79]

Marya Vladimirovna seems to have decided at an early age that she would not marry and instead seek a career on the stage. The first mention we have of this is in a letter she wrote to her uncle on 20 April 1867, when she was nineteen years of age, telling him of her decision and saying that she would be appear under the stage name "Konstantinova."[80] This in itself is suggestive of an unusual closeness, as several of Leontiev's works on Eastern affairs appeared first under the pseudonym "Konstantinov." She reiterated her ambition the following year in reply to her uncle's invitation to visit him in Tulcea and also stated that it was her firm intention never to marry.[81] In a letter to her uncle of 18 January 1868 she explains this decision, in language redolent of Chekhov's heroines: "I can comprehend family life, in the full sense of the idea, only if it means spending my life with the man I love, but not just in order to live free from want and raise children. There are other goals for which I would join my life to the man I loved; I wouldn't be afraid of poverty, if that were necessary, provided that by my living with this man we wouldn't be wasting our lives."[82]

It is evident from these letters that the man Marya Vladimirovna loved was not in a position to marry her. Were they then a veiled declaration of love toward her uncle? The clearest evidence that her relations to her uncle were more than those of a devoted niece and that she herself may not have been merely the passive recipient of forbidden and unwanted advances comes in a letter dated 7–9 July 1869. In this she writes from Ioannina to tell her father that she intends to spend a whole year there with her uncle, despite the fact that this will lead to her missing her debut on the professional stage, which was planned for February 1870. She is doing this, she explains, to escape the "drab life I have been living for the past five years since uncle went away."[83] She insists that her health is the reason for remaining in Epirus and that "nothing and *no-one* is keeping me there."[84] If her uncle asked her to stay for his sake, she continues, she would *refuse for his sake.*

Describing herself as "guilty, oh how guilty," Marya Vladimirovna begs her father's forgiveness and declares: "The only reason I want to be an actress, and independent, is so that in my new position of freedom I can belong completely to him, if that is what he wants." Her initial impulse to go on the stage, she continues, was to obtain freedom and independence, but now "the only reason is so I can give my freedom and independence to him, and him alone, if he wants them." Declaring that she feels she has the talent to become a good actress and that she will enjoy the stage, she nonetheless insists that: "I regret the past five years, not only because of the stage, but because I have not been living during that time. I have had no strong passions, and as to enjoyment the least said the better. Now I want both. I am to blame for the emptiness of the years of my youth. I don't want to go back to that, it is time to wake up. As uncle would say, I look on Epirus as a glorious recreation."[85]

This first part of the letter was composed on 7 July. Two days later, she changed her mind. "I can't stay here," she declares on 9 July. "My heart is breaking and time is going by . . . And the last two days! I had conversations with uncle."[86] She reiterates her desire to become independent as soon as possible for: "He says that he doesn't feel himself justified in allowing himself anything in regard to me until I am on my own feet, in the first place because of his moral duty toward you, and second because he simply doesn't want to give free rein to his passions which are, he says, not fierce in him at the moment . . . Now you know, father, what he means to me and I'm sorry not to have told you sooner."[87]

Following his religious crisis Leontiev left Salonika, intending to seek ordination on Athos, and Marya Vladimirovna returned to Russia. The next time they would meet would be in 1874 in the family home of Kudinovo and from that time on there is no indication that their relations were anything other than platonic. It appears that Marya Vladimirovna had resigned herself to the inevitable, albeit "with a heavy heart,"[88] more or less immediately after the crisis and what appeared to them both to be the divine intervention of the Virgin.

In due course Marya Vladimirovna would become the prototype of Sofia Lvova, the protagonist of Leontiev's unfinished novel *Girlfriends* of 1889–90, and another heroine in the Chekhovian mold. When Sofia's first love, her first cousin Aleksandr, tells her he does not reciprocate her feelings but hopes they may still be friends, Sofia "considers it her highest and most sacred duty to serve him from afar."[89] She does this by managing the estate Kureyevo, where she dreams of becoming, for Aleksandr's sake, a tragic actress. Though not especially religious, she prays to God to "cool this tormenting passion in me for this man. My passion is no use to him, if we ever met again I'd be just a burden and a grief to him."[90]

On the evidence available then it seems reasonable to conclude that as a young girl Marya Vladimirovna developed an erotic attachment to her uncle and that this was reciprocated by him but only up to a certain point.[91] It is also more probable than not that he never gave full rein to any sexual impulses he felt toward his niece. This would explain the change of tone of Marya Vladimirovna's letter to her father from Ioannina of 1869, veering suddenly from the enthusiasm expressed on 7 July to the near despair after her "conversations with uncle." It also throws light on Matveyev's mental struggles over whether he had the right to make Sonya his mistress, which end by him concluding "that of all women he had the least right to do so with her."[92] Finally, it would also go far toward explaining some enigmatic remarks made by Marya Vladimirovna to Durylin at their meeting in 1925. "He [Leontiev] could not arrange the family life that he wanted," she told Durylin. "The way he wanted to arrange things is impossible in a family . . . Nobody could arrange a family that way."[93]

The concluding third part of *Two Chosen Women* was not published, but Leontiev gave an outline of the denouement in a letter of 24 October 1883 to

V. G. Avseyenko, newly appointed editor of *Sankt-Peterburgskie Vedomosti*, according to which Matveyev's plans go awry and after much discord he and the "chosen women," his wife Lina and the repentant nihilist Sonya, go their own ways, leaving Matveyev nowhere to turn to but God for consolation.[94] As with Matveyev, so with his creator. By the time his confrontation with death arrived in July 1871, it seems that Leontiev was primed, physically, psychologically and emotionally, for the cataclysmic change which was about to engulf him.

It is possible that deep in his psyche Leontiev had been conscious of the possibility of such an outcome for a long while before Salonika. His 1851 essay "A Few Words about Three Characters from the Gospels" contains sketches of the Disciples Peter and John and of the Apostle Paul. The description of Paul's conversion to Christianity uncannily prefigures Leontiev's own Damascene experience on his sickbed ten years later: "Blinded by the dazzling light of truth he submitted, as must submit the will of every strong and noble human soul which is set on the path of falsehood when he hears a righteous, forgiving and sorrowful reproach."[95] It seems that Leontiev's gift for prophecy was with him from an early age.

PART TWO

A Prophet in His Own Country

CHAPTER 5

Russians, Greeks, and Slavs

We have now arrived back at the critical watershed in Leontiev's life, his existential crisis on his sickbed in Salonika. Following his physical recovery and what he styled his "inner rebirth" and *"violent conversion to personal* Orthodoxy," Leontiev spent a year in the Orthodox monastic community on Mount Athos seeking ordination as a monk.[1] As he was aware, this was a particularly bad moment for a serving Russian diplomat to be there since it was at the height of a passionate religious dispute between the Greeks and Bulgars, which meant that his presence on the Holy Mountain was bound to be interpreted by the former as Pan-Slavist intrigue, and indeed it caused a furore in the Greek Press in Constantinople.[2] Leontiev later recalled that this aroused the fury of the Russian foreign minister Prince Alexander Gorchakov and brought him under suspicion of unsuitability for service. As Gorchakov put it: *"Nous n'avons pas besoin de moines"* ("We have no need of monks").[3]

The elders of Athos refused to accept Leontiev for ordination, as they considered him to be of "too passionate a nature" and not yet ready for such a step, an assessment he later acknowledged to have been correct at that time. "It was through gritted teeth and not from genuine acquiescence that I accepted the idea of renouncing the world and welcoming death," he later recalled, "I didn't resign myself to it, I was thinking more of saving my body than of saving my soul."[4] Indeed attachment to the things of this world remained strong in Leontiev's breast for a long while after Salonika; in October 1875 he wrote to Gubastov from the Monastery of Saint Georgy at Meshchovsk declaring he had gone there "to drown my longing for life and the good fight, to drown it."[5]

Leontiev accordingly set off on a harrowing thirty-three-day journey to Constantinople overland via the Balkan Mountains and Thrace.[6] On 1 January 1873, shortly before his forty-second birthday, he formally retired from the diplomatic service after having accused the Russian ambassador to the Sublime Porte, Count Nikolay Pavlovich Ignatiev, to his face of betraying the Orthodox faith by conniving with Bulgar efforts to set up an independent national Church in defiance of the Ecumenical Patriarchate in Constantinople.

With a pension of only 600 rubles a year, a wife to support, and a mountain of debts accumulated during his service days, Leontiev now found himself in much reduced circumstances. He settled for the time being on Halki, modern Heybeli, one of the Princes Islands near Constantinople, which had the advantage of being both cheap and near to his friends in the embassy and yet affording him peace and quiet in which to work in the invaluable proximity of an Orthodox hermitage. To supplement his meager resources he negotiated with the conservative editor Mikhail Katkov a retainer of 100 rubles a month for articles he was to write on Eastern affairs for the latter's journal *Russkii Vestnik*. These articles, "Pan-Slavism and the Greeks," "Pan-Slavism on Athos," and his masterwork *Byzantinism and Slavdom*, written in 1872–73 under the pseudonym Konstantinov, contain both the essence of Leontiev's mature thought on the vexed question of Russia's future relationship to her Orthodox brethren in the Balkans and an idiosyncratic theory of the rise and fall of civilizations. They are among his most important legacies to posterity.

Before turning to an examination of these works, we should first take a look at the genesis of Leontiev's political thinking, which takes us back once more to the early 1860s and the novel *A Place of One's Own*. Leontiev's unhappy sojourn in Petersburg had not only crystallized his "aesthetic morality," it stimulated the development of his political consciousness, notably his ideas on the future course of Russia, Orthodoxy, and Slavdom. We can see this unfolding in the novel in the views of Likhachov, the provincial Marshal of Nobility. Likhachov laments the state of alienation from their roots into which the landed gentry had fallen in comparison with their forefathers. Unlike the old nobility, who remained in touch with the spirit of their native soil, the current generation, in their haste to flee the land and chase the latest European fashions, were in Likhachov's eyes turning the heartland of Russia into a desert and sacrificing their native culture and originality. "The spirit of the nation is the yoke," Likhachov contends, "to which, willingly or unwillingly, even the most unbridled hearts must submit. A people is only of any use to other nations by being different from them!"[7]

Likhachov is a conservative but no reactionary; he welcomes the emancipation and sees the salvation of Russia in an awakening of the national consciousness. But why he asks should Russians follow at the heels of Europe when Russia already enjoyed everything that Europe had to offer but in much greater abundance? "Ethnic variety," he eulogizes, "wealth of temperaments, diversity of customs, climates and degrees of development, what scope there is here for evolution!"[8]

For all her rich possibilities, for Likhachov the Russian spirit lacked a focus, a sense of unity and purpose, in the absence of which Russia had achieved power but had not realized her cultural potential. This deficiency could only be supplied, in the marshal's opinion, if Russian society returned to its roots and imbibed the life-giving force which lay hidden in the ordinary Russian. "I do not expect anything from our society," he declares, "unless it returns to the common Russian people, devoted, rough-hewn and self-reliant as they are . . . Our native genius is dormant; it lies buried in the common folk, instinctively, in embryo . . . It is our task to fan these native sparks, to sow the wheat that has slumbered for millennia in the tombs of Egypt."[9]

Likhachov's views here are readily identifiable as reflecting the ideas of that school of Russian thought known as the "Pochvenniki," the "men of the soil," whose chief representatives were the brothers Dostoevsky, the philosopher and publicist Nikolai Strakhov, and the poet and critic Apollon Grigoriev. Like the marshal, these thinkers were possessed of a passionate belief in the virtues of the Russian "folk," they generally welcomed the reforms of the emancipation, and they held that the Russian gentry had lost touch with its native roots. Unlike the Slavophiles, who preached the outright rejection of all things European, the Pochvenniki sought a reconciliation of the divided nation, to be achieved by the Westernized upper classes coming to an appreciation of the common people and returning to the "land," a convergence of opposites which in the eyes of the men of the soil was the absolute prerequisite for the flowering of a distinctively Russian national culture.[10]

That Pochvenniki views should appear as the first expression of Leontiev's political thought is unsurprising. He became acquainted with Strakhov in Petersburg in the early 1860s and for several years the two men kept up a frequent correspondence, while in the spring of 1863 he met Apollon Grigoriev, whose writing he had admired since his youth. And the eulogizing of the diverse virtues of the common people by the Pochvenniki is strongly redolent of Milkeyev's dictum in *A Place of One's Own* that "Beauty is unity in variety." That Leontiev's thoughts were already tending in the same direction is evidenced by one incident from his time in Petersburg. As one of his "disciples," Anatoly Aleksandrov, later recalled, Leontiev fell into conversation with one Ignatiy Antonovich Piotrovsky, a literary critic and contributor to *Sovremennik*, near the Anichkov bridge, which carries Nevsky Prospekt over the Fontanka River (the surroundings have altered over time). Leontiev extolled the aesthetic virtues of the contrast between nearby palaces (representing the state), churches (faith), and fishermen's cottages (the folk). Piotrovsky countered that he would have them all torn down to make way for utilitarian dwellings for the people,[11] and Leontiev afterward represented the incident as one of the chief reasons for him turning against liberalism. "The poetry of *real life*," he wrote, "is impossible without that *diversity* of *social position and feeling* which comes from inequality and competition . . . *Aesthetics saved the civic consciousness in me*."[12]

Toward the end of the 1860s Leontiev was invited by Strakhov to submit some articles for the journal *Zaria*, the editorship of which the latter had recently assumed. This resulted in Leontiev writing two "letters" to Strakhov, which may be regarded as his first definitively political essays: "Literacy and National Character" (written 1868–69, published 1870), and "Some Reminiscences on the Late Apollon Grigoriev" (written in 1869, never published).

The later, and shorter, of these articles is, as its name suggests, an appraisal of Apollon Grigoriev from a personal standpoint; yet it also serves as a window on the development of Leontiev's own thoughts at a relatively early stage in his career. Grigoriev himself is generally regarded as a morally ambiguous figure in Russian letters, but for Leontiev he seemed to embody in his person that reconciliation of the opposing elements in the Russian soul that was the central plank of the Pochvenniki program. Leontiev admired what he saw as Grigoriev's "preference for breadth over the purity of spirit" and found "something secretly corrupt" in his writing. Far from regarding this "impurity" in a negative light, Leontiev saw it as giving voice to the hidden poetry of the Russian folk, "a poetry of revelry and debauchery, not foisted on us by the West but living in the very bowels of the common people," a poetry which, as it did not conform to the fashionable liberalism of the day, was generally ignored, to the detriment of the "wholeness" of Russian culture.[13] Grigoriev had been, in Leontiev's eyes, a standing corrective to this cultural bias and might therefore be forgiven his moral shortcomings. "It is not vice we should fear today," Leontiev declared (as he had had Milkeyev declare in *A Place of One's Own*), "we should fear mediocrity and indifference!"[14]

In a wholly italicized passage in "Apollon Grigoriev" Leontiev summarizes what he understood to be Grigoriev's (and by implication his own) view of the future of Russia. "*What we want for Russia is a future which is rich and lavish and above all distinctive. In the light of this distinctiveness our half-European recent past will pale and appear of little value. However we cannot but feel warmth toward this recent past. There are elements within it that are indispensable to a rich national culture and life. All we want is for these elements to take on more Russian patterns."*[15]

The anti-European, anti-Western outlook that was to become the hallmark of Leontiev's later political philosophy begins to peep through here. As this quote demonstrates however it was a considerably more complex phenomenon than the knee-jerk xenophobia exhibited by certain of his contemporaries, notably among the Pan-Slavists. To the end of his life Leontiev was ready to admit that Western, Romano-German and Catholic culture had been "immeasurably more fruitful than that of either Classical Rome or Byzantium."[16] It was what he saw as Europe's decline into mediocrity that provoked his indignation, not her great age of cultural flowering, and he was ever at pains to draw a distinction between the two. "I'm not speaking about the Europe of Byron and Goethe, Louis XIV, and even Napoleon Bonaparte," he insisted, "but about the Europe that *came after*, the Europe of railways, banks, chambers of deputies, in a word about the present caricature of Europe with its self-delusion and prosaic fantasies of universal welfare."[17]

But for Leontiev Europe's great days were behind her now and decay, or worse, was staring her in the face. "We don't need to fear the decay of Europe," he argued, "decay is horrible but can be fruitful. Europe is threatened by necrosis via a different route: ossification of the soul."[18] As to contemporary Europe, the passionate anti-Westerner that Leontiev had become by the close of the 1860s finally emerges into rather startling relief toward the end of his Grigoriev essay: "Russians are barbarians, you say, who prate about the latest European ideas without a glimmer of understanding? Thanks for the compliment! Let them be barbarians, but of the stamp of Suvorov, Potemkin, and the rest of *Catherine's Eagles*, and of our peasantry, Ostrovsky's heroes and Tolstoy's Cossacks . . . The nation stands to gain more from such barbarians than from our Westernizers and scribblers, the rabble that defiles Nevsky Prospekt with its fawning imitation of Europe."[19]

This was altogether too strong stuff for Strakhov, whom Leontiev was later to refer to as *Le Bien Nommé* ("strakh" in Russian means "fear, fright"), and he refused to publish the essay; it disappeared until its rediscovery in 1915.[20] Leontiev was most unhappy with Strakhov over this episode. His letter to him of October 1869 is full of reproaches, perhaps an early indication of his later tendency to attribute his literary failures to the treachery of those he regarded as his natural allies.[21] Strakhov though may have been influenced in his decision by Fyodor Dostoevsky, whom we can see in his letters to Strakhov of 1870 opposing the placing of "Apollon Grigoriev" in *Zaria*, apparently on personal grounds: Dostoevsky appears to have felt that Leontiev had in this essay "distorted facts" relating to his editorship of *Vremya* and *Epokha* and also his financial relationship with his brother Mikhail.[22]

After lengthy delays and anguished correspondence, Strakhov did publish Leontiev's other essay, "Literacy and National Character," the starting point of which is his consideration of the perennial European jibe about Russia that it was "barbarism armed with all the latest weapons of civilization."[23] Leontiev was only too happy to agree. "This is the truth," he wrote, "but it is by no means a bitter one. Yes, there are a lot of illiterate people in Russia, indeed there is a lot of what is described as 'barbarism.' *That is our good fortune and no cause for sorrow!* Don't throw up your hands in horror, I beg of you! My point is only that our illiterate peasants, more than we ourselves, preserve the national character, without which it will be impossible to build an original civilization."[24]

The admonition not to get upset is apposite. In fact, "Literacy and National Character" is more measured and considerably less confrontational than the study of Apollon Grigoriev and cleaves more consistently to the Pochvenniki ideal of the reconciliation of the classes. Its core thesis is that their very lack of education had preserved the peasantry from the creeping Europeanization which had robbed the educated classes of their national identity. Significantly, Leontiev argues for the first time here that this was true not only in Russia but, drawing directly on his experiences in the European provinces of Turkey, in every society where the native intelligentsia came into contact with European ideas. "In the East," he claimed, "the educated classes *lack all idealism, whether personal, religious, philosophical or poetic.*"[25] By contrast the peasantry had everywhere preserved the national character, and to the extent that serfdom and the peasant commune (*obshchina*), its post-emancipation successor, had helped to immunize the common people against infection from the West they were to be applauded as the cornerstone of Russia's rural and administrative life.

The new Russia of the emancipation had, Leontiev concluded, grown organically from the old and represented a "union of autocracy and the commune." This outcome might mean *"bloody revolution"* in the West; for Russia it was the cherished ideal of *"monarchy and the faith of our forefathers"* (such a union of autocracy and commun-ism is an early instance of an idea which will bulk large in Leontiev's later writing).[26] In the face of pressure to adopt Western values, the salvation of Russia's national individuality lay for Leontiev in the harmonious synthesis of her conscious principles with the elemental attributes of the common people: *"If we are to accept what Europe offers us we must make every effort to transmute it within ourselves, in the way that a bee transmutes the nectar in a flower into a wax that does not exist outside its own body."* [27]

These quotes from "Literacy and National Character" and "Apollon Grigoriev" sufficiently illustrate Leontiev's debt to the Pochvenniki. Yet his association with that school was to prove brief enough and, like so much of his earlier writing, the theory of "reconciliation" was not to survive his spiritual crisis of 1871. Well before the onset of that cataclysm though his thoughts had been turning toward the search for a source of the spiritual discipline which would unite the disparate peoples of the Christian East and at the same time preserve them, and Russia herself, from what he regarded as contamination by western liberal ideology.

One possibility appeared to lie with Slavophilism. During his Pochvenniki period Leontiev had already begun to observe in himself "the green shoots of Slavophile inclinations." There were difficulties however. While Leontiev instinctively sympathized with the Slavophile point of view, he harbored reservations about their political program. In particular, he disliked their strong ethical stance on political questions and what he saw as their tendency to "impose their personal morality on the customs of our common people," an attitude he felt to be in its own way as potentially destructive to the future of Russia as that of the nihilists. [28]

In addition, by the time of Leontiev's sojourn on Athos the cultural Slavophilism of the 1840s, to which he was drawn, had been largely superseded by a political and racial Pan-Slavist movement which aimed ultimately to unite all the Slavic peoples then dispersed predominantly among the Ottoman and Austro-Hungarian empires in an Eastern federation under Russian hegemony. This change of direction and emphasis among Russian Slavists [29] was to have far-reaching consequences for Leontiev himself; in his various postings in Turkey-in-Europe he found himself located in precisely those areas which were of greatest significance to Russian Pan-Slavism and increasingly possessed of local knowledge denied to those who might perhaps be regarded as the abstract theorists of that movement.

This disparity of experience and point of view would eventually lead Leontiev into a head-on collision with the leading voices of Russian Pan-Slavism. For the present though this was some way off and the actual catalyst for Leontiev's thinking on the Eastern question was an obscure but fateful initiative taken by the Turkish government in response to the nationalist sentiment which had been growing among the Christian peoples of European Turkey through most of the nineteenth century, notably among the Greeks and Bulgars. Part of Greece had attained independent statehood in 1832, but the

Bulgarian diaspora was widely dispersed across the Balkans, with the result that by the 1860s Bulgar national feeling was focused less on geographic independence than on the establishment of an ethnic Bulgarian Orthodox Church free from domination by the Greek Patriarch in Constantinople and the Greek bishops appointed by him. Naturally, Greek opinion was wholly opposed to this aspiration.

In an attempt to break the deadlock, and exasperated at its inability over nearly ten years to reconcile the conflicting religious demands of the Greek and Bulgar populations within its jurisdiction, the Sublime Porte issued a decree in February 1870 establishing a Bulgarian Exarch, who would appoint, initially, thirteen Bulgarian bishops. Anxious to show even-handedness and appease Greek opinion the Porte further decreed that the Exarch should not assume the title of patriarch and would be subordinate to the Ecumenical Patriarch in Constantinople.

It is a feature of attempts at a compromise that they tend to aggravate rather than appease, and the decree of 1870 was no exception. The Patriarch of Constantinople entered a formal protest against the decree on the basis that canonical tradition did not provide for the overlap of two jurisdictions and that the civil authorities had trespassed on what was essentially a Church matter. A Council of the Orthodox Church held at Constantinople two years later formally indicted the Bulgarians of the heresy of *Phyletism*, or attempting to organize their faith on ethnic, rather than ecumenical, lines. Regardless of this the exarchate flourished and was eventually formally confirmed as the national Church after the Principality of Bulgaria was established following the Russo-Turkish War of 1877–78.

While these events were unfolding in Constantinople, Leontiev was in the throes of his spiritual crisis in Salonika and on Mount Athos. Foreseeing potential complications for Russia in the Greco-Bulgar dispute, however, and noting with dismay that the affair was going largely unnoticed in Russian intellectual circles, Leontiev accused his countrymen of letting their lamps go out like the foolish virgins in the parable and determined to enter the fray.[30] He could hardly do otherwise, as the issue of the Bulgar exarchate had come to encapsulate for him the very essence of the problem of the future course of development for the peoples of the Christian East and for Russia.

Leontiev's first intervention began in an uncharacteristically low key. Greek intellectual circles had long been suspicious that Pan-Slavist elements in Russia were fomenting religious discontent among the Bulgars, and certainly the interventionist policy pursued by Leontiev's chief in Constantinople, the Ambassador Nikolai Ignatiev, on behalf of the Christian peoples generally and the Bulgarians in particular, gave them some grounds for apprehension. Against

FIGURE 6. The tomb of Ali Pasha, the "Lion of Janina," modern Ioannina, Epirus, where Leontiev served as a consul in 1869.

this backdrop Leontiev's essay "Pan-Slavism and the Greeks" had, ostensibly at least, the dual aim of allaying this morbid fear of Pan-Slavism among the Greeks and of reconciling Russian public opinion, insofar as it was aware of the issue at all, to the apparent hostility to Russia displayed in the Greek Press. Thus we find Leontiev aiming at even-handedness toward Bulgars and Greeks alike, accusing both sides of "falling into the error of *Phyletism*, that is the intrusion of national issues into Church questions and the abuse of religion for political ends."[31]

Evidence that Leontiev's initial even-handedness in this dispute was genuine is provided by his sympathetic portrayal of a Bulgar monk, Father Parfeny, in his novel *Aspazia Lampridi* of 1870.[32] However he soon came to view this impartiality as "an error, and a foolish one." In later life Leontiev regarded his "unmasking" of the true intentions of the Bulgar nationalists as one of his most important achievements.[33]

Leontiev continued his attempt at peacemaking with some observations on Russia calculated to give Ignatiev (fortunately by the time of publication in 1873 his *former* boss) an attack of apoplexy. "Russia has never been a purely

Slav power," he assured the Greeks, "her western and eastern possessions, broadening and enriching her cultural spirit and her secular life, have constrained her Slavism in various ways." Seen in this light Pan-Slavism became as much of a danger to Russia as to Greece. "The formation of a unified and entirely pan-Slavic state would usher in the fall of the Russian Empire," he declared. "The coalescence of the Slavs into a single nation would herald the dissolution of Russia; confluence with the 'Slav streams' would drain the 'Russian Ocean.'"[34]

In the passages that follow these dramatic assertions, there emerges for the first time Leontiev's particular concepts of the nature of the state and of government. Racial homogeneity or "blood" plays little part in these, rather it is the formative idea that lies behind the outward appearance of the state which is all important to him, and in his view this "idea" lies beyond the domain of human emotion. By way of example he considers the notion of pacifism: "There are humane people, but humane governments do not exist. Humanity may dwell in the heart of this or the other ruler, but nations and governments are supra-human organisms. Organisms indeed they are, but of a different order; they are ideas made incarnate in particular social organizations. The idea does not have a humane heart. Ideas are inexorable and cruel for they are nothing other than the clearly or dimly understood laws of nature and history. *L'hommes'agite, mais Dieu le mène* (Man proposes but God disposes)."[35]

The influence of Hegel is very apparent here, notably his view of "the individual state as self-referencing organism . . . i.e. the unfolding of the idea to its particularities," from which it follows that "the wellbeing of a state has a completely different validity to the wellbeing of an individual."[36] And two fundamental components of Leontiev's political outlook are plainly evident in the above quote on pacifism: organicism and determinism. For Leontiev the state, culture, and the whole of history are to be explained in terms of an organic development actuated by specific inner laws that give expression to a determining idea and which lie above and beyond the will of the individual. It follows that from his perspective "no amount of pacifism and no amount of ingenuity and determination can guarantee to alter, in its essentials, the course of historical destiny."[37]

What then is the "idea" that would inform the greater Slav state so feared by the Greeks? The answer, replies Leontiev, is that there is *no* common idea that might unite the Slav peoples in the way in which, for example, the German people had recently been united. "The Germans are a nation," he declares, "the Slavs are a tribe, differentiated into individual nations by language, customs, past history and hopes for the future. The Germans were able to unite in a single federal state (État confédéré). The Slavs would be at best a confederation of different states (Confédération d'États)."[38] And such a union of fundamentally different nations without a common, unifying "idea" would, in Leontiev's view, contain within itself the seeds of constant discord and strife: "A union of this kind might show considerable unanimity in response to external pressure or conflict with Western interests. But can it be guaranteed that it will always be unanimous at bottom? Each of the nations will have its own particular interests in which it will diverge from the others, and especially from Russia."[39]

Whatever the Pan-Slavists might aim at, and in apparent defiance of Russia's Eastern policy since at least the time of Catherine, Leontiev insisted that it had never been the aim of Russia herself to seek the downfall of Turkey-in-Europe, an eventuality he argued would be in no one's interest since the existence of Ottoman rule simultaneously protected the Greeks from Pan-Slavism and the Bulgars from Pan-Hellenism. "Writing these lines I do not in any way desire the fall of Turkey," Leontiev declared. "On the contrary, as I will try to show, we need Turkey, she is necessary to us all, Russians, Bulgars and Greeks alike. It seems to me that in certain circumstances she might even become our most natural and reliable ally."[40]

By these "certain circumstances" Leontiev had in mind chiefly the existential threat posed to the Orthodox Christian East by Austro-German encroachment from the North and West, which he felt must sooner or later unite Russians, Turks, and Greeks in a climactic struggle for cultural survival. In the face of such a menace, Leontiev saw no contradiction in a union of Orthodox Christians and Mohammedan Turks, for the Ottomans were no threat to the cultural ideals of their Christian subjects, however much they might exploit them economically and oppress them politically. As he recalls a Bulgar acquaintance putting it: "Germany with her higher civilization, founded in Christianity, can cause us much greater spiritual harm than the Turks ever could. A great religious gulf divides us from the Turks. They may cause us material harm, but what of it! You have to put up with some inconveniences for the greater good."[41]

In "Pan-Slavism and the Greeks" we can see in embryo the essential elements of Leontiev's mature political thought: a deterministic view of historical development and the rise and fall of nations and cultures as an organic process independent of the human will; the crucial importance to a culture of a central unifying "idea" which can allow for and bind together the greatest possible variety in its expression; and the insistence that racial homogeneity, "blood," is not in itself a sufficiently unifying factor, which must be sought rather in the spiritual than in the physical sphere.

Leontiev expands on these ideas in the 1873 essay "Pan-Slavism on Athos." Here he repeats his assertion that both Greeks and Bulgars had been wrong to pervert their faith to national political ends and that the latter had more to gain by cultivating the Porte than by hatching Pan-Slavist conspiracies. He describes the severe difficulties in which the monks of the Russian monastery of Saint Panteleimon found themselves as a result of the Pan-Slavist hysteria which gripped the Greek laity following the celebration of the Bulgar Exarchate liturgy on 6 January 1872. All this political discord was entirely alien to Athos, Leontiev insisted, as Athos was an ascetic, spiritual community which had but little to do with the affairs of this world and certainly eschewed all national interest: "The majority of its inhabitants, Russians, Greeks and Bulgars alike, live as they have always lived, their life is specifically that of Athos, not Russian, not Greek, not Bulgar."[42]

For Leontiev it was its multinational ethos that prevented the Holy Mountain from coming under the sway of any particular national grouping, a feature of the monastic community which he believed must be preserved at all costs, even if this meant the maintenance of Turkish power over the peninsular. "By a strange constellation of political events," he wrote, "the real interests of Orthodoxy (spiritual, not political) are closely linked to the continued rule of the Muslim state. The power of the descendant of the Prophet is now the guarantee of preservation and independence for Christian asceticism . . . The political power of the Turks, religious subordination to the universal Greek Patriarch, enduring financial assistance from Russia, this is the threefold dependency which contains in itself the surest pledge of inner freedom for the Holy Mountain."[43]

A great variety of expression, but always subject to the single unifying "idea." This is Leontiev's conception of Athos, and it is a conception that is central to his social and political views in the wider sphere as well. In his eyes the great enemy of "unity in variety" was ethno-nationalism, and it was from this curse in particular that he would have the monastic community escape. "National exclusivity," he wrote, "it matters not whether Russian, Greek or Bulgar, would destroy the life of Athos and deprive her of her reason for existence."[44] Should the Ottoman state finally crumble and the cohesion provided by Turkish power be lost, there was only one answer in Leontiev's eyes, the application of the only viable alternative source of stability, as given poetic expression in his novel *Aspazia Lampridi* by Khristaki Lampridi, a representative of the Greek trading plutocracy in Epirus. "It is only the two-headed eagle," declares Lampridi, "that can shelter under his wings and reconcile the cross of Hellas and the moon of Islam. Only Russia can answer for the Greeks to the Turks and for the Turks to the Greeks."[45]

One of the minor characters in *Odysseus Polichroniades* sees no limits to the unifying potential of Russia: "It seems to me that Russia can hold sway over the Muslims, the Orthodox, the Buddhists and the followers of Confucius" declares the merchant-adventurer Deli-Petro (madcap Peter). "There may be a huge preordination of historical destiny in this. We've seen Count Amursky, there will be a Count Transamursky, there will be a Count Brahmaputrsky."[46] The time was not yet ripe for Russia to assume the role of protector, however, and Leontiev concludes these first forays into the complexities of the Eastern question by counseling caution in Russia's policy in the Balkans: "A *gradual, cautious* nurturing of those Greeks and Southern Slavs in the domains of the Sultan, fostering of good relations with the Turks and with more or less all Eastern Christians, especially in the event of a threat appearing from the West."[47] He also makes an urgent appeal to the Greeks not to despise the link of faith, rather than blood, which existed between Greece and Holy Russia, as the latter would always support all her Orthodox brethren and be "the staunchest friend of *legitimate Hellenism.*"[48]

By *legitimate* Hellenism Leontiev meant of course not Greek nationalism but support for the Greek Orthodox Patriarch as a buttress against the toils into which he believed Western civilization had fallen and which were now threatening to engulf the Ottoman lands. As he has Akiviad Aspreas, the hero of *Aspazia Lampridi,* recognize, the antidote to pan-Hellene nationalism and to the debased Europeanism of much of the Balkan bourgeoisie lies in the words of his own father: "All political wisdom, all farsightedness, the whole history of the struggle between the East and Europe, was contained in the simple words of this ancient patrician: 'We bow our heads before the Greco-Russian Church, my son.'"[49]

CHAPTER 6

The Social Organism

In his famous work *From the Other Shore* the Russian thinker and political writer Alexander Herzen threw down a challenge to his contemporaries: "Of course, the laws of historical development do not contradict the laws of logic, but neither do they correspond in their pathways to the pathways of thought, just as nothing in nature corresponds to the abstract norms constructed by pure reason. Knowing this, shouldn't we be striving toward the study and discovery of these physiological influences? But do we do this? Has anyone seriously investigated the physiology of social existence or approached history as a genuinely objective science? Nobody, not the conservatives, nor the radicals, nor the philosophers, nor the historians."[1]

We have seen from "Pan-Slavism and the Greeks" that Leontiev viewed peoples and nations as supra-human organisms possessing features akin to those of organisms in the natural world. It is not improbable that in constructing his major socio-political treatises of the 1870s Leontiev believed he was rising to Herzen's challenge. He does not specifically refer to the passage quoted above, but he was clearly well acquainted with the *Other Shore* since his work is peppered with references to what he regarded as Herzen's post-1848 repudiation of the European ideal of "progress."

Perhaps the best and most detailed example of this occurs in a letter to Iosif Fudel' of July 1888 in which Leontiev asserts that Herzen espoused an essentially "aesthetic" worldview that allowed him the freedom to attack in a fashion untrammeled by moralistic self-censorship the "shallow, gray and lifeless order of absolute equality" eulogized by Proudhon in his *Justice in the Revolution and in the Church*.[2] As we have seen from Milkeyev's declamations in *A Place of One's Own*, and from his own verbal clash with Piotrovsky, Leontiev's view of the human condition was fundamentally aesthetic, seeing beauty as the "chief measure of things" and the "only reliable yardstick," and his detection of similar values in Herzen greatly enhanced his regard for a man whose radical leanings made them anything but natural bedfellows.

At this point a word is necessary on Leontiev's sources. Leontiev tends toward an extreme eclecticism in his use of authorities, and one finds scattered through the pages of his works a galaxy of thinkers and writers, sociologists, historians, political essayists and novelists, of every complexion and point of view. As authorities on Byzantine history, we find François Guizot and Augustin Thierry rubbing shoulders with Dmitry Rostovsky, while in the political sphere, among many others, Thomas Carlyle, John Stuart Mill, and Wilhelm von Humboldt vie with Proudhon, Charles Fourier, and Étienne Cabet. Typical of his method is the first of his *Letters from Athos* of 1872 where he describes his writing table bearing simultaneously volumes by Proudhon, King David, Byron, John of Damascus, Goethe, Khomyakov, and Herzen.[3] (It is interesting that, apart from Herzen and Apollon Grigoriev, Leontiev hardly ever looks to contemporary Russian writers. For example, his thought runs parallel to Dostoevsky's in many respects, but he hardly refers to him except late in life. This is perhaps indicative of the essential European-ness of much of Leontiev's thinking, despite his anti-European rhetoric.)

Notwithstanding his impressive array of sources, Leontiev was at best an indifferent scholar, and his main works are considerably and sometimes glaringly under-researched. As he admitted in later years in a letter to Aleksandrov, in the context of German philosophy: "I do hate drudgery, my preference is to flit around the blossoms of someone else's mind, and the German language is not made for flitting . . . it requires you to be an 'honest toiler,' which is something alien to my frivolous nature and my habits, though in extremis I suppose I could read the original works in German."[4]

Thus the many expressions and turns of phrase Leontiev borrows from his multifarious sources have the advantage, or defect, depending on one's point of view, of lending his works a greater semblance of academic rigor than they actually possess. And it cannot be said that this eclecticism worked in general as a forming influence on his thought at a deep level. The notion of "flitting," butterfly-like, around the heavy tomes of philosophy and social history is a favorite motif with Leontiev and one of the most important keys to understanding his thought processes. His strength was as a fearless and original

thinker rather than a painstaking researcher, and with one or two notable exceptions it is clear that from each of the authors he quotes he uses only that
which supports his particular thesis and, as we have seen with Belinsky's aesthetics, discards or ignores anything which seems to argue in the opposite
direction. As he himself put it: "Although I'm not wholly incapable of comprehending abstractions I very quickly tire of that *toilsome and alien weightiness
and interminableness* into which philosophy drags me. For the most part I just
flit through the pages of philosophy books, although my flitting has its own
hidden agenda . . . I am *seeking* when I flit."[5]

Leontiev's aversion to excessive academic toil was well known to his contemporaries. His service colleague Gubastov, who knew him well, declared
that "he lacked bureaucratic capability, staying power and appetite for work."[6]
And Strakhov, who as we have seen harbored reservations about Leontiev as
a man, believed that intellectual laziness contributed to his lack of public success. "His thoughts were a cat's cradle," Strakhov wrote to Rozanov, "he had
talent, taste and education but he lacked spiritual purity and the faculty for
conscientious work."[7]

One particular exception to this practice of "flitting" was that Leontiev
came early on, even if possibly largely at second hand, under the powerful and
enduring influence of the German idealist philosophers, Schelling, Fichte and,
above all, Hegel.[8] Strakhov expressly linked Leontiev's organicism and theory
of historical development to Schelling and Hegel, and there can be no doubt
that Leontiev was acquainted with Hegel's thought, at least in its basic con-
figuration, as a young man.[9] The protagonists of two of his early novels are
expressly described as disciples of Hegel: the radical aesthete Milkeyev from
A Place of One's Own of 1864, who derived much of his radical thinking from
Hegel and Leibniz; and the young official of German extraction, Gersfeld, in
"Second Marriage" of 1860. And the structure of Leontiev's works of fiction,
including the long novels *Podlipki* and *A Place of One's Own*, is decidedly dialectical, with the action proceeding from an initial clash of opposites toward
the final resolution on a higher plane.

In "Pan-Slavism and the Greeks" we saw Leontiev subscribing to Hegel's
view that individuals and states are on the one hand conscious of their individual aims and interests but on the other subject to historical processes over
which they have no power, being even unaware of the wider perspective, a
diagnosis that clearly suited his inherently deterministic bent and provided a
theoretical framework for his view of historical development. It is an outlook
intriguingly reminiscent of Tolstoy's theory of history, as expounded in *War
and Peace*, as a chain of events the causality of which is so extensive as to be
beyond the grasp of the players, such as Napoleon, who are called upon to

enact its effects. Leontiev first came across *War and* Peace in Tulcea on the Danube in 1867 or 1868, some four or five years before the appearance of "Pan-Slavism and the Greeks," and read it avidly,[10] so it is not impossible that his theory of history may have been influenced by Tolstoy's. There is no direct evidence for this in Leontiev's writing however—Tolstoy's historiography plays no role, for example, in his discussion of *War and Peace* in Leontiev's acclaimed study "Analysis, Style and Tendency" of 1889–90—so it is probably safest to regard it as another example of the convergent evolution we saw in our discussion of Nietzsche. Leontiev was trained as a doctor and spent two and a half years on the Shatilov estate in the Crimea and with the Rozens in Nizhny Novgorod Province where he was able to devote his considerable spare time to an intensive study of literature, the natural sciences, and philosophy.[11] It seems probable that his own observations of nature and of society, superimposed onto the fundamental tenets of Hegel and the other German idealists with which he became acquainted at an early stage, were more than sufficient to plant the seed of his view of societies and cultures as organic entities developing along predetermined lines.

Having once come to regard society as an organism, subject to malign influences in the same way as organisms in the natural world are subject to infection and disease, Leontiev quickly concluded from his own personal observations of Russia and the Christian East that the gravest danger to the health of the social organisms in those places was the seemingly unstoppable rise of the Westernized bourgeoisie, "wise as serpents but no doves."[12] In search of an antidote to this menace, he turned for consolation and support to a veritable pantheon of writers who seemed to him to harbor similar reservations about the course of nineteenth-century "progress." Thus he makes free use not only of Herzen but also, among others, of John Stuart Mill's warning against the rise of "collective mediocrity" and the "tyranny of numbers" in democratic government, and Alexis de Tocqueville's analysis of the dangers inherent in the universal drive toward egalitarian rule.

At first sight it appears paradoxical that Leontiev, the confirmed monarchist, should make common cause with Herzen, the great opponent of autocracy, or with Mill or de Tocqueville. The latter were primarily passionately concerned with human freedom and their critique of bourgeois society was informed by what they saw as the threat to freedom posed by the processes of leveling and indifferentiation demanded by the new industrial age. But like them Leontiev perceived the rise of the bourgeoisie as a threat, although for him the threat was of a different kind, a threat to the maintenance and preservation of human culture. Leontiev is indifferent to individual "juridical" freedom, or to be more exact he identifies it as precisely the prime mover of the bourgeois worldview, an outlook which in his eyes must, paradoxically, result in its exact opposite, universal tyranny, with the additional defect that it will have destroyed culture in the process. Leontiev is in this respect more logical than these libertarian thinkers who, viewed from his cultural standpoint, were seeking a cure in what was the source of infection. It is for this reason that, notwithstanding that he described Mill as "the greatest among contemporary writers,"[13] he repeatedly refers to him in particular as "illogical" and "inconsequential" in his positive conclusions, however incisive he might have been as a critic of contemporary trends.[14]

Unlike many of Leontiev's other "sources," whom he drew on liberally as supporting evidence for conclusions he had already reached, it is certain that Herzen also exercised a considerable influence on the development of his ideas. For one thing, Herzen's writing on history is deeply permeated by just that "organicism," which would later characterize Leontiev's own. Society is for Herzen, as for Leontiev, an organism and like all organic life subject to the processes of change and decay. Herzen's pose is often that of a doctor examining the ills that afflict the social organism; as such he adopts the role of dispassionate observer and diagnostician, exactly the role Leontiev, a doctor by training, was to assume for himself. And after 1848 Herzen's diagnosis for Europe and for Russia was not encouraging. "Russia," he wrote, "seeing Europe vanquished and writhing in the dust, is herself sweating at every pore that poison of which she has already drunk deep and which will destroy her. She will fall apart and decay from the same cause. I don't know if even God himself has a remedy for this universal disintegration."[15]

Characteristically, Leontiev sees Herzen's rejection of the bourgeois ideal as an *aesthetic* reaction: "This ideal is so utterly simplistic, unpoetic, dry, coarse and gray, that Alexander Ivanovich Herzen, a *genuine* Moscow nobleman, refined in taste, an idealist by upbringing, had no option but to turn away in disgust."[16] Leontiev referred to Herzen (following the latter's hint) as "a Janus, with his best face turned back toward the *old Russia of gentry and peasants,* not toward democratic revolution."[17] What he may have had in mind by the reference to Janus was that, from his point of view, Herzen was indecisive in not bringing himself to see that rejection of the European bourgeoisie could lead to positive results. Like Leontiev, Herzen had largely come to believe that the great European culture to which he still adhered was now doomed but, unlike him, in the face of imminent dissolution Herzen had adopted a quietist stance. Akin to the pagan philosophers before the onset of the Christian era he chose, instead of hopeless struggle, a dignified withdrawal and passive contemplation of the tragedy in the hope that a bright new day might eventually dawn for future generations "on the other shore." In his doctor role, Herzen's advice to his contemporaries was not to attempt to cure the terminal illness of a moribund society but to take their cue elsewhere. "What does a priest do at the bedside of a dying man?" he asked. "He doesn't try to cure him, he doesn't excite him to delirium, he reads him the last rites, accords him extreme unction."[18]

Leontiev, by contrast, was not prepared to abandon the search for a cure and made it his business to seek out the remedies that God might have available if only they could be discovered. To this end he adopts and adapts many of Herzen's formulae: his passionate condemnation of the European bourgeoisie; his laments about the degenerate condition of modern Europe; his attacks on the intelligentsia for their condemnation of the common people for not living up to the idea the former had invented for them. For the Leontiev of the late 1860s and early 1870s, seeking a framework within which to express his own contempt for the modern European, certain of Herzen's more radical and far-reaching conclusions must have been truly inspirational, as when the latter declares that: "the petty proprietor is the worst bourgeois of all," or: "if the proletariat were a bit better off they wouldn't give a fig for communism," or "the notion that man is born free and is everywhere in chains— what nonsense!"[19]

For all the differences of outlook that existed between Leontiev and Herzen, the two men therefore had more in common than might at first glance be supposed, both of them warning Cassandra-like against the apparently inexorable rise of the petty bourgeois ethos and its stultifying effects on the once-mighty civilization of Europe. Unlike Herzen though, Leontiev was too aware of his debt to the great edifice of European civilization to stand by and watch its destruction without attempting to intervene; and as a Russian concerned with the future of his motherland he was a hundred times less inclined to play the passive spectator. Which brings us to the point at which, bearing in mind Leontiev's debt to Hegel and to Herzen, we can turn to an examination of his magnum opus *Byzantinism and Slavdom*.

Leontiev's political testament is relatively concise for a work of its type and the age in which it appeared, running to less than a hundred and fifty pages in his collected works, yet it contains in distilled form the bulk of his mature thought on social and cultural issues. He claimed to have worked out the central thesis in the autumn of 1871 on his way, as he thought, "to die" on Athos,[20] while the bulk of the work seems to have been completed in 1873 while he was living on Halki.[21] The controversial essay was rejected by Katkov for publication in *Russkii Vestnik* and only saw the light of day in 1875 in the obscure journal *Chteniia v Imperatorskom obshchestve istorii i drevnostei Rossiiskikh pri Moskovskom universitete* (*Proceedings of the Imperial Society for History and Russian Antiquities*). Katkov's reasons for rejecting the work are not entirely clear. The politician in him may simply have woken up, following his publication of "Pan-Slavism and the Greeks" and "Pan-Slavism on Athos" to the fact that Leontiev's ideas were not entirely consonant with his own on the question of Russian policy in the Balkans (as Dostoevsky, for one, realized was the case).[22] Or else Katkov the astute entrepreneur may have been influenced by the publication four years earlier of Nikolai Danilevsky's *Russia and Europe*, which treats of similar themes. Either way, his reaction on receipt of Leontiev's manuscript was dismissive: "One can ramble on about this sort of thing till the cows come home."[23]

Katkov's discouragement notwithstanding, and despite its small size and arcane provenance, *Byzantinism and Slavdom* caused a furore amid Slavist circles in Moscow and began a controversy over its author's exact place in the history of Russian thought that has lasted to this day. The work is divided into twelve chapters and may be characterized as having two aims, one general, which is the development of a theory of history, of the rise and fall of political and social systems, of "cultures"; and one particular, the application of the lessons of this theory to Russia, with reference to her European "rivals" and to her Slav and Orthodox brethren.

In 1887, as part of a campaign to obtain an enhanced pension following his second retirement from government service,[24] Leontiev epitomized the aims of *Byzantinism and Slavdom* in the following condensed terms:

> The essence of the author's view is that the *democratisation of society is nothing less than the beginning of its decline and fall; that liberal egalitarianism has already destroyed beyond recall whole cultural worlds; and that after the onset of a leveling of rights and the reduction to a single type of all particular conditions of persons only those states can survive for any length of time which contain within themselves the possibility of a re-stratification of society and where beyond their borders there is the potential for expansion and the conquest of new lands which are original in terms of customs and of spirit.*[25]

These ideas clearly need a considerable degree of unpacking, and perhaps the best place to begin is in chapters 6 and 7 which, despite their position in the middle of the book, offer a natural starting point as they develop the notion of the organic nature of cultural systems we have already come across in "Pan-Slavism and the Greeks." They were also the opening chapters of Leontiev's original working manuscript *Progress and Development*, largely worked out while he was staying at the Zograf Monastery on Athos in 1871. Still believing himself to be of their party, Leontiev was anxious that this theoretical component of *Byzantinism and Slavdom* should be disseminated in Slavophile circles as quickly as possible.[26]

Chapter 6, "What Is Meant by Progress?," begins with a critique of the term *razvitie*, which in Russian covers the ideas of "progress" and "development." Leontiev notes that the word *razvitie* is often used loosely to describe a number of activities which might more accurately be styled "diffusion" or "spread": "The *spread* of drunkenness, the *spread* of cholera, the spread of morality, of sobriety, of politeness, the spread of railways, and so forth." Whatever these processes may be, for Leontiev they are not "progress" in the true meaning of the word. "In the exact sciences," he declares, "from which it was transferred into the historical sphere, the idea of progress or development properly corresponds to a *particular complex process*, a process, be it observed, which is *frequently diametrically opposed to the process of spreading, of diffusion*, a process as it were hostile to the latter."[27]

The notion of development, Leontiev continues, was originally taken from organic nature, where it signifies: "*A gradual ascent from simple to more complex forms,* a gradual individualization and *segregation, on the one hand, from the surrounding environment; on the other from similar and related organisms, from all similar and related phenomena* . . . a gradual movement away from achromatism, *away from simplicity and toward individuality and complexity* . . . a gradual elaboration of the component parts, an *increase in their inner diversity* and at the same time a *strengthening of their unity*."[28]

Properly understood, Leontiev continues, development in the natural world corresponds to the life process, which demonstrates the principle of "unity in variety" to the greatest possible degree: "Thus the *highest level of development*, not only in organic bodies, but in all organic phenomena, means *the highest degree of complexity bound together by some form of inner and despotically unifying constraint*."[29] For Leontiev everything that can be viewed as an organism is subject to this force: "Not only whole organisms, but *all organic processes*, and each and every *part of an organism*, in a word, all organic phenomena are subject to this law."[30]

The foregoing definition of "progress/development" is so central to Leontiev's conception of the historical process that we must dwell on it at some length. By way of illustration he takes an example from his medical background and describes how the illness pneumonia gradually "progresses" from simple initial symptoms common to many illnesses until it achieves the maximum degree of complexity and individual differentiation, following which one of two things may happen. It either subsides into a new simplicity and disappears; or else the sufferer dies, and in dying gradually loses the features which marked him out from his fellows, subsiding first into the quasi-anonymity of a dying man, then into the greater anonymity of a corpse, until finally the physical elements of his body dissolve and fuse chemically with the soil and all trace of the individual disappears.[31]

This last phase of the process, the "freeing" of the constituent parts from the "constraining idea" that held them together is one to which Leontiev devotes particular attention: "Before the final demise individualization weakens, of the parts as well as the whole. The dying man becomes less clearly defined, more a part of the things around him, more akin to other cases related to his own, which is to say *more free.*"[32] More free, that is, of the "idea" in which his individuality was bound: it is in this light that, for Leontiev, the concept of "progress," much vaunted by the positivists and materialists, is to be judged: "*The complexity of the unfolding of the progressive process* is similar to the *complexity of some horrid pathological process*, step by step leading the *complex organism toward the secondary simplification of a corpse, of a skeleton, of dust.*"[33] (In passing, the irony of Leontiev's choosing the course of the illness pneumonia as his primary example of the undesirable pathological consequences of "progress" has not been lost on his commentators: in November 1891 he was to die of the illness at the Troitse-Sergiev Monastery near Moscow.)

Seen in this light, progress is a neutral term and can be good or bad according to the position of the organism in the cycle of birth, flowering, and death. And what is true of the individual, Leontiev continues, is true also of the higher unities, the species and the genus, which at their highest pitch of development all show the same maximum degree of variety bound together by a central unifying idea: "Everything is simple in the beginning, before becoming more complex, then simplifying for a second time, *initially leveling down inwardly and amalgamating,* then simplifying even more with a falling away of the individual elements leading to general disintegration and the transition to inorganic *Nirvana.*"[34]

This is the essence of what Leontiev called his "Triune Process," the discovery of the mechanics of which he counted as among his greatest achievements. He summarizes its three phases as: "a) the period of original simplicity; b) the period of flowering complexity; c) the period of *amalgamation,* the transition to secondary simplicity, to decay and replacement by other things."[35]

Applied to natural phenomena these ideas are perhaps relatively unexceptional, but Leontiev unhesitatingly goes one step further and applies the same deterministic formula to human social and cultural organisms: "On further reflection we find that this triune process is not confined solely to that world which is usually regarded as organic, but is possibly applicable to everything which exists in time and space . . . perhaps the works of man as well, for it can be seen clearly in the history of the development of the arts, in schools of painting, in musical and architectural styles, in philosophical systems, in the history of religion and, last but not least, *in the life of peoples, state organisms and whole cultural worlds."*[36] (A far-reaching contention perhaps, though it is interesting that in the mid-twentieth century the Russian-American sociologist Pitirim Sorokin, founder of the Harvard department of sociology, would make a heroic attempt to demonstrate the truth of it in his monumental work *Social and Cultural Dynamics* of 1937–41. Sorokin certainly knew of Leontiev, and the basic premises of his work are remarkably, though possibly coincidentally, similar to Leontiev's schema; it is not possible to say how far, if at all, he was stimulated to his effort by a reading of *Byzantinism and Slavdom*.)

In chapter 7, "On the Form of the State," Leontiev expounds on this idea, urging us to "regard peoples and nations, for clarity's sake, as instruments of ideas and causes."[37] And if states are subject to the triune process, Leontiev insists, then their development must be marked by a gradual unfolding of their particular state-form, followed by the gradual decline of this form into the homogenous mass of its surroundings. Thus a state, like an oak tree from its acorn, develops inexorably according to those inherent features which informed its fundamental nature right from its first appearance on the world-stage. For Leontiev this is the universal "expression of an inner and higher law of existence, as immutable as all the other laws of nature" and the only genuinely realistic view of human affairs.[38] *"Whoever wants to be a true realist where it matters,"* he maintains, *"must examine human societies from the same point of view."*[39]

In Leontiev's eyes, the prevailing ideology of the nineteenth century, the liberal belief in continuous "progress," accompanied with what he regarded as its humanistic posturing and a complete disregard for the organic nature of society, was not only an absurdity but the absolute negation of all cultural development. *"The liberal-egalitarian process,"* he declared, *"is the antithesis of the process of development* . . . its notion of progress, which is to struggle against every kind of constraint, whether that of class distinction, of corporate bodies, of monasteries, even of wealth, is *nothing other than the process of disintegration,* of that secondary *simplification of the whole* and the *amalgamation of the parts* of which I have spoken earlier."[40] Thus the rise of liberalism is equated by Leontiev with the decay of an organism, the loosening of the parts and their "liberation" from the unifying force of the whole, as in the thawing of ice or the disruption of the human system by a fatal infection such as cholera, or as Leontiev calls it: *"the triumphant cholera of democracy and universal welfare."*[41]

At the beginning of the life of a state, Leontiev argues, the social organism is comparatively simple, the predominant feature being the general freedom and equality of the parts. As the organism grows and approaches its period of "flowering complexity," power becomes vested in ever smaller numbers of these parts, and there is a gradual spread of inequality and differentiation of persons and classes, a process which is accompanied by a broadening and deepening of culture. "There is," he wrote, "an increase of wealth for some, of poverty for others, on the one hand the possibilities of satisfaction diversify, on the other this diversification and refinement (development) of feelings and demands gives rise to more suffering, more sorrow, more errors and more great deeds, more poetry and more humor."[42] It is at this point that the particular state-culture becomes most highly differentiated, most typical, and most itself: *"The governing form of every nation*, of every society, is entirely *its own*; it is unchangeable in its basic outline right up to its historical demise, although its constituent parts may change, slowly or faster, from the beginning until the end."[43]

Leontiev was fully aware that there existed widespread resistance to this view of human affairs as determined by an immutable quasi-organic process, but he attributed this to the obsession of his contemporaries with looking at all questions from the moral-humanist standpoint of freedom, equality and "welfare." He notes that such considerations are meaningless in nature and suggests, in the kind of trenchant language which was to bring him lasting notoriety, that they merely serve to furnish the social investigator with blinkers that make impartial observation impossible. "What have I to do," he asked, "in a more or less abstract investigation, not only with the inconveniences of others, but even with *inconveniences of my own*, with *my own suffering and groans*? . . . Suffering is present equally in the process of growth and development and in the process of decomposition. Pain is the natural condition of humankind."[44]

Accordingly, the social theorist, for Leontiev, is not concerned with either pleasure or pain; instead, he must seek to discover under what conditions a state or culture can achieve the optimum state of "flowering diversity." To this end he analyzes various cultures from the point of view of the basic "idea" that informed them and gave them durability, from ancient Egypt and Persia, through classical Greece and Rome, to modern European states. As long as their "idea" maintains its vitality, he finds, the cultural organism is preserved; once it is no longer strong enough to suppress the centrifugal impulse of the parts, the organism begins to disintegrate. In the case of modern Europe this weakening of the idea had coincided, during the last two hundred years, with the so-called Enlightenment, when *"the liberal and egalitarian process everywhere began to reveal itself."*[45]

Leontiev's verdict on contemporary Europe was intensely pessimistic. As was the case with previous civilizations, he argued, the fatal process of dissolution in Europe was being accompanied by a simplification of the social organism and a tendency to homogeneity among its parts—which didn't stop the parts regarding themselves, under the influence of the prevailing liberal philosophy, as on the high road to a new and better world. "These days (in the nineteenth century)," he declared, "they want to regard this fatal *disease* as the ideal of future *hygiene!*"[46]

It is all in vain: undifferentiated among themselves and "liberated" from the idea that gave their existence meaning, this atomized collection of individuals which was once a cultural whole is doomed to be swept away by the tide of history. It may perhaps be objected that Leontiev's thinking here is paradoxical in that it is both highly deterministic yet seems at the same time to make social coherence depend on the will of the component parts of the organism. There is more than a little truth in this, but as we have seen Leontiev is less concerned with maintaining internal consistency in his arguments, more with getting his message across, and if his thinking is marked by paradoxes there is no disputing the semantic power of the metaphors in which he expresses them: "The separate cells, fibers, tissues and members of the organism become stronger in their egalitarian impulses than the power of the internal regulating and constraining idea . . . the atoms of the globe no longer wish to form a globe! The cells and fibers of a cut and withering tree either *burn up or dry out* or rot away but *everywhere they renounce their individuality*, celebrating the *coming simplicity* of their organization and not noticing that this *indifferentiation* is the fearful moment of the transition to the *inorganic simplicity* of open water, of lifeless dust, of uncrystallized, liquefied or crumbled salts."[47] (Recalling Leontiev's debt to Hegel, it is interesting that the self-elevation of particularity over the interests of the whole, as in this example of the atoms of the globe no longer wishing to form a globe, constitutes for him the very definition of evil.)[48]

From Leontiev's point of view this process is not subject to ethical considerations, and if the observer has a moral choice to make at all, it is only this: while the social organism is growing to maturity, he must take a progressive stance and encourage the emergence of new forms and ideas; from such time as the point of maximum flowering is reached, he must shift to the side of conservatism and react against innovations which can only be destructive: "*Up to the moment of flowering* it is better to be a sail or steam boiler; after this *point of no return* has been reached one should become an anchor or brake for peoples rushing down the slippery slope."[49]

Here we have another iteration of the same paradox: the process of disintegration and decay of the organism is inevitable, in Leontiev's analysis, and the constituent parts in their blind rush for emancipation only serve to hasten the end, yet the onset of the final breakdown may, by the action of at least some of these same constituent parts, be slowed down. It is tempting to see this paradox as the outcome of a tendency visible in Leontiev's fiction, a desire to cut through difficult ethical problems but at the same time an inability to evade them. In the case of his fiction, the ethical knot is severed by the application of an overriding aesthetic criterion; in his theory of history, this is achieved by a rigorous determinism which admits of precious little room for moral action. However that may be, in the teeth of the remorseless internal logic of his system Leontiev held that retardation of the process of decay and secondary simplification *was* possible, that one might indeed become "an anchor or a brake."

How this might in practice be achieved was a question that was to occupy him for the remaining two decades of his life.

CHAPTER 7

Blood Is Not Enough

Chapters 6 and 7 of *Byzantinism and Slavdom* contain the essence of Leontiev's theory of the state and his view of the history of culture. Had the essay contained no more than this, it would be of limited significance, one more doom-laden prediction about the inevitable demise of Western liberalism, one more theory of the rise and fall of civilizations that so fascinated the nineteenth century, cobbled together from bits and pieces of German romanticism and Hegelian dialectics, strongly redolent of Auguste Comte's influential "law" of the three stages of social development, overlaid with a veneer of Schopenhauerian pessimism and legitimized by a host of metaphors taken from the natural sciences.[1]

Worse, had his book been taken more seriously in Moscow intellectual circles Leontiev might have been hard put to it to escape a charge of plagiarism. For he was by no means the only Russian in the 1860s to respond, consciously or unconsciously, to Herzen's challenge, cited earlier, to "seriously investigate the physiology of social existence and approach history as a genuinely objective science." In 1869 a treatise by an unknown author was published in the journal *Zaria* which was eventually to achieve international fame and for decades exert a profound influence on the development not only of Slavist and nationalist thought in Russia but of the academic discipline of historicism worldwide. This book was *Russia and Europe*, and the author Nikolai Yakovlevich Danilevsky, known ever since as the man who brought science to Slavophilism.

The principal aim of *Russia and Europe* is, as its subtitle suggests, an examination of *the Slavic World's Political and Cultural Relations with the Germano-Roman West*. Danilevsky by no means confines himself to the relations between Slavdom and the West, however, but like Leontiev expounds a fully fledged historicist view of human social and political development from the time of the ancient Greeks and Egyptians to the unification of Germany by Bismarck, which was in full swing at the time of writing.

At least at one level, that of style and readability, it would be hard to imagine two books ostensibly about the same subject as dissimilar as *Russia and Europe* and *Byzantinism and Slavdom*. Where Leontiev's essay is incisive, paradoxical, and highly entertaining (and can be read as much as a work of literature as a political treatise), Danilevsky's great work, five times its length and much better researched, comes across to the modern reader as something of an overblown and pretentious tract. Nonetheless, it has to be said that there is little in Leontiev's theories of the state and historical development, and in his attitude toward the West, which is not foreshadowed in *Russia and Europe*, which he first read in 1869 while he was consul in Ioannina in Epirus. Given that Leontiev admitted to developing *Byzantinism and Slavdom* between 1871 and 1873 it is difficult to escape the conclusion that, to put it mildly, he borrowed heavily from Danilevsky in constructing the socio-historical framework for his own work.

Recent commentators in Russia have tried hard to exonerate Leontiev from the charge of plagiarism. Olga Fetisenko cites A. V. Yefremov's description of him as "an independent scholar" who took forward Danilevsky's ideas, and states that "the majority of contemporary scholars cleave to the notion of parallel development."[2] If by "parallel development" is meant "convergent evolution" of the kind we have seen with reference to Nietzsche and Tolstoy and will see again with Herbert Spencer and Lev Tikhomirov, then the present writer must demur. Leontiev may have been thinking along similar lines to Danilevsky in general terms before he came across *Russia and Europe*. Indeed, Stanislav Khatuntsev has pointed out that the organic process of growth, flowering, and decay that forms the basis of Leontiev's "triune theory" is foreshadowed in his essay "From the Danube" of 1867, two years before he became acquainted with Danilevsky's work.[3] But this isolated example (of an apple progressing from original green simplicity through flowering diversity to secondary uniformity of decay) is a long way from a fully worked out theory of the rise and fall of peoples and cultures, and the textual similarities between many areas of Leontiev's magnum opus and his predecessor's are so close as to make it difficult to accept that the one was not taken out of the other.

Upon publication *Byzantinism and Slavdom* received only one review, a fairly lukewarm appraisal by Strakhov in *Russkii Mir* in May 1876. In his letter to Rozanov of 21 May 1891 Strakhov suggests that Leontiev took his basic ideas from Danilevsky as well as from Schelling and Hegel. "Take a look at *Russia and Europe*," he tells Rozanov, "Chapter Six, 'The Relationship of the National to the Universally Human.' Leontiev is very gifted and stylish, though his tastes are a bit perverse, but he has no ideas of his own, in the strict sense of the word idea, none." As this extract tends to confirm, Strakhov may have been influenced by extraneous matters discussed above.[4] Stanislav Khatuntsev, by contrast, cites the German physiologist and botanist Karl Gustav Karus (1789– 1869) and the Russian medieval historian T. N. Granovsky (1813–55, interestingly a follower of Hegel and noted Westernizer) as especially influential in the development of Leontiev's theory.[5]

If indeed Leontiev had worked up his triune theory to an advanced stage of development before he first read *Russia and Europe* in 1869, then it must have come as a considerable and rather unpleasant shock to discover that another had got in first with a book containing virtually the same ideas. We get a hint of his reaction in a letter he wrote to Strakhov in March 1870 where Leontiev claims that an "unnamed gentleman" in Petersburg had commiserated with him that his ideas had appeared in another's book before he had a chance to publish them himself.[6] This claim has a rather hollow ring to it, although the possibility of Leontiev and Danilevsky contemporaneously arriving at similar conclusions on the evolution of societies and cultures does have a striking precedent in Charles Darwin and Alfred Russel Wallace independently reaching similar conclusions a decade earlier regarding natural selection in the animal and vegetable kingdoms. The theory of evolution was clearly "in the air" in the mid-nineteenth century, and all four men had a background in the natural sciences.[7]

Fetisenko would seem to be on firmer ground when she cites the view of R. A. Gogolev that "Leontiev only 'utilized' the intellectual framework of *Russia and Europe* in an attempt, at bottom, to express his own ideas," a view that aligns precisely with Leontiev's general way of working. She is also clearly right when she cites Yefremov's observation that Leontiev was alone among Danilevsky's contemporaries to see the deficiencies in his notion of Slavdom.[8] The "utilization" was extensive, but that Leontiev "developed" Danilevsky's ideas is beyond dispute; it was his unique contribution to Russian thought, and it brought him considerable grief.

Many points of similarity exist between the ideas in Danilevsky's magnum opus and those in Leontiev's but mention of only a few of them is needed to bring the latter's debt to *Russia and Europe* into sharp relief. Danilevsky, too, viewed the state or "cultural type" as a supra-individual organism, and his work is thickly strewn, as is Leontiev's, with biological, especially botanical, metaphors. For Danilevsky, as for Leontiev, the state is subject to organic change, growth, and decay, which leads naturally to his viewing of cultural development and historical change as a living process. "Geology and paleontology show us," wrote Danilevsky, "how for different types, species and genera of living creatures there is a time of germination, of maximum development, of gradual decline, and finally complete disappearance . . . History says the same about peoples, they too are born, attain different levels of development, age and become senile, and die."[9]

From ideas like these Danilevsky developed a theory of the rise, change, and fall of "cultural types," which preceded Leontiev's triune process by several years and, apart from being somewhat looser in form (reflecting its author's penchant for verbosity), is in essence identical to it. Danilevsky sees the social organism, much as Leontiev did, as consisting in numerous parts held together by a central unifying force or "idea": "The development of cultural-historical types . . . reaches the greatest fullness, power, and magnificence in a certain relationship between the demands of unity and the diversity of the constituent elements."[10]

The weakening of this unifying idea through decay—Danilevsky calls it "ferment"—that is, progress in the Western liberal sense, leads inexorably to dissolution. "All fermentation is dissolution," declares Danilevsky, "that is, transformation from complex forms of organized matter into more simple forms approximating to inorganic forms of amalgamation . . . Where there is ferment there is the dissolution of forms, whether of material aggregations or of the life of societies. In order for a new organic form to arise from such dissolution into disparate elements the presence of a formative principle is essential, under the influence of which the elements can come together in a new whole endowed with an inner vitalizing idea."[11] If this "idea" loses its unifying vitality, the parts are "liberated" from the whole and the organism of the state or culture sinks into death and decay.

This organic view of society is not the only point of resemblance between Danilevsky and Leontiev however. A second close similarity is their deterministic, anti-millenarian view of the historical process as unfolding without a final purpose and without regard to the well-being of humanity. As Danilevsky put it: "Nations have a historical instinct which leads them in directions they do not comprehend; in its main outlines history is beyond the disposition of man, although to man is reserved the execution of its designs."[12]

For both Danilevsky and Leontiev the state organism is by its nature bound to space and time and may only realize itself in these two dimensions, rendering idle any consideration of final goals in history. From this flows logically the conscious resistance of both thinkers to all attempts to burden the study of history with moral imperatives and to subject the working of nature to what they considered the meaningless abstractions of "universal humanity" and "eternal progress," or as Danilevsky's puts it: "to cloud one's reason with absurd humanitarian nonsense which doesn't even possess the dignity of sincerity and impartiality."[13] Leontiev wholeheartedly agreed. "The state psycho-mechanism, so to speak," he wrote, "cannot be guided simply by 'moral' considerations or predilections, the actions and reactions in the natural struggle between nations must be founded as little as possible on personal sympathies and enthusiasms, even those of whole multitudes of people."[14]

In the optimistic atmosphere of the mid-nineteenth century this was thinking on cold and inaccessible heights which few were willing or able to scale. It took the cataclysmic upheavals of the twentieth century for Danilevsky's work to escape the narrow confines of Moscow Slavism and bring its influence to bear internationally on the likes of Oswald Spengler, author of the influential treatise *Decline of the West* (1918–22), and Pitirim Sorokin. For Leontiev it brought with it an opprobrium that endured for well over a century. It is a stern and unbending reasoning from cause to effect which, coupled with the rejection of secular teleology, seems to foreshadow *Beyond Good and Evil* and Nietzsche's "new philosophers," in his words "searchers to the point of savagery, reaching with bold fingers for the ungraspable, sharpening their teeth and exercising their guts on the most indigestible nutriments, ready for anything that calls for acumen and sharp senses . . . prepared to venture all."[15]

For Leontiev, the appearance of *Russia and Europe* was a defining moment in the development of his political thought. His niece Marya Vladimirovna recalled in her memoirs that in Ioannina in 1869: "Uncle read it himself and then made me read it aloud to myself. He found almost everything in it to be the truth."[16] It was a debt Leontiev was always ready to acknowledge. As he wrote some years later:

There is one man who, though not recognized by every Slavophile as one of their own, set out the essence of the Slavophile worldview more clearly than any of the devotees of that doctrine. His name is *Nikolai Yakovlevich Danilevsky*. He wrote only one book, but that book, *Russia and Europe*, revealed for the first time that true Slavophilism is not *simple Pan-Slavism* and not *love for the Slavs* at all costs, but the aspiration for an *original culture* (whether achieved by love or force, despotism or liberty matters not), the aspiration for a *distinctive civilization* (not modeled on Europe), which will swallow and digest Europeanism in the same way that Europe swallowed and digested the ancient Roman, Greek and Byzantine civilizations. In essence, Danilevsky is the *living interpreter* and *freethinking pupil* of Kireyevsky and Khomyakov; compared to him these older Slavophiles were simply forerunners.[17]

A rather glowing assessment, but one needs to be careful about accepting it at face value, for Leontiev is being more than a little disingenuous. His description of Danilevsky's thesis in this passage is a deliberate reinterpretation made to distance him as far as possible from racial Pan-Slavism and to place him in what Leontiev still believed to be the mainstream of cultural Slavophilism. Danilevsky, as Leontiev well knew, was at least as close to the doctrine of racial Slavism as he was to Leontiev's program of cultural renewal, if not more so. And although Leontiev was heavily influenced by Danilevsky, he believed that in his predecessor's adherence to the doctrine of racial Slavism he had discovered a fundamental defect in his reasoning which, if allowed to go unchecked, might have fatal consequences for the future of Russia. He felt it his bounden duty, in the name of Holy Russia and of the older, cultural Slavophilism to which he believed he owed allegiance, to expose this flaw while there was still time to apply a corrective. In so doing Leontiev set a course that would lead to social and political ostracism in his homeland but at the same time redeem *Byzantinism and Slavdom* as a social and political treatise of the first importance and ensure his place in the history of Russian thought.

Danilevsky unswervingly insists that the only reliable basis on which a distinctive historically determined culture may develop is that of racial and linguistic affinity, which he regards as "the root principle on which the state must be founded" and "the highest political principle."[18] For Danilevsky, as for Leontiev, the state is an organism, and an organism can only flourish if it contains within itself a "life-giving idea." But it is fundamental to Danilevsky's analysis that "by this formative, unifying, life-giving and life-saving idea of the state we can have only nationality in mind," in other words, "the ethnographic principle which is really the only lasting foundation of the state system; it alone gives it true meaning and significance."[19]

Danilevsky accordingly looks forward to the creation of an "all-Slavic federation with Russia at its head and its capital at Czargrad, the sole rational and considered solution to the great historical problem which has come to be known as the Eastern Question . . . because it alone provides the solid ground which will allow the original development of a politically independent, outwardly strong, inwardly diverse, Slavic cultural-historical type."[20] In Danilevsky's eyes this union of related but independent peoples under Russian hegemony will both guarantee the long-delayed flowering of the Slav cultural type and provide a bulwark against what he sees as an aggressive crusade on the part of the Romano-German world to become the sole and universal culture, a crusade which aims at the reduction of humankind into a "single humanity which is emptying out all its content."[21]

"And so," Danilevsky concludes, "for every Slav: Russian, Czech, Serb, Croat, Slovene, Slovak, Bulgar (and I would like to say Pole)—following God and His Holy Church—the idea of Slavdom must be the highest idea, above freedom, above science, above enlightenment, above every earthly good, since not one of these can be obtained without it, that is without a spiritually, nationally, and politically independent and distinct Slavdom."[22]

For Leontiev this was Danilevsky's fundamental error. However much he owed to Danilevsky for providing the framework within which he could crystallize the thoughts he had been developing during his time in the Christian East, Leontiev's conclusions were different, both about the nature of the Eastern Federation and about the kind of unifying idea needed to keep it together. This clash of values is foreshadowed in Leontiev's earlier works, especially "Pan-Slavism and the Greeks," but to appreciate just how different from orthodox Slavism his views had become, we need to turn to the first two chapters of *Byzantinism and Slavdom*, where the key to Leontiev's concept of the "idea" which he believed had once informed, and must inform again, the Russian state-culture lies in the chapter headings: "Ancient Byzantinism" and "Byzantinism in Russia."

"What is Byzantinism?" Leontiev asks at the outset of chapter 1, and then goes on to give the answer: "Byzantinism is a particular kind of civilization or culture possessing its own distinguishing features, defining principles which are common, clear, sharply defined and comprehensible, and having a specific historical aftermath."[23] He then defines the basic characteristics of Byzantinism: autocracy, Orthodox Christianity, a pessimistic morality based on a rejection of "exaggerated" individualism and the hope of creating a paradise on this earth, and its own inimitable notions of aesthetics. The period of Byzantine culture proper Leontiev defines as lasting from Constantine the Great (r. 306 to 337) to Charlemagne (r. 768 to 814), after whose reign the West formed its own unique and initially feudal Romano-German culture while Byzantium gradually declined until "the fifteenth, sixteenth and seventeenth centuries saw the full flowering of European civilization and the complete eclipse of the Byzantine state on just that soil where it was born and nurtured."[24]

FIGURE 7.   Konstantin Leontiev, ca. 1880, aged about fifty.

The final sentence is key to Leontiev's argument. Byzantine culture may have been all but extinguished by the Turk in the former Eastern empire, yet it was just this Byzantine culture, flowing west after the fall of Constantinople and uniting with the already highly developed Romano-German culture, which helped Europe achieve the brilliant period which goes under the name of the Renaissance, a misnomer in Leontiev's view. According to his classification, this was precisely the period of that flowering complexity which is the high-water mark of every culture: *"The epoch of profound and many-faceted development, bound together by the highest spiritual and temporal unity of the whole and the parts."*[25]

Unlike Western Europe, Leontiev argues, Russia did not achieve her cultural peak at that time, for whereas Western society was highly advanced before her injection of Byzantine culture, Russia had only just started to emerge from her subjugation to the Mongols, which lasted from the thirteenth to the late fifteenth century, the period known as the "Tatar Yoke." On the virgin soil of Russia, the Byzantine principle did not simply act as a catalyst; it became the Russian principle. For the beginning of the Russian "renaissance" or period of flowering complexity Leontiev suggests that one must look to the end of the seventeenth century and the reign of Peter, when Byzantine culture began to come again to Russia refashioned in the likeness of Europe; in other words, with the emphasis on its classical Roman, juridical, side to the detriment of its religious element. The synthesis of these two versions of Byzantinism, Leontiev continues, initially sparked off the Russian cultural flowering, but since Peter this new tide of "Europeanized" Byzantinism from the West had become a flood, bringing with it the grave danger that it might entirely displace the original "pure" Byzantinism which had become naturalized in Russia. For Leontiev this process was already dangerously far advanced, although he felt it improbable that it would ever succeed in completely eradicating the "true" Byzantinism which had set its roots deep in the Russian psyche and the Russian soul." It is all too clear," he warned nonetheless, "that Russia is very quickly losing her Byzantine face."[26]

The Byzantine principle, Leontiev continues, was heavily indebted to Classical Rome for the idea of "Caesarism," the state embodied in one all-powerful figurehead. Yet this alone could not explain the durability of the Byzantine system; there was something else at work, the principle of the coalescence of Caesarism and Christianity in the anointed Orthodox emperors. In Leontiev's view this synthesis of the material and the spiritual, aided by the discipline engendered by the bureaucracy established under Diocletian, gave Byzantium a stability in the whole, however erratic in the individual, that was unprecedented in history, a stability which enabled her to outlive her Western sister by more than a millennium. "With the accession of the Christian emperors," Leontiev declared, "to the new bureaucratic authority was added another, incomparably greater mechanism of social discipline, the power of the Church, the authority and privileges of the episcopacy. Ancient Rome did not possess this resource; she did not have this privileged sacerdotal caste. This new and extraordinarily beneficial medium of discipline first arose in Christian Byzantium."[27]

It was this fusion of Roman Caesarism and Orthodox Christianity, imbuing Byzantium with such power of endurance, that in Leontiev's eyes gave Russia the strength to endure and finally shake off both the Tatar yoke and Polish incursions, and later on to repel the Swedes and survive the ordeal of 1812. This Russian "Caesarism," coupled with the limitless facility of Russians to subject themselves to its authority, was for Leontiev the great pillar of its social edifice, which Russia had inherited directly from Byzantium: "Our own Caesarism, which has been for us so fruitful and redemptive, consolidated under the influence of Orthodoxy, under the influence of Byzantine ideals, of Byzantine culture."[28]

In summary, "Byzantinism" is held up by Leontiev as carrying the "idea" on which the Russian state-organism depends and without which, like all such "organisms," it would cease to exist as a coherent whole. Typically, he expresses this in a biological metaphor: "The Byzantine spirit, Byzantine principles and influences, like the complex web of a nervous system, permeate the whole of the Great-Russian social organism."[29] This was Leontiev's Rubicon. It was with this insistence on the essentially spiritual nature of the "idea" which informed the Russian state that he was led inexorably to part company with those who held that race or "blood" is sufficient grounding for the state and its cultural identity.

In the eyes of orthodox Pan-Slavism this elevation of Byzantinism to the place of the Slav bloodline as the ideal principle of the Russian state was simple heresy. Danilevsky does acknowledge, as he could hardly fail to do, that by adopting the Orthodox faith the Slavs, and specifically the Russians, had assumed the mantle of Byzantium: "The empire of Philip [of Macedon] and Constantine was reborn on the wide plains of Russia . . . in the restoration by Ivan the Great, Ivan the Terrible, Peter the Great and Catherine the Great of the Eastern Roman Empire of the Slavic nationality."[30] He also rather grudgingly accepts that, for simple reasons of geography, and future Slav federation will contain non-Slavic peoples, the Greeks and Romanians. Yet for Danilevsky this is as far as it goes. Byzantium fails to appear among the ten cultural types he identifies as constituting the core of world history (a fact Leontiev was never able to comprehend). Further, it was a central tenet of Danilevsky's theory of history that "the political forms produced by one people are suitable and beneficial only to that people and cannot be suitable and beneficial to another people."[31] Therefore any attempt, such as that undertaken by Peter, to graft onto the "Russian rootstock" by attaching foreign principles of a foreign civilization to the Slavic tribes generally and to Russia specifically must be just as unsuccessful as all other such attempts: if it produced anything at all, it produced noxious outgrowths of Westernization.[32] In Danilevsky's view the future Slav cultural flowering would be, like all previous flowerings in world history, essentially "autochthonous"; that is, it would arise as and of itself from the ethnological material inherent in the Slav race. An example of this was the Russian commune (*obshchina*), "by historical right ours, as sacred and inviolable as any other form of property."[33] For Danilevsky there was no need for Russia or Slavdom to look to foreign examples: "We have material in abundance and all by ourselves are organically taking shape under the influence of inherent founding principles, with no need for any fanciful blueprints."[34]

For the Pan-Slavists, to whom Danilevsky had assumed the dimensions of a prophet or seer, by suggesting that the basis of the Russian state and the future Slav federation should be Byzantinism rather than ethnic Slavism, Leontiev was proposing just such a "fanciful blueprint," an unnecessary, Quixotic, and doomed attempt to transfer the principles that informed one people and one civilization onto another. On this his central thesis Danilevsky is firm from beginning to end: blood and blood alone will count and "peoples that are not connected by racial affinity cannot form a lasting federation."[35]

Typically, Leontiev responds to this assertion in a way that neither seeks quarter nor gives any. "What is a people without its system of religious and social ideals?" he demands to know. "Why should one love it? For blood? But blood, remember, is on the one hand seldom pure, and God knows whose blood you are loving when you suppose you are loving your neighbor's. But what is pure blood anyway? Spiritual sterility! All the great nations have very mixed blood . . . To love a people as a people - an affectation and a lie."[36] And what was true of community of blood was for Leontiev true also of community of language: "Language? But what exactly is language? Language is precious particularly as the expression of our closest and dearest ideas and feelings. The splendid *anti-European* aphorisms of Herzen writing in French produce a *more Russian* impression than the "progressive" Petersburg press writing in their native tongue."[37]

It is difficult to believe that Leontiev could not have known that in denying the primacy of linguistic and racial affinity as the basis for the "idea" informing a civilization or culture, he was making a direct attack on the holiest tenets of Russian Slavism. Indeed, it has been a matter of dispute ever since whether he should be regarded as belonging to the Slavophile camp at all. Yet Leontiev considered himself and his doctrine of Byzantinism as being the true inheritance of the Slavophiles of the 1840s. He believed that his experiences in the East had given him a unique insight into the true nature and condition of the Southern Slavs, an insight denied to those Slavophiles who might perhaps be described as armchair theorists and to academic researchers like Danilevsky whose personal acquaintance with the non-Russian Slav peoples was limited or nonexistent. And with this insight came a burning need to warn his contemporaries of the fearful mistake he believed they were making in courting the Slavs without regard to the degree to which their Slav-ness had been supplanted by Western liberal ideas.

For Leontiev, nationalism, which was the inevitable outcome of a social theory based on racial or linguistic affinity, meant the exact opposite of cultural diversity.

> The idea of nationalism is nothing else than that liberal democracy that has long been laboring over the ruins of the great cultural communities of the West . . . Equality of persons, equality of classes, equality (i.e. monotony) of provinces, of nations—all this is one and the same process . . . The idea of purely racial nationalism in the form in which it appears in the nineteenth century is in essence a fully cosmopolitan idea, inimical to the state, inimical to religion, possessing considerable destructive, and no creative, power, incapable of forming a cultural nation, for culture is nothing other than individuality and individuality is today everywhere dying pre-eminently from political freedom. Individualism is killing individuality, of people, of regions, of nations.[38]

If there were any doubt about Leontiev's relevance for our time then surely it would be laid to rest by this impassioned denunciation of a process which now goes by the name of *globalization*. But where did it leave the Slavs? At the beginning of *Byzantinism and Slavdom*, immediately after ascribing to Byzantinism a high degree of organization, Leontiev describes "Slavism," challengingly, as the absolute opposite, as "a sphinx, a riddle . . . a kind of amorphous, elemental, unorganized vision, similar to those large faraway clouds you see which, depending on your distance from them, you can take to represent the most diverse things."[39] It is to clearing up this riddle that he turns his mind in the third, fourth and fifth chapters under the heading "What sort of thing is Slavism?"

The short answer to this question, for Leontiev, was that there was no answer. Unlike Western Europe, where there was a common cultural heritage of a distinctly "European" kind, there was nothing about the Slav group of peoples that might provide the crucial underlying "idea" which would imbue the notion of "Slavism" with meaning. "Slavism can only be understood as an ethnographic, a tribal, abstraction," he wrote, "as the concept of common blood (though not altogether pure) and related languages."[40] In other words, the only things the Slavs had in common were those Leontiev had just dismissed as meaningless from the cultural standpoint.

Of all the Slavs it was the Bulgars who most concerned Leontiev. In Bulgar "Phyletism," in what he regarded as their perversion of religion for nationalist ends, as well as in the minds of Russian Bulgarophiles, Leontiev saw the horrid spectacle of a people locked in a struggle to the death with its own "idea," the results of which were potentially disastrous for Russia too. "For the *first time since the very beginning* of our history," he wrote (as he was later to emphasize when he met the leading Pan-Slavist Ivan Aksakov face to face), "the Bulgar question has caused the two forces which make up the Russian idea of the state, ethnic Slavdom and ecclesiastic Orthodoxy, to come into conflict in the heart of a Russian."[41]

Leontiev feared that if left unresolved this conflict posed an existential threat to the cultural future of Slavdom. "The might of Russia is indispensable to the existence of the Slav peoples," he argued. "Byzantinism is indispensable to the strength of Russia. Whoever shakes the authority of Byzantinism is undermining, possibly without realizing it, the foundations of Russian power. Whoever fights against Byzantinism fights indirectly, and without realizing it, against the whole of Slavdom, for what is racial Slavdom without theoretical Slavism?"[42] As far as Leontiev could see no other powerful principle of discipline was to be found among the widely dispersed Slav peoples; like it or not, for good or ill, the Byzantine principle was for him the only trustworthy pillar of security not only for Russia but for the whole of Slavdom.

The danger to Russia was therefore clear and present. "The closer to us peoples are by blood and tongue," Leontiev insisted, "the more we need to keep them at a safe remove while maintaining our contacts with them. Our ideal ought to be, not union, but gravitational pull from a calculated distance."[43] As things stood, Leontiev suggested, a Slav federation based on racial affinity could only be a vehicle for spreading Western liberal notions which the Slav peoples had already half digested, and this at the time that Western liberalism was digging its own grave by willfully ignoring the laws of "progress" which were discernible in the natural world but which did not accord with the new "religion of eudaemonism," the doctrine of universal welfare that had become the great new faith of modern man. But whether Europe continued on the path of slow indifferentiation and became a bourgeois federation, or simply dissolved into anarchy and chaos, either way Russia would need all her strength to resist being drawn after. To this end Russia must husband those sources from which her strength grew, Byzantine Orthodoxy and social discipline. "One way or another," Leontiev wrote, "Russia will need her inner strength; vigor in organization, vigorousness of spiritual discipline."[44] Russia should therefore stand fast against the infection of new Europeanism and hold herself in readiness for the defense of the old European ideals to which she owed a genuine and profound debt: *"To preserve all that is old in order to merge it organically with the unavoidable new."*[45]

Leontiev concludes *Byzantinism and Slavdom* by driving this message home, appropriately, with a biological metaphor. "It is not the foreign enemy," he warns, "on whom we continually turn our frowning gaze, which is dangerous to us, it is not the strong and impetuous rival, casting in our face the bloody gauntlet of ancient enmity . . . it is not the German, the Frenchman or the Pole, half brother, half adversary . . . more terrible than them all is our close brother, our younger and apparently defenseless brother, *if he is infected* with that fatal condition which may, through negligence on our part, prove lethal for us as well."[46]

"Danilevsky," wrote Leontiev, "gives us a solid foundation in Orthodoxy, Autocracy and the peasant commune. But he doesn't forbid us from building on this foundation *in our own way.*"[47] The way in which Leontiev chose to build on Danilevsky's foundation was to lead to the second great crisis of his career, his rupture with Pan-Slavism. Yet to the end of his days Leontiev believed himself to be not the antagonist of Danilevsky but his collaborator and the developer of his ideas. In 1888, three years before his death, he wrote the essay "Vladimir Solovyev versus Danilevsky," a spirited defense of his mentor against Solovyev's criticisms. In this essay he refers to *Russia and Europe* as the "catechism of Slavophilism" and styles the older Slavophiles as "mere dreamers" compared to Danilevsky and his "scientific" approach.[48] He excuses Danilevsky's liberalism as natural in a "man of the 1840s" and, his continued disagreement with the racial basis of Danilevsky's Slavdom notwithstanding, emphasizes the latter's great merit in having devised a scientific basis for the development of the Slav cultural type. Coming from a man who by that time had endured fifteen years of isolation, rejection, and vilification from those very circles most sympathetic to Danilevsky's views this was a generous tribute indeed.

CHAPTER 8

The Tide of History

"Those who cannot remember the past," so runs the famous aphorism of the philosopher George Santayana, "are condemned to repeat it." If there is truth in this statement, and it seems intuitively unlikely that a study of history will give us *no* instruction about the human condition which might help us avoid repeating past mistakes, then it is difficult to escape the conclusion that there are patterns in the historical record which may, with diligence, be discernible to human intelligence and which will furnish us with both an explanation of past events and, perhaps, a guide as to the future course of history. Many thinkers, of varying degrees of mental acuity, have attempted to isolate these patterns and draw conclusions from them, thus contributing to the academic discipline which became known as historicism, the search for explanations for the rise and fall of civilizations and cultures in the past and, building on those insights, for guidance about their rise and fall in years to come.

Historicism reached its zenith in the late nineteenth and early twentieth centuries, the apex being perhaps Oswald Spengler's famous work *The Decline of the West*, but in recent times it has had an increasingly bad press and now finds itself, if not entirely discredited, at least considerably out of fashion. Indelibly linked with the name of its most famous exponent, Karl Marx, it has shared in the eclipse of the now widely ridiculed Marxian doctrine of the historical inevitability of the triumph of the proletarian revolution. Even before the collapse of communism however thinkers such as Isaiah Berlin and Karl Popper were making devastating assaults from both the logical and the moral standpoint on the propensity of historicism to fall into a deterministic view of human affairs which diminishes or even eliminates the possibility of moral choice and the exercise of free will and tends to justify evil and suffering as part of the "inevitable" course of historical development.[1]

Leontiev counted himself very definitely among the disciples of historicism. We have seen that his approach to history is markedly deterministic and that he owes a considerable debt in this both to Danilevsky and to Hegel, that most deterministic of thinkers whose dialectics are visible beneath the surface of most if not all historicist systems. In particular, Leontiev took from Hegel (and Leibniz) the notion that everything that exists is rational and used it as the means of justifying the inevitability of evil in the world and of reducing the significance of moral choice in human affairs, thus falling neatly into the critique of historicism put forward by Berlin nearly a century later. Yet Leontiev would have given such criticisms short shrift. He believed firmly in what he styled "prophecy via common-historical induction" and held that the science of history "cannot confine itself to explanations of the past, it has to provide definite forecasts of the future, even if that means the very near future."[2]

Of course the ghastly results of historicist determinism in the twentieth century make the criticisms of Popper, Berlin, and others all too comprehensible and they excite our instinctive sympathy. But Leontiev was using Hegelian quietism for a *reason*. He was concerned above all with identifying the conditions under which human culture could achieve its greatest possible flowering, as in fifth-century Greece or the European Renaissance, and he had established to his own satisfaction that the world-improving humanist and socialist doctrines which appeared to be gaining ground everywhere in Europe in the mid-nineteenth century represented the absolute negation of any possibility of the emergence and development of high culture. If the world, and in particular Russia, were not to collapse into a stultifying, if materially comfortable, uniformity, this process must be stopped, and if possible reversed, and if not that then at least slowed down. Desperate times require desperate measures, and for Leontiev the times were indeed desperate.

The first seven chapters of *Byzantinism and Slavdom* we have examined so far contain the essence of Leontiev's theory of history and of the rise and fall of states and cultures and also his doctrine that the salvation of Russia and Slavdom must be a return to the principles of Byzantinism. It is perhaps a pity that he did not stop there. This, his greatest essay, is primarily an attempt to articulate a feeling about the conditions that are necessary for the health of a culture and what weaknesses bring about its decline, and such an attempt is bound to bring about a general theory. His mistake is then to implicate this general theory in particular instances. The remaining chapters, "On the Longevity of States," "On the Growth of European States," and "A Comparison of Europe with the States of Antiquity," measure the theory against the known historical facts and extrapolate the best means of ensuring the survival of the Russian state and the "true" Slav culture after Western liberalism had come to grief. As such they serve mainly to highlight the contradictions inherent in any deterministic theory of history, especially one that not only explains what has been but also predicts what is to come. In one sense, as an interventionist political essayist with an apocalyptic sense of the abyss confronting his homeland, Leontiev was bound to make the attempt, but in doing so he gave his multitude of critics, then and since, the comparatively easy task of exposing the inevitable paradoxes in his ideas.[3]

It is not difficult to construct a critique of these ideas. Obviously, the validity of Leontiev's—and Danilevsky's—chief methodological approach, the drawing of deductions about human society from an examination of biological processes, is questionable. Notable critics of Leontiev's historicism have included Nikolai Berdyaev in his *Sub specie aeternitatis* of 1907; the philosopher P. E. Astafyev; the liberal historian Pavel Milyukov; the theologian Vladimir Solovyev; and the philosopher and theologian Sergei Nikolaevich Trubetskoy.[4] (Ironically, the post-1917 essay by a Berdyaev presumably chastened by events is a much more objective and less hostile study and still one of the best introductions to Leontiev's thought.)[5]

Further, as we noted in connection with his use of sources, Leontiev's procedure is highly selective and he has a marked tendency simply to ignore data incompatible with his main argument. Nonetheless, if his theory is shown to be defective in particular ways, by the same token his critics have surely erred in the opposite direction by attacking him in detail while ignoring the overall significance of his thought. Leontiev was all too aware that this was likely to happen, as he noted in a letter of 1879 to a female friend: "Byron wrote even more inconsistently in particulars, but then that was in a poetic age! People knew then how to comprehend the spirit of the times, they placed more value on the reflection of reality in the soul of a chosen individual than on reality itself."[6]

In brief, Leontiev reviews the great cultures of history and concludes that it is difficult, if not impossible, for the life of a state to exceed 1,200 years. Even here though he is forced to concede that China and Egypt constitute apparent exceptions, exceptions he finds it impossible to reconcile with his theory. Undeterred, he states that, although the culture produced by a state may outlive the demise of that state, "in general" the state as such, as an independent organism, cannot last longer than twelve centuries. The significance of this figure may be seen when Leontiev fixes the rise of the modern European states from the time of Charlemagne, that is from the ninth century; thus Europe, after achieving crystallization in the Middle Ages and cultural flowering in the Renaissance, is fast approaching the fatal threshold beyond which she may not go.

The apparent parallel between the position of modern "egalitarian" Europe and the "period of decline" of all state cultures, especially those of classical Greece and Rome, is a constant theme with Leontiev in this essay, in which all too obvious doubts about his methodology and conclusions need to be set off against the expressive force of the imagery he deploys to frame them. "Flowering diversity," for example, implies harmony, but for Leontiev this does not mean an absence of rivalry, rather the contrary: "Harmony does not mean peaceful agreement, but a pregnant and fruitful, if at times violent, conflict."[7] That such a concept of harmony should not disintegrate into anarchy requires a unifying force, and he accordingly sees the hallmark of the Renaissance as "a lavishness of substance, constrained by diverse forms of despotic discipline."[8] (For an example of such lavishness without a sufficiency of constraining discipline, he directs the reader's attention toward the disintegrating Ottoman Empire.)

Leontiev regards contemporary Europe, facing her incipient decline, as no longer able to tolerate formal discipline; it is the European individual, the "bourgeois everyman," who must reign supreme and unconstrained: "Organization is hardship, is constraint, we no longer want constraint, we no longer want elaborate organization!"[9] At a superficial level nineteenth-century Europe might appear to be a tremendously complex society, but for Leontiev this is only skin deep, masking the uniformity of striving which lies beneath. "The methods of egalitarian progress are complex," he insists, "but the goal is crudely simple in its conception, in its ideal, in its influence, and so on. The goal is simply the average human being, the peaceful bourgeois among millions of equally average and peaceful people exactly like him."[10]

Whether or not he convinced others, Leontiev seems genuinely to have convinced himself that his 1,200 years limit for the life of a state-culture was correct, with many states not even achieving the millennium. This, combined with the view that Russia was not so young as certain Slavophiles believed—she had by the time he was writing (1873) already existed 1,011 years since Rurik built his settlement near Novgorod, or 885 years since the conversion of Vladimir—imbues his prose with a markedly apocalyptic flavor. It also leads him to seek a way of avoiding imminent disaster, which he finds all the more inevitable as his study of history has taught him that simple conservative reaction to the process of democratic fusion and secondary simplification is doomed to failure. His solution lies in the revitalization of the organism of the state by the assimilation of fresh cultural material from abroad. Citing the examples of the British and ancient Roman empires he concludes that: "The conquest of undeveloped peoples is the only salvation once the process of secondary simplification has set in."[11]

One of the cultures that fascinated Leontiev was that of ancient Iran. He was particularly struck by the way in which the Persian Empire had been able to renew itself after its conquest by Alexander. He attributed this capacity for renewal to three things: the assimilation of fresh blood from abroad in the shape of the Parthians; the vigor of the Zoroastrian religion; and the fact that the Persian state-form was a monarchy supported by a hereditary aristocracy, which Leontiev held to be the most durable of all political systems. "Precisely those societies have proved historically more fruitful and more powerful than the rest," he wrote, "in which, cleaving to the monarchical principle, the native aristocracy endured most steadfastly."[12] Under the right circumstances, Leontiev believed, an absolute monarchy could through the acquisition of fresh cultural material arrest the process of "secondary fusion," even at quite an advanced stage.

Leontiev admitted that he possessed limited data about the successive Persian empires and modern historians would doubtless find his method of lumping them together crude. Since his main criterion for the state-cultural "idea" is a spiritual one however, the continuity of the Zoroastrian faith in Iran until the Muslim conquest would seem to lend some support to his thesis. Yet regardless of the extent to which his analysis was grounded in romantic supposition, his vision of the multinational, highly variegated, durable, and self-renewing Persian Empire, united in the person of the all-powerful and semi-divine emperor, seems to have caught Leontiev's imagination as a possible blueprint for the Eastern Orthodox culture of the future. But where to look for the "fresh cultural acquisition" that might slow or even stop the dissolution ushered in by the spread of liberalism and make cultural renewal in the Christian East a real possibility? For Leontiev this could mean only one thing: the acquisition by Russia of Constantinople, "Czargrad," the semi-mythical entity that combined in itself the cultural heritage of "New Rome" and the strategic advantage of controlling the outlet from the Black Sea into the Mediterranean. The need for Russia to obtain this city as a center for cultural renewal was to become something of an idée fixe for Leontiev during the next decade. It was to have formed the second part of *Byzantinism and Slavdom*, but this never materialized. Instead, the second major crisis of Leontiev's middle years intervened: his disastrous collision with the Moscow Slavists.

In the spring of 1874, with *Byzantinism and Slavdom* still in manuscript form, financial exigency compelled Leontiev to leave the Bosphorus and return to Moscow to regularize his journalistic work for Katkov. The real sadness Leontiev felt at having to abandon his beloved Constantinople, coupled with the necessity of undertaking journalistic work, which he called "the scullery, worse, the drains, the watercloset of literature," was offset by his keen anticipation at the prospect of a meeting in Moscow with the doyen of "second generation" Slavophilism, Ivan Aksakov.[13] At that time Leontiev considered himself "a disciple of Khomyakov and an adherent of Danilevsky" and was convinced that he and Aksakov were both firmly in the same camp.[14] He anticipated a comradely exchange of views, as he recalled in his autobiographical reminiscences: "I needed a reality check. I had been living and thinking so long in remote provinces of Turkey that nearly all my conclusions about the Slavs, Europe, and the East had matured independently and unaided. I even lacked a sufficiency of books, and there was no possibility whatever of conversations and discussions with the leading figures of that doctrine among whose disciples I counted myself."[15]

By now Leontiev had been away from the centers of Russian, and especially Muscovite, intellectual life for a considerable time, since his first diplomatic posting to Crete in 1863. He had subsequently spent nearly all his time at Constantinople and various outstations in European Turkey and when he finally got back to Russia in 1874 he had been away for a total of eleven years, interrupted only by four months leave in 1868 which he spent in Petersburg. Yet Leontiev did not consider that his time of exile in the Ottoman domains had been wasted. Far from it, it had been midwife to the birth and development of his most cherished political ideals. In 1869 he had written from Ioannina in Epirus that "far from the Motherland I see her more clearly and appreciate her more highly . . . the land in which I am now living is especially adapted for me to grasp in its whole breadth the historical calling of Russia."[16]

This belief would bring momentous consequences in its train. As we have seen, Leontiev's experiences in the Christian East had convinced him, in direct opposition to Danilevsky, that there were two fundamental flaws in the Pan-Slavist agenda: their emphasis on the tie of blood, which in his view was too weak and unreliable to serve as the basis for a new Eastern Confederation; and what he regarded as their naive unawareness that the Southern Slavs, at least the leading educated classes among them, were already so far infected with Western values that in courting them, unless strict prophylactic measures were employed, Russia would be exposing herself directly to the selfsame virulent liberal contagion.

Once possessed of the conviction that he, and he alone, had discovered these dangerous weaknesses in the Pan-Slavist program, Leontiev felt it his duty to proclaim them to the world, and especially to the Slavists, not as an attack on Slavism but rather in an attempt to save it from succumbing to its own internal contradictions and ending in catastrophe. In so doing he was to suffer the fate that has befallen so many thinkers who have said the right thing at the wrong time: he was to be vilified, ostracized, and ignored. Yet he returned to Moscow in blissful ignorance of the reception that awaited him. Seeing himself in the role of a favored son returning from exile, he expected a warm welcome from the leading figures among the Pan-Slavists since he considered both them and himself to be the heirs of the "first generation" of Slavophiles. "I regarded the Slavophiles *as my fellows*," he wrote, "*as fathers, as noble elder relations*, who could not but rejoice to see their younger disciples advancing their teachings ever further, even when the actual course of advancement brought these disciples to unexpected conclusions, like mine for example."[17]

Unfortunately, during the eleven years Leontiev had spent deliberating with himself in his Turkish seclusion, the cultural and religious Slavophilism of Khomyakov and Kireyevsky had mutated into a militant political and racial Pan-Slavism of which Ivan Aksakov (1823–86) was a leading representative. Taking his words at face value Leontiev would appear not to have noticed this evolution. It would soon be made all too clear to him however, as the "unexpected conclusions" to which his solitary musings had brought him were not such as were likely to appeal to a man like Aksakov, for whom racial Slavism was the cornerstone of his political program.

It is a consistent feature of Leontiev's career that he appears to have been possessed of an alarming degree of naivety regarding the effect of his controversial views on a succession of sacred cows of the Russian intelligentsia of both liberal and conservative persuasions. A striking example of this is that despite his violent disagreement with Ignatiev, the Russian ambassador to the Ottoman Porte, on the occasion of his resignation from the service, Leontiev nonetheless appears to have considered dedicating *Byzantinism and Slavdom* to him and got as far as writing a draft in which he declared that Ignatiev would surely have nothing to do with that "simplistic and inept political Pan-Slavism of which people writing from afar with little understanding of the complexities of Slav and Eastern affairs regard you as the representative." It is not clear whether Leontiev had a blind spot here, or was merely being disingenuous, but such "political Pan-Slavism," whether or not simplistic and inept, was (as he should have known better than most) precisely Ignatiev's policy in the Slav provinces of Turkey.[18]

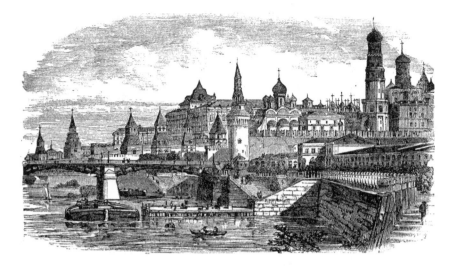

FIGURE 8.   A mid-nineteenth century view of the Kremlin and the Moscow River.

Thus it was with Aksakov as well. "It is not so much *the Slavs themselves* that are important for Slavophilism," Leontiev told him when they met at the Aksakov's house in Moscow, "it is what is in them that is specifically Slav and sets them apart from the West . . . the true Slavophile is bound to love, not the Slavs themselves, unconditionally and in *whatever state* he finds them, but that *special quality of cultural* Slavness."[19]

This "unexpected conclusion" held little appeal for Aksakov, who had played a pivotal role in the transformation of the Slavophilism of the 1840s into the Pan-Slavism of the 1860s and to whom the distinction Leontiev was attempting to draw between racial and cultural Slavism was essentially meaningless. At first sight indeed it appears extraordinary that Leontiev could have believed that these views would elicit a positive response in Pan-Slavist circles. When we recall his earlier approaches to the literary world of Petersburg, however, the matter appears in a different light. In both cases Leontiev seems to have believed that his message was consistent with, or rather a logical development of, the philosophical foundations on which his contemporaries were building, in the present case Slavophilism, in the former the aesthetics of Belinsky, but both having their roots in the 1840s.

Leontiev receives support here from Andrzey Walicki, who asserts in *The Slavophile Controversy* that his idealism was much closer to the aspirations of the original Slavophiles than were the political expediencies of Danilevsky and Aksakov, to say nothing of Katkov. Walicki notes that Aksakov had a foot in both camps, quoting his statement to the police in 1849 that "the greater part

of these Slavic peoples are already infected by the influence of barren Western liberalism which is contrary to the spirit of the Russian people and can
never be grafted onto it."[20] That Leontiev should have expected a warm welcome from the Aksakov of 1849 is accordingly understandable; that he should
not have noticed the changes of the intervening quarter of a century considerably less so.

Given Leontiev's preoccupation with Eastern affairs, however, is it not possible that he was being disingenuous when he claimed that he could not distinguish between the older Slavophiles and the direction of their Pan-Slavist
successors? Perhaps there is an element of disingenuousness here, but one of
the things that marks Leontiev out, in an age dominated by idealists and system builders of every hue, is that he was a consummate realist who, whenever a theory collided with reality, chose reality. Thus it was for Leontiev on
the question of Russia's relationship to the Slavs. As he told Aksakov:

> I have often thought that if it were possible to bring Khomyakov or
> Kireyevsky or your own brother back from the grave and ask them in
> all conscience what they would rather have: a merging of the Russians
> with the Southern Slavs and with it the final loss of the cultural indi-
> viduality which distinguishes us from the West; or a union, an associa-
> tion, some kind of blending even with the Turks, the Tibetans or the
> Hindus, precisely in order to create something particular of our own,
> something organic, under their influence, even if only indirectly, then I
> believe all the older Slavophiles would prefer these Asiatic peoples to the
> Slavs. *The importance lies in one's culture, not in the Slavs themselves.*[21]

All of this was anathema to Aksakov, and understandably so since Leontiev's firsthand and realistic assessment of the spiritual condition of the Southern Slavs constituted an attack on the former's idealized and sentimental
Slavism more deadly, coming from a supposed ally, than any assault from the
Westernizing camp could ever be. And in addition to their differences over Slavism, Leontiev's deterministic view of the relation of the individual to the
state organism appears to have offended Aksakov's essentially liberal political
orientation. "You completely annihilate the importance of the *individual*," Aksakov fulminated, "you leave out of account the free and private activities of
human beings. Your theory of development and secondary simplification is a
fatalistic process, despotic, inexorable . . . why should we strive for anything,
why write? You are Jeremiah, weeping over the ruins . . . To hell with the state
if it coerces and maltreats its citizens. Let it perish!"[22]

Leontiev's fatal interview with Aksakov took place at one of the latter's
Thursday evening "at homes" in company with Madame Aksakova and the

Slavophile prince V. A. Cherkassky. Leontiev was initially welcomed as the "Konstantinov" who had written the articles about Russia and the Greeks, but this was evidently insincere. He was subjected to what one might call a "polite grilling" and left apparently oblivious of what was to follow, even though Mme Aksakova had accused him of "defending iniquity," to which he retorted, "Yes, I prefer Jesuits to Liberals!"[23]

Not content with attacking Leontiev's political views, Aksakov became personally hostile and even defamatory, styling Leontiev a "fanatical Phanariot" (a reference to the Greek aristocracy of Constantinople, residents of the Phanar, modern Fener, district, from whom were drawn the Ecumenical Patriarchs of the Orthodox Church), a "slave of the Greeks," and "bringer of discredit on God."[24] He even went so far as to suggest that a personal disposition to sexual sadism lay behind Leontiev's often rigorous political doctrines.[25] Cruel and unjust as these allegations were, they had the effect of rendering Leontiev persona non grata among the people he had looked to for sympathy and ended whatever hopes he may have had of establishing himself in literary Moscow. It was, as he described it, "a horrible disaster, a total literary debacle, losses in the Courts, pursued by creditors, in peril of losing my last shirt and coat, sudden flight to a monastery, and one other humiliation it is painful for me to think of even now."[26]

Leontiev does not elaborate on the nature of this further humiliation. But his flight from Moscow in the autumn of 1874 for the Nikolo-Ugresh Monastery, where he was known as Brother Konstantin, ushered in probably the darkest period of his life, six years of wanderings between his crumbling family estate and various monasteries, occasionally wintering in Moscow, heavily in debt and suffering constant ill health, until in November 1880, following his all too brief spell as assistant editor of the *Warsaw Diary*, he at last found a degree of financial security through his appointment to the Moscow Censorship Committee, a post he held until his retirement through ill health in 1887.

The longer perspective of history suggests that Leontiev was not entirely isolated in his quarrel with Aksakov. He receives support from Michael Boro Petrovich, who notes in his *Emergence of Russian Pan-Slavism* that Leontiev's doctrine of Pan-Orthodoxy, as opposed to Pan-Slavism, was by no means entirely idiosyncratic, having had a historical precedent in the Eastern policy of Catherine II.[27] And Ivan von Kologrivov, following a hint from Gubastov, throws an interesting light on the dispute, suggesting that Leontiev's Byzantinism brought about his isolation from the Slavophile and Pan-Slavist camp in much the same way as Peter Chaadayev's advocacy of Roman Catholicism had isolated him four decades previously.[28]

The unfortunate episode with Aksakov had one positive outcome: it made Leontiev once and for all aware of the gulf that separated him from the mainstream of Slavism. "After a few months I saw clearly," he wrote in his memoirs, "that on matters of state, of politics, and even, to my astonishment, of religion I would never be of one mind with the excessively liberal Moscow Slavophiles. For I became convinced, and witnessed with my own eyes, that take from them the colorful velvet and brocade of their dearest ideals then underneath you will find clinging to them the usual gray bourgeois liberalism which is no different in essence from Western egalitarian freedom-worship."[29]

If the Russian Pan-Slavists had caught the contemporary European disease, Leontiev reflected, perhaps it was no wonder that they should be so willing to embrace the Slavs further West. The lesson was clear. "Whoever seeks *cultural Slavophilism*, distinctiveness or Slav-ness," he declared, "should shun *political Pan-Slavism*, for it is too close to the egalitarian-republican ideal, to the West."[30] For the future, Leontiev determined to make no bones about where he believed the true path of Slavophilism lay. As he wrote in a later article: "True *Slavophilism*, which is to say a Culture-philism which facilitates our distinctiveness of life, spirit and institutions, *must become the deadly enemy of reckless, purely political Pan-Slavism*." If the Slavophiles did not wish merely to repeat the liberal errors of Khomyakov and Danilevsky they must now serve the "*highest and purest ideal, a genuine and original nationalism which furthers and strengthens our spirit and our ways of life . . . the ideal of an Orthodox-cultural Russism*, original, noble, rigorous, traditional."[31]

The immediate aftermath of Aksakov's rebuff was a period of silence from Leontiev on political issues. Then came the Russo-Turkish War of 1877–78, which ended with the spoils of victory, most notably the Greater Bulgaria envisaged by the Treaty of San Stefano, snatched from Russia's grasp at the Congress of Berlin. These events drew from Leontiev's pen a series of articles in which his ideal of a great Eastern Orthodox Alliance under Russian hegemony acquired its most definite shape. It is in these articles also that the symbolic significance of Constantinople, "the City of Caesar," comes fully into prominence.

Leontiev was by no means the first, nor the last, Russian to become obsessed with the "Second Rome." Danilevsky, for example, devotes a whole chapter to it in *Russia and Europe*. And the subject has a long history—aesthetic, spiritual, and practical. Prior to his choice of Eastern Orthodoxy as his state religion, Vladimir the Great's ambassadors had seen the cathedral of Hagia Sophia, and their master's decision to accept Orthodox baptism in the year 988 was doubtless deeply influenced by their report. "We no longer knew," they said, "whether we were in heaven or on earth, nor such beauty, and we know not how to tell of it." Then in 1472 Ivan III had married Sophia, niece of Constantine Palaeologus, last emperor of Byzantium, and taken the double-headed Byzantine eagle as his emblem, from when onward the conviction grew that Moscow should assume the mantle of the "Third Rome" and the princes of Muscovy the position of the defenders of Eastern Orthodoxy which had fallen vacant in 1453. And side by side with theology, from the time of Peter the Great, at least, and especially under Catherine, the strategic importance to Russia of the Bosphorus as her exit from the Black Sea into the Mediterranean had exercised a fascination over Russian policymakers.

Yet for Leontiev Constantinople was of something more than religious or political significance. The city was of course the fountainhead of that Byzantine principle which he believed must be at the heart of Russia if she were to survive as a state and as a culture. But just as his views on the Eastern Question had been colored by his personal observation of the Southern Slavs, Leontiev's attitude toward Czargrad reveals a curious coincidence of the political and the personal, his vivid awareness of the symbolic and strategic issues surrounding Constantinople heightened by a deep personal affection for the city where he had spent some of his happiest years, and his letters of the late 1870s give an eloquent account of what amounted to persistent homesickness. This strong feeling of loss at leaving the Bosphorus, which had long lain dormant in Leontiev's breast, was reinvigorated by the deteriorating situation in Russo-Turkish relations following the Bosnian uprising of 1875 and the Serbo-Turkish War that broke out in 1876. In a letter to Gubastov of August of that year Leontiev openly envied his diplomatic friend's increasingly problematic situation in Constantinople and expressed a desire to change places with him.[32] In the spring of 1878 he agreed with Katkov to return to Constantinople as his correspondent, but got only as far as Kiev before being forced by ill health to abandon the enterprise, incidentally driving himself even further into debt.

It is in a letter of December 1876, written in Moscow at the height of the agitation for Russian intervention in the Balkan conflict, that Leontiev first enunciated his views on the political future of Constantinople. After reiterating his highly deterministic concept of the interplay of historical forces, he went on to consider the watershed upon which Russian policy now seemed to him to stand: either she would grasp the nettle and endure a "difficult period" of perhaps bloody wars, which he compared to the wars of Napoleon against the whole of Europe, but in the confident hope of final victory; or she would miss the moment and begin her inevitable and irretrievable decline. "A time of trials perhaps—but Czargrad and the Dardanelles will be in Russian hands; or wretched self-immolation—that is Czargrad as a free city open to the whole of Europe, in other words a powder keg of as yet unheard of inter-national radicalism, next to the all-consuming flames of which the conflagra-tions of the Paris commune will seem mere insignificant sparks."[33]

In another letter to Gubastov of August 1877, after the outbreak of the Russo-Turkish War, Leontiev remained optimistic, asserting that things were moving "with mathematical precision" not only toward the fall of Turkey in Europe but also toward the collapse of Austrian power in the Balkans as well.[34] As the conflict unfolded however, and especially as the likelihood grew that the outcome would be decided by a European peace conference, which he was convinced would not be favorable to Russia, his letters take on an increasing note of fatalism and pessimism. His fears were realized when the Treaty of Berlin was agreed by the Great Powers in June 1878, abolishing the Treaty of San Stefano of February 1878, signed by Russia and Turkey, which had con-cluded hostilities.

The main provision of San Stefano had been the creation of a unified and autonomous Principality of Bulgaria which, crucially from Russia's perspec-tive, would have access to the Mediterranean, opening up the prospect of the use of Bulgarian ports by the Russian navy. However the size and configura-tion of the Principality was unacceptable to the rest of the Great Powers, es-pecially Great Britain, and San Stefano was annulled at the Conference of Berlin and replaced by the Treaty of Berlin under which the Greater Bulgaria envisaged under San Stefano was reduced in size and partitioned, thus ren-dering void most of Russia's objectives in its creation.

At the time of the negotiations leading to the Treaty of Berlin, Leontiev made his contribution to the growing tide of indignation in the Russian press over the terms, which were almost universally perceived as a sellout of Rus-sian interests and her sacrifices during the war. This was the short article "Mosque and Church," which was published in the conservative journal *Grazh-danin* in March 1878, the first of a series of articles Leontiev was to publish there.

As the title suggests, "Mosque and Church" is mainly to do with the fate of the cathedral of Saint Sophia in Constantinople, and it shares the generally anti-Western, especially anti-English, tone of the times. With his usual clear-sightedness Leontiev realized that, despite Russia's victories in the field, "some-thing crucial to us is once again slipping through our fingers."[35] For Leontiev this was not Greater Bulgaria but the possession of Constantinople and the adjacent Straits of the Bosphorus and the Dardanelles. Of course the city and the straits were very much in Russia's long-term strategic interest; indeed they became a primary war aim for Russia in the Great War, agreed to by the West-ern allies in 1915, and they were also a key part of the Pan-Slavist program, but for Leontiev the vision of Czargrad assumed importance all of its own on a much higher, more symbolic, almost mystical plane.

If Russia were to create anything on the ruins of European Turkey, Leontiev argued, she would need the discipline of her Orthodox faith, which in turn presupposed a reconciliation of all those peoples who professed this faith, whether Slav or not. As ever, he could not resist taking this point to its logical conclusion: "If somewhere or other in Tibet or Bengal there existed Orthodox Mongols or Hindus with a wise and solid hierarchy at their head, then we ought to choose this Mongol or Hindu hierarchy over a million Slavs headed by *a liberal intelligentsia à la Gambetta or Thiers,* we should choose them to provide firm discipline to the Slavs themselves!"[36]

The very minimum that Russia must demand, insisted Leontiev, was that those Constantinople churches that had been turned into mosques since the Muslim conquest be restored to Orthodoxy. This applied particularly to the great edifice of Saint Sophia, which for Leontiev had an even greater symbolic significance. "On Orthodox soil," he wrote, "there is 'neither Hellas nor Judea,' neither Russian nor Bulgar nor Greek, and the universal, so to speak, temple of Saint Sophia must stand on the shore of the Bosphorus as an external symbol of the great Eastern Orthodox Federation. The Bosphorus must become from now on the center of peace, brotherhood and unity for all Christians of the East under the direction of those among them who are stronger, more experienced and therefore more just."[37]

Thus Russia was to become "first among equals" in the Orthodox (not purely Slav) Eastern Federation, with Czargrad and Saint Sophia representing the supranational, Orthodox-Byzantine "idea" that must inform the Eastern Federation and give it, and through it Russia, the strength to endure and to flourish. Holding particular nationalist aspirations to be fatal to this idea, Leontiev returned to the defense of the Greek Patriarchate which, despite the acknowledged shortcomings of its individual members, represented the universal Orthodox Church. "Russian influence or Russian power in this great metropolis must have no tinge of exclusivity," he wrote, "neither Southern Slav nor Greek; Russian power or Russian influence must acquire in these lands a universal character . . . And to this end the Patriarchate in Czargrad must become the most stable and powerful support for the conciliating influence of Russia . . . It is not the nationality or the behavior of the individual clergy that counts; it is the prestige of the Patriarchal throne."[38]

Few things demonstrate more clearly the difference between Leontiev and the Pan-Slavists than their respective attitudes to the question of Constantinople and the Straits. In Leontiev's scheme of things Czargrad must in no circumstances become a national capital, nor the capital of a purely Slav federation, nor, as we have seen from his letters to Gubastov, should she be designated a "free city"; rather, she must become the capital seat of the Eastern *Orthodox* Union, in which sense she would be "free" in the only acceptable sense, "free only for the members of the Union."[39]

As an aside, given what we know of Leontiev's attitude to nationalist aspirations, it is unsurprising that he does not even mention the alternative role for Constantinople envisaged by the Greek irredentists as the capital of a "Greece of Two Continents and Five Seas" comprising all the ethnically Greek areas under Ottoman rule including the Southern Balkans, Asia Minor, and Cyprus, the so-called Megali Idea. But Danilevsky does and dismisses it out of hand: "Even if Constantinople were made its capital the small Greek people could never revive the Byzantine Empire. The Empire of Constantine, Theodosius and Justinian could come to life only in the form of a Slavic-Greek federation and only in this way could Greece take part in its glory and its greatness."[40]

Alas, the vision of Czargrad was never to become reality, not as the Pan-Orthodox metropolis dreamed of by Leontiev, not as the epicenter of ethnic Slavdom envisaged by the Pan-Slavists, not as the strategic prize of imperial Russian foreign policy, not even as the embodiment of the "great idea." Leontiev's premonition that it was "slipping through Russia's fingers" proved all too correct, the obstacles all too insurmountable, and the dream foundered on a plethora of reefs and shoals: British and French suspicion of Russian imperialist ambitions, irreconcilable differences between Greeks and Southern Slavs (as Leontiev had foreseen), the October Revolution and the Bolshevik repudiation of Russian war aims, the patriotic resolve of Atatürk. For two centuries it had seemed that the dream of the erection of the Third Rome on the foundations of the Second was at times palpably, achingly close to coming to fruition, yet it remained, in essence, a dream. After 1917 it was no longer even that. The tide of history had ebbed.

For Leontiev the dashing of the hopes of Czargrad raised by Russian victories over the Turks, however ephemeral these hopes may have been, signaled the end of all optimism about the future prospects for Russia and the Eastern Federation. As he wrote: "Neither an exclusively Slavic union with Russia at its head, nor a more natural and stronger great Eastern union, membership of which would include willy-nilly, thanks to the racial and political kaleidoscope of the East, the Romanians, Greeks and Armenians, neither the one nor the other confederation is conceivable without the federal capital in Czargrad."[41]

A further blow came when the constituent assembly of the fledgling Bulgar state met for the first time in the ancient capital of Tirnovo and adopted a secular and extremely liberal constitution based on universal manhood suffrage and the guarantee of what would now be called "basic human rights," including freedom of speech, freedom of assembly, freedom of the press and so forth. This "liberal-bourgeois" construct appeared to Leontiev to confirm his greatest suspicions about Bulgar intentions and Bulgar duplicity. It was a hard morsel for the lonely idealist to swallow, the final and crushing blow to his hopes for spiritual renewal in the Christian East.

Leontiev's response was the evocatively titled *Letters of an Anchorite*, published in the magazine Vostok in 1879. These "letters" show us a man almost prostrate with despair at the course of events, supported only by the knowledge that his warnings of the past decade had been vindicated. The very title of the first of these letters, *Our Bulgaromania*, sets the tone. Why, Leontiev asks, must Russians decry and abuse everything, especially themselves, while the Bulgars get off Scot-free solely because they share the same Slav bloodline? Blood, Leontiev repeats for the thousandth time, is the least durable of ties and cannot substitute for an ideal relationship: "An Orthodox bishop of even the harshest stamp or the most depraved character, of whatever race, even a baptized Mongol, is more precious to us than any twenty Slav demagogues and progressives."[42]

This whole piece is written in a tone more bitter and more outraged than anything we have yet seen from Leontiev's pen:

> To be a voice crying in the wilderness would be bearable if you could look forward to the advent of someone who would see things even clearer than we do, who would be stronger and more forthright than us, who would exert more influence in our favor. But when you see everything moving further and further to the left without anyone apparently noticing, when you see, for example, a worthless bourgeois-Belgian constitution foisted on the remotest and most patriarchal of Slavic lands, recently liberated by us, when you see the archaic and pastoral Bulgar folk delivered into the hands of lawyers, Europeanised merchants and conceited pedagogues . . . well, is it possible not to despair?[43]

The Moscow Slavophiles of the older generation—the Kireyevskys, Khomyakovs, and elder Aksakovs—had deceived themselves, Leontiev continued, believing that their ideal of a self-dependent Slav culture, founded as it was on the beliefs and values of hereditary nobility, could appeal to a bourgeois Bulgar demagogue, yesterday's peasant, who had received a European education. If any group in the East, besides the Turks, showed signs of nobility, then for Leontiev it was the Greek aristocracy of Constantinople, the "Phanariots," who might be despised in some quarters as collaborators with the Porte but who had nonetheless preserved the sacred Byzantine tradition and were therefore of incomparably more value to Russia than the Bulgar bourgeoisie.[44]

It is in these *Letters of an Anchorite* that Leontiev finally makes clear that it was his personal experiences of the Christian East under Turkish rule which separated him from the theoretical Pan-Slavists: "I arrived in the East some fifteen years ago as a pupil and disciple of the cultural Slavism [of the first generation of Slavophiles] which seemed destined to grow and flourish luxuriantly on the ancient and unshakeable rootstock of Orthodoxy . . . But alas! Living in Turkey I soon came to understand something truly terrible: I understood with grief and horror that it was only thanks to the Turks that anything truly Orthodox and Slavic was left in the East."[45]

This was one point on which Leontiev and Danilevsky were in accord. As the latter put it: "The general idea or essential meaning of Islam lies in its involuntary and unintentional service to Orthodoxy and Slavdom, protecting the first from the pressure of Latinism and saving the second from absorption into Germanic-Latindom."[46] Leontiev was of course not blind to the fact that an Orthodox Slavdom underpinned and kept free of Western influences solely by the alien power of Islam could not endure indefinitely in the face of resurgent nationalism and the waning power of Ottoman Turkey. But what was to take the place of this power? In answering this question Leontiev signals his final departure, not only from any possibility of rapprochement with Pan-Slavism but also from any correspondence of views with actual Russian policy in the Balkans.

"A truly national policy beyond our borders should support not naked, so to speak, ethnicity," he declared, "but those spiritual principles which are rooted in the history of the race, in its strengths and in its renown. A policy based on the Orthodox spirit is more desirable than one based on Slav blood, on agitation of the Slav 'sinews.'" For Leontiev, nationalism without the leavening of religion was nothing other than a stalking horse for the principles of 1789, for the canons of universal freedom and equality. "Pan-Slavism is unavoidable for us," he concluded, "but Orthodox Pan-Slavism is our salvation whereas liberal Pan-Slavism means destruction above all for Russia."[47]

Leontiev's experiences in the Christian East had taught him the painful lesson that the leaders of the Slav nations under Turkish rule hungered for one thing above all else, which was national statehood in the guise of Western European liberal ideals. In his eyes the newly independent democratic Bulgaria was one more manifestation of that Proteus of cosmopolitan destructiveness, which he viewed as the ultimate threat to the individuality of peoples and cultures, and which was never more dangerous than when it adopted the guise of a fanatical ethno-nationalism which led not to the individualization and flowering of culture but to its total loss of identity in "secondary simplification" and its reduction to amorphous homogeneity. Leontiev's final, pessimistic testament to his countrymen was that this was the fate that surely awaited Russia if she followed the path of racial, rather than religious and cultural, Slavism.

Once one accepts Leontiev's premises, his logic is impeccable: "The power of Russia is necessary to the whole of Slavdom; the strength of Orthodoxy is necessary to Russia; indispensable to the strength of Orthodoxy is a close union of Russia and the Greeks, for they are the trustees of the holy places and the occupants of the four great patriarchal thrones . . . Whoever loves the Slavs in the broadest sense . . . must therefore side with the Greeks in Church affairs."[48]

Unfortunately, whether in the early 1870s or in the turbulent year 1878, the racial Slavism of Danilevsky held the ring, and there were few in Russia who were prepared to accept either Leontiev's premises or his conclusions. His magnum opus *Byzantinism and Slavdom* caused barely a ripple upon publication, receiving only the sole, and equivocal, review by Strakhov noted above. It took more than ten years for the work to begin to gather some more favorable responses, notably from the philosopher and psychologist P. E. Astafyev and the theologian Vladimir Solovyev, but even after that elapse of time Aksakov still could not resist responding to the latter with a renewed condemnation of Leontiev's attack on Bulgar nationalism at the expense of church unity.[49] Leontiev was typically more forgiving. On Aksakov's death in January 1886 he told Gubastov: "I long ago forgave him his base injustice toward me in 1875. Who is not sinful before God! It was an error!"[50] It is one more proof that Rozanov was all too right in his assessment that "Leontiev himself loved others more than he was loved by them."[51]

"In me," wrote Leontiev in 1888, "I won't go into details *how*, the Slavophiles, Danilevsky, Katkov, Herzen and to an extent Solovyev are all accommodated. To me personally *all* this is clear and connected by a living, organic thread. Whether my ideal is clear to others—I can't say."[52] It may have been clear to Leontiev, but in the late 1870s few others would have shared his view. He was now truly a voice crying in the wilderness, his warnings denigrated or simply ignored in influential Pan-Slavist and governmental circles in Moscow and Petersburg. Yet he did not completely lack personal sympathizers. In December 1879, he received an offer from Prince Nikolai Nikolaevich Golitsyn of the post of assistant editor of the latter's Russian-language newspaper, the *Warsaw Diary*. Here at last was the possibility, albeit on a small circulation provincial newspaper, of a mouthpiece for his views, as well as some much-needed financial support. Leontiev did not hesitate, and by the new year he was in Warsaw.

PART THREE

Toward the Abyss

CHAPTER 9

The Beginning of Wisdom

The spiritual crisis of 1871 in Salonika and the flight to Athos marked the end of Leontiev's attempt to live according to the dictates of his aesthetic worldview. What he now styled his "beautiful but vaguely pantheistic mirage" of a life based on the creation and contemplation of the beautiful and on the search for self-fulfillment in external things had proven unsustainable in the face of imminent annihilation.[1] Something more durable was needed, something that might outlive the flesh. Toward the end of his life Leontiev recalled that at the age of forty *"the advent of personal faith* suddenly completed my political and artistic education."[2] The last twenty years of his life, following this "inner rebirth," would be characterized by an attempt to live according to the dictates of an Orthodox Christianity of a severely ascetic and mystical temper, the highest ideal of which, he tells us repeatedly, was to be found in the words of Christ: "My kingdom is not of this world."[3]

We have seen that the 1870s were a time of trials for Leontiev, of a semi-nomadic existence in search of a reliable means of sustenance, of servicing his debts and seeking to rescue the family estate of Kudinovo. His letters of this period reveal the onset of something akin to clinical depression: by 1878 he is ready to compare himself to a crippled dog he once saw in the Crimea, "a creature tormented by itself and by its calamities." To his other difficulties were added periodic resurgences of chronic illness, a relic of his time in the

East, which made him feel like "a mutilated corpse" or "a man whose skin has been all but flayed."[4]

To Leontiev's general reasons for pessimism in his later years may be added two particular trials. One was a worsening of his wife's mental condition, which left the once vivacious Liza Pavlovna in a state of "peculiar idiocy, coupled with repellent dirtiness and slovenliness."[5] There is evidence that Leontiev made the best of things and even toward the end of his life found a kind of happiness in his domestic arrangements, but we may assume he was speaking from experience when he told Rozanov that although marriage is often regarded as a bed of roses, "there is nothing worse than the pricking of the thorns!"[6]

On top of this the 1880s saw a deterioration in Leontiev's already precarious state of health. In 1884 he suffered a severe attack of catarrhal dysentery that brought him close to death, along with an affliction of the larynx and the urinary tract.[7] The following year he experienced an especially acute worsening of his general medical condition, which again brought him close to death in the spring of 1886; his symptoms included fever, inflammation of the bowels, a skin infection, and ulcers on his hands and feet.[8] He was ill again in 1887 but "very quickly recovered" after writing to the famous miracle worker John of Kronstadt.[9] But his symptoms persisted and even shortly before he died of pneumonia in 1891 he still feared a "terrible death" from ischuria, constriction of the urinary canal.[10]

Under the impact of these difficulties, from about the mid-1880s, five years before his actual death, we see Leontiev beginning to acquire to some degree that "resignation" and scorn for the things of this world, which he had so manifestly lacked at the time of his failed attempt to become a monk on Athos fifteen years earlier. As he described his state of mind: "My one consolation is what an elder told his spiritual son in response to the question: When can we expect the sins of our former life to be forgiven? The answer: When we begin to hate them!" He goes on to confess that his most recent illnesses "had made me so desperately hate my former life, and not only my earlier life which was more or less godless, prodigal, arrogant and complacent, but also my more recent, when on Athos (fifteen years back) I gradually began to be imbued with the light of truth yet, due to my shameful carnality, my faith and the fear of God and love of the Church still could not eradicate in me the subtle and deeply ingrained roots of vice, frivolity, vainglory, temper, self-justification and *literary gibberish*."[11]

The net result of his accumulating problems was to induce in Leontiev a feeling of depression, fatigue and apathy that comes across in his letters of the mid-1880s: "What I call 'inward tonsuring,' a kind of invisible monasticism.

Reconciliation with everything except my sins and my deplorable past. Indifference. Quiet and passionate prayers for peace and the forgiveness of my sins. The strongest wish not to be writing."[12] In these circumstances his lately acquired religious faith became an indispensable crutch for the ailing thinker, and we should now examine it more closely, not least because it would serve to form the basis of Leontiev's later concept of the ideal secular polity as well. And like much else in the life of this complex man it was anything but a straightforward phenomenon.

In the first place Leontiev interpreted Christ's declaration that His kingdom was not of this world to mean that the only road to salvation lay in rejecting the things of the world absolutely and following the spiritual example of the elders of Athos. Only by cleaving to the precepts of monastic asceticism, he insisted, might the penitent soul focus his thoughts on the only true reality, that of the life to come, and attain "as far as possible that *highest degree of self-abnegation in Christ which is known as spiritual enlightenment.*"[13] For Leontiev, this became the mystical center of gravity of Orthodox Christianity: "Faith in the divinity of He of Nazareth, who was crucified under Pontius Pilate, who taught that everything in this world is shifting, paltry and ephemeral, but that reality and eternity will stand after the destruction of this world and everything in it: this is that *tangible-mystical fulcrum* on which has turned and turns to this day the mighty apparatus of Christian doctrine."[14]

Second, it was all too clear to Leontiev that his personal "enlightenment," his insight into what he now saw as the true nature of reality, had been imparted to him through horror at the prospect of his own imminent destruction, through the sudden and overwhelming awareness of the absolute incommensurability between the might of God, expressed in His universe, and the weakness of the human individual. As he vividly recalled: "Confronted by invisible and chastening forces I suddenly came to a realization of my own helplessness and was seized by pure animal terror, after which I felt myself utterly vanquished in my own eyes and in need of help, not from man but from God . . . It was not just fear, but horror, at one and the same time horror of sin and horror of death."[15]

Unsurprisingly then it is dread—"*dread* of sin, dread of punishment, dread of God, dread in the soul"—that becomes the central tenet of Leontiev's religious outlook.[16] "I had crossed a Rubicon," he recalled, "I began to fear God and the Church (as His manifestation). With time my physical fear subsided, but my spiritual dread remained and grew apace."[17] This is an outlook which recalls vividly Psalm 55, verse 5: "Fear and trembling come upon me, and horror overwhelms me" and which forms the background to "Fear of God and Love for Mankind," Leontiev's critique of the approach to Christianity of

Leo Tolstoy.[18] One is also inevitably reminded of Kierkegaard and indeed, as noted above, Leontiev has been viewed as a forerunner of twentieth-century existentialism. No evidence exists however that Leontiev knew or was influenced by the writings of Kierkegaard, and as far as Leontiev can be called an existentialist, this applies rather to his earlier views, at the time of *A Place of One's Own*, than to his later religious period. The striking similarity in language between Leontiev and Kierkegaard is in fact restricted largely to their common concept of dread as the natural response of the individual to the immensity of God and His creation.

Leontiev's dramatic and personal experience of existential terror in Salonika issued in a notable consistency in his writings on matters of faith and dogma; they varied remarkably little between the mid-1870s and his death in 1891, his most common and oft repeated formulation being: "Fear of God is the beginning of wisdom; love is the fruit."[19] For Leontiev this fruit was not easily to be garnered: "That love of God which is so perfect that it banishes dread is accessible only to a very few."[20] For most mortals the fear, the original impulse to faith, must suffice. Leontiev continually stresses that the desire to believe is more important than any results it may bring in this world, which explains his insistence that monasteries, for example, should be regarded as an ethical end in themselves, with no need of further justification in "works."[21]

Based as it was on existential dread, faith for Leontiev now meant strict adherence to the tenets of the Orthodox dogma and, more than anything else, the avoidance of sin: "The ideal of the monk is above all to end each day without having sinned. This should also be the highest ideal of every Christian. We should listen to the prayer in church: 'Please Lord keep us this day without sin.'"[22] As Leontiev was only too well aware, the passions of the flesh must be torn out while they are small, like saplings; for him they are the source of sin and once they take firm root nothing will shift them. And at the root of the passions lies the will, which must be subdued. "Our will must be whipped out of us at all costs," he insisted, "we must learn submission, we must humble ourselves."[23] Only by such drastic methods could the sinner find salvation and true bliss, "the inexpressible sweetness of repentance and even tears."[24]

The attempt to eliminate the very possibility of sin led directly to what for Leontiev was the quintessence of Orthodox Christianity, the ascetic rule of the monastic life as he had experienced it during his time on Athos. This "ascetic heroism" of "voluntary martyrs" now becomes for Leontiev the "science of sciences," ousting all secular philosophy.[25] Its adepts, the monks, whom he compares to artists or soldiers of the faith, point the way to that ascetic denial of the things of this imperfect world which was for Leontiev the "basis of all true Christianity."[26] The rigors of the monastic life, which Leontiev's uncertain health prevented him from personally enduring for long when he stayed at the Nikolo-Ugresh Monastery in 1874–75, are well documented in his article "Easter on Athos." In this he describes how the physical torments of the long hours of prayer, kneeling, and fasting are forgotten and replaced by the purest joy on Easter Sunday when the triumphant cry is heard: *"Christ is risen from the dead, vanquishing death by death."*[27]

Rejection of the world and its pleasures and cares accordingly lies at the heart of Leontiev's concept of Orthodox asceticism. Yet personal experience had taught him that the flesh is tenacious and not so easily mortified and that the susceptible individual can hardly hope to achieve mastery over his passions alone and unaided. Conscience was not to be relied upon, being influenced by self-esteem, moral pride, and so forth; reason, too, was a false guide: once you passed a certain point in the acquisition of faith, your very knowledge made you aware of its deceptiveness, and even collective human reason could not guarantee to avoid the subjective distortions of the collective human ego (in his later writing Leontiev often employed the rubric *Credo quia absurdum*—"I believe *because* it is impossible"—a formulaic rejection of the human faculty of reason in which he had lost all confidence).[28] Thus the soul in torment needed more robust support, and this it might achieve, Leontiev suggests, by submitting itself in all matters to the spiritual hegemony of an elder.

In his later years Leontiev found much consolation in submitting himself to the spiritual control of his own guide and master, Ambrose of Optina Pustyn; he would latterly refuse any undertakings not expressly sanctioned by his elder. He discourses at length on the institution of elders in his biographical study of one such spiritual counselor, Father Konstantin Karlovich Zedergol'm, an Orthodox convert from a Lutheran background (his father was a noted authority on German philosophy), whom Leontiev came greatly to admire after the two met at Optina. The study is typically subjective in tone and constitutes perhaps the best introduction to Leontiev's religious ideas.[29] From this and other sources such as his *Four Letters from Athos* it becomes plain that submission to such a "doctor for the soul" had become an absolute need for Leontiev. "Have you any idea," he asks, "what a pleasure it is to submit one's perceptions, one's scholarship, one's vanity to the directions of a simple but practiced and honorable elder? Have you any idea how much *Christian will-power* is needed to suppress in oneself the *other, the worldly, will?"*[30]

And the response the disciple may expect from his elder—"affection coupled with dire admonitions, the demand for renunciation alongside indulgence toward the repentant sinner"—mirrors Leontiev's conception of the relationship of man to God, also a mixture of fear and love (and in this we can see the germ of Leontiev's later secular polity beginning to emerge).[31]

"Downplaying the divinity of Christ," he wrote, "may come step by step to eradicate in a Christian the feeling of spiritual awe and dread; but reducing His *humanity* and concentrating solely on His divinity may cut at the root of that *love to Christ the Man* which we presently feel, believing that He, like us, hungered and thirsted, became weary and slept, grieved, even feared death in the final hours (let this cup pass, etc.)."[32]

Leontiev's concept of Christianity was thus in essence a rigorous and uncompromising ascetic Orthodoxy predicated on a love of God stimulated by dread of incurring His wrath. But his religious concept is by no means wholly circumscribed by this framework, and it is worth considering what other strands of thought contributed to its development. For which we need to look eastwards. Leontiev described Orthodox asceticism as *"the spiritual triumph of the East over the West."*[33] The description is apt enough, as the roots of Leontiev's faith extend considerably further to the East than the world of Orthodoxy and contain elements which are not, properly speaking, Christian at all.

"Christianity," Leontiev asserted, "contains within itself everything that is strong and good in all other religions."[34] We should not be surprised then if at the heart of Leontiev's version of Christianity, in his absolute separation of this world and the next, of good and evil, fear and love, we find a polarity which seems to echo the dualism for which the teachings of Zoroaster are perhaps most famous and which we saw to be an integral part of Leontiev's earlier aesthetic morality. For Leontiev such a dualistic outlook stood in no inherent contradiction to Orthodox asceticism. In Christianity, he asserted, there "is the answer to all questions, consolation for all afflictions; and where there is no consolation there is punishment and coercion."[35]

The emphasis Leontiev places on submission and the annihilation of the will is indicative of a further strand in his religious outlook, one that is at least as significant to his intellectual makeup as Manichean dualism: his admiration for Islam. The literal meaning of Islam is submission, humbling oneself, obeying commands, and heeding prohibitions without objection, and in this sense there is indeed much that is Islamic in Leontiev's Christianity.

During his diplomatic service in the East, Leontiev had of course had ample opportunity to become acquainted with the Islamic faith and, as it would seem, to fall under its spell. In *Father Kliment Zedergolm* he speaks of his admiration for the Koran, while his story cycle *Scenes from the Life of Christians in Turkey* is peppered with passages friendly to individual Turks. But perhaps the best example of Leontiev's Turcophilia is put into the mouth of one Koevino, a Greek physician and one of the chief protagonists of the long story *Odysseus Polichroniades*. "I love the stern simplicity of this idealistic, warlike and secretly voluptuous religion," declares Koevino, "I love it when the call of the muezzin 'Allahu Akbar' resounds from the minaret on a dark winter's night! And polygamy? Oh, I'm well disposed to that! I'm a devotee of secret and immoral sensuality!"[36]

The very religious fanaticism to which he describes the Turks being prone actually predisposes Leontiev in their favor as being supportive of their faith, any faith being in his eyes preferable to European rationalism. As he told his friend Terty Ivanovich Filippov: "If people can't be good Orthodox Christians, it's better they should be good Muslims, good Buddhists, Skoptsy, Mormons, Khlysty, anything rather than the usual industrious Europeans gathering for some liberal conference or other."[37] He noted, prophetically enough, that Islam would be resistant to Western ideas. "Liberalism," he cautioned, "emanated specifically from Christian countries, as the *antithesis of spiritual, ascetic and stringent* Christianity, and not from the mountains of the Caucasus or from Mecca. Liberalism will find it hard to make inroads in the lands of Islam."[38]

In the Islamic world the doctrine of *qismah* holds that the overall fate of human beings is governed by the foreknowledge of God.[39] This does not absolve the individual from the necessity of moral choice, but it can issue in a tendency to fatalism, which is another aspect of that faith almost designed to appeal to a man of Leontiev's cast of mind. His material position improved considerably in the 1880s with his appointment as a censor in Moscow, a position he jokingly compared to the "life of a well-fed pig scratching itself on the corner of its stye," the work itself being "the laundering of other people's (mostly soiled) underwear."[40] Yet the cumulative effect of the long series of emotional trials and professional disasters he had gone through, added to an enduring lack of positive critical response from those he regarded as his closest allies, had resulted in a marked disposition in Leontiev's political writing toward a fatalistic interpretation of events, as well as in an exacerbation of an incipient paranoia in his thinking which manifested itself in a tendency to see treachery in the acts, or in the failure to act, of individuals he regarded as close to him: "Something which I am sometimes disposed to call the churlishness, the obtuseness and the slavish adherence to European ideas of our reading public, but which I regard in other, more idealistic, moments as the avenging hand of God requiting my years of sin, in a word, something outside of myself."[41]

The increasing tendency to fatalism found expression toward the end of Leontiev's life in a belief, amounting to an obsession, that the years around the turn of each decade had held momentous (and usually negative) import for him. In a letter to Anatoly Aleksandrov of January 1890 he stresses that the turn of the decade had always been fateful for him and that now "something is approaching, if not death, then a new, difficult and significant change in my life. Already signs of the end are revealing themselves one after another."[42] And in a letter to Iosif Fudel' of September 1891, when he had already moved from Optina Pustyn to Sergiev Posad, he elaborates at some length on the "fateful" events which transpired in his life at the turn of each decade from 1841 until the date of the letter, intimating that he now had nothing to wish from life but peaceful and Christian death.[43]

In particular, following the collapse of the *Warsaw Diary* in 1880 the Islamic side of Leontiev's religious outlook, what Leibniz called "Fatum Mahometanum," gave him a key to coming to terms with his travails: "It was *necessary* that I should be reworked, and both in my friends and in my critics that end was served by Russian indolence, ubiquitous egoism, an *intellectual* timidity which is especially Russian, and a Russian type of disloyalty which does not always emanate from malice, but more often from lethargy and frivolity."[44] In all this Leontiev saw a "*teleology* of spiritual readjustment,"[45] which he had first discerned in the series of "accidents" and "chance combinations of events" that had led to his sickbed in Salonika. The higher logic behind these apparently unconnected things was, as he told Rozanov: "The thread by which the Lord draws men out of the labyrinth of their personal passions and intellectual meanderings."[46]

It is interesting here to compare Leontiev's view of the workings of fate before and after his religious crisis. Of his feelings before 1871 he recalled: "At that time I had a mystical feeling (which alas did not proceed from Orthodox belief) that an invisible and omnipotent power was watching over me and that everything that happened to me would turn to my advantage, even perils."[47] By 1876 the wheel had come full circle. "It was God's will," he told Gubastov, "that everything I tried turned out second rate, so that I became more depressed than happy and found myself in the highest state of indifference possible in this world. And that was as well . . . *It was the will of God that I should be crushed.*"[48] This belief became essential to Leontiev's peace of mind in the face of his repeated failures; without it, he told his friend Filippov three years later, he "might as well put an end to everything."[49]

If then with Leontiev it is hard to determine just where Christian belief in Providence ends and "Fatum Mahometanum" begins, a further twist to his religious thought appears in his attraction to Buddhism. The teachings of the Buddha became a source of very personal consolation for Leontiev in his later years. "Buddhism," he declared, "while not acknowledging a personal God, is in the opinion of its own disciples closer to Christianity in all other respects than any other religion. For example, in its teaching of meekness, compassion toward others and severity (asceticism) toward oneself."[50] And at times Leontiev's is a version of Christianity that seems really to approximate to the teachings of the Buddha and the aspiration toward a state of nonbeing, as experienced

by Ladnev in *The Egyptian Dove*: "Silence! A soundless, passionless, mute obliviousness among eternal snows."[51] Like his hero, Leontiev himself did now and
then achieve forgetfulness and a kind of peace, although the relief was all too
short-lived. "The pity is," he lamented, "that this exquisite Nirvana—even if it
is more physical than ascetic—only gives me a few enchanted moments of
oblivion."[52]

The element of Buddhism that finds the greatest echo in Leontiev's thought
is its pessimism toward the things of this world. "All positive religions," he argues, "which have influenced, directly and indirectly, the formation of the
great cultures of the world, were doctrines of *pessimism, sanctioning* the suffering, insults and injustices of earthly life."[53] Given this predisposition, it is
not surprising that we find Leontiev late in life turning to the German philosopher Arthur Schopenhauer, and to his disciple and the disseminator of his
ideas in Russia, Eduard von Hartmann, to try and make some sense of the
increasing despair and pessimism which were casting lengthy shadows over
his declining years.

Schopenhauer is famous as the supreme advocate of a pessimistic philosophy that sees the universe and everything in it, including man, as nothing more
than manifestations of the universal will to existence, a will that has no other
purpose or end in view than its own insatiable striving for self-realization. Since
this striving is eternal and can never be satisfied, the natural condition of all
created beings, as particular instances of the universal will, is a feeling of dis-
satisfaction and suffering.

This worldview is closely akin to that of Buddhism. Like Leontiev, Schopenhauer took an unusual interest in Eastern philosophy and the influence in
particular of Buddhism on the development of his thought is clear and well-
documented. There are indications in the novel *A Husband's Confession*, and in
one or two other places, that Leontiev was acquainted with Schopenhauer as
early as the late 1860s,[54] but it is not until he assumed editorship of the *Warsaw Diary* in 1880 that we find him using Schopenhauerian motifs in a constructive way. Perhaps the most striking example is contained in an article
written for that newspaper titled "What Do We Mean by Connecting with the
People?"

This article is essentially a return to the themes of *Literacy and National
Character* of 1868. The "people" are the bearers of the seed of the true Russian
cultural ideal, and the Europeanized educated classes should therefore tread
warily in "connecting" with them lest they spoil everything by destroying this
ideal and turning the "folk" into a pale imitation of themselves. Unlike in the
earlier article though, Leontiev introduces themes from Schopenhauer to illustrate his arguments. For Leontiev, the Russian people had always been

FIGURE 9. "Silence! A soundless, passionless, mute obliviousness among eternal snows."
From the novel *The Egyptian Dove*.

possessed of an innate wisdom which had been largely overlooked and denigrated by the intelligentsia. In particular, the folk had always been aware of certain key truths of existence which had only recently been discovered by philosophy: "An awareness of the inevitability in life of suffering, wickedness, abuses, disappointments and even horrors, and the *impossibility* of rectifying all this through *reason, science and human rights,* an awareness even of the *enormous indirect benefit* of all these evils, an awareness which . . . even has its proper *designation* in the sphere of philosophical thought: it is called *pessimism*."[55]

We have noted Leontiev's method of "flitting" through the works of philosophers and social theorists to find supporting evidence for his ideas. He now lights upon Schopenhauer's critique of optimistic ideology, that the idea of progress is a dream bound in the long run to be brought to ruin by the essential insatiability of the needs of the will and the paradox that each need satisfied and each goal achieved only gives rise, hydra-like, to new needs and new goals to torment humanity. This view of the nature of existence provides Leontiev with a theoretical underpinning for the thesis that pessimism is the only possible attitude for anyone who has penetrated to the real nature of things. Seen through this prism, the end result of all progress must be mankind coming to an awareness of the true poverty of its achievements and returning to religion for consolation. "In soil *thoroughly prepared* by the teachings of *pessimism,*" Leontiev suggests, "*all positive religions* could freely flourish and gather a splendid harvest, for who would wish to live long by dismal *negation* alone, negation of all bounty, *both in this world* and (as Hartmann supposes) *in the next?*"[56]

Of particular interest to Leontiev is Schopenhauer's discovery that the root of unhappiness lies in man's nature, not in the conditions in which we exist: "Universal happiness will not come about, for suffering is *in us*, and not in external circumstances. Boredom will grow in proportion to the increase in material comforts . . . A Christian may usefully exploit this intelligent aspect of pessimism for the strengthening of his outlook on life."[57] Indeed Leontiev had by now come to regard the German philosophic tradition from Leibniz and Kant to Schopenhauer and Hartmann as "broadening and deepening the mystico-religious principles of the future."[58] The support he finds in this tradition for his conviction that the power of evil in human affairs is enduring and ineradicable becomes for him one more weapon in what was effectively his life's crusade: to affirm, in the teeth of nineteenth-century progressive optimism, the totality of human life and human history in all their aspects: "*Truth* is not to be found in rights and freedom, but in something else entirely, something which will bring no cheer to those who seek peace and reason in earthly affairs, but which is entirely bearable and even pleasing if you view life as a swiftly passing dream. Pessimism regarding the *whole of mankind* and personal faith in divine providence and in our fragility and ignorance, that is what reconciles a man with his own life, with the *power of others*, with the awful and eternally tragic face of history."[59]

Thus Leontiev, the self-styled "cosmic pessimist," reconciles belief in this "worst of all possible worlds" with faith in divine providence.[60] This method, which he styled "optimistic pessimism," is a key element in his later politics as well as his religious outlook. He starts from the premise that the terms *optimism* and *pessimism*, as usually understood, are too nebulous: "It seems to me we will be more exact if we set that complex notion of optimism, which is to say *continuous improvement* of a *progressive-eudaemonistic* kind, against philosophical and theological pessimism: *that evil is inevitable* and, who knows, perhaps *everything* on earth is *worsening* and tending toward annihilation."[61] At first sight these propositions would seem to be irreconcilable opposites, but Leontiev finds a synthesis in ascetic Christianity: "All Christian thinkers have been pessimists in their way. They even found that evil, abuses, grief were in the highest degree *beneficial* to us, even necessary, so that from this point of view it is possible to describe the Christian worldview as *optimistic pessimism*."[62]

Thus Leontiev arrives at the conclusion that "the worse, the better," for the greater the remoteness of earthly happiness, the more likely it is that mankind will seek solace in transcendental faith and thus return to true values. The example uppermost in Leontiev's mind here is Saint Augustine in his retorts to the pagans after the fall of Rome: no matter how great the sufferings of individuals, they are useful to them in bringing them to an understanding of their sinfulness and the greater durability of the things of the next world over those of this. Curiously, the career of Saint Augustine of Hippo bears an uncanny resemblance to Leontiev's. Both men eventually came to Christianity under the influence of an Ambrose, in Augustine's case Saint Ambrose of Milan, in Leontiev's Ambrose of Optina Pustyn. And like Leontiev, Augustine too was a reformed sensualist and for a time attracted to Manichean dualism as a solution to the problem of evil—though he later fiercely condemned it—comprehending evil as necessary to the world for the sake of harmony, like dissonance in music or shadow in a painting. In this he anticipates both Leibniz and Leontiev.

As the other side of the coin, so to speak, of "optimistic pessimism," Leontiev develops what he calls "pessimistic teleology," the view that, under prevailing conditions, all historical and social movement, which the nineteenth century viewed as "progress," would end in general destruction. This process of disintegration is inexorable according to Leontiev's "Triune Theory," but he felt it might be slowed if science and philosophy were to adopt the pessimistic approach of Schopenhauer and St Augustine, for "it is only pessimism of this kind that can lead human *reason* into truly new channels."[63] By these channels Leontiev meant the teachings of Orthodoxy, which for him were always *"closer to the true nature of existence than crude and prosaic dreams of progress."*[64] If men could only be led to comprehend this truth, Leontiev argued, then perhaps the world might yet be saved.

In this overview of Leontiev's religious views we can see the components of his vision of the future of mankind gradually falling into place, even if the blueprint was not yet quite worked through and an encounter with another remarkable thinker would be required before his legacy to his countrymen achieved its final form. Before examining his later political thinking, however, including the fruitful synergy and surprising outcome of his relations with Vladimir Solovyev, we should examine his spiritual views in a little more depth, as they shed particular light on some of the foremost religious thinkers of his day.

CHAPTER 10

The Grand Inquisitor

By the end of his life Leontiev knew that he would not attain the highest state of renunciation of the things of the world, what he called the condition of the "spiritual man." In a letter of May 1888, just over three years before his death, he is still referring to himself as a "Hellene" and "a sinful, an iniquitous aesthete," while in other letters around this time and earlier he mentions various ideas for novels.[1] However his poetic muse appears to have been hamstrung by the crises of 1871 and 1874. His fictional output in the last fifteen years of his life is restricted to the religious fable *Child of the Soul* of 1876, two further stories from Greek life, "The Sfakiot" and "Yadez" (Game of Bones) of 1877, the unfinished *Egyptian Dove*, published in 1881, an epilogue to *Odysseus Polichroniades*, published in 1882, and the revised but still unfinished *Two Chosen Women*, published in 1885. In his later years it seems he had simply lost the ability, if not the impulse, to write novels; indeed he had come to view the métier with a degree of disgust. "I am still tied to the world," he lamented, "I have the vile habit of scribbling, and suffer from the great misfortune of being a Russian writer."[2]

All too aware of his pariah status in Russian intellectual circles, in 1882 Leontiev wrote an essay titled "Where to Seek Out My Works after My Death." In it he ruthlessly condemned his pre-Athos stories, especially *A Husband's Confession*: "Audacious and well written but in the highest degree immoral, a sensual, pagan, diabolical work, subtly corrupt and *containing no shred of*

Christianity, a faithful portrait of a deeply depraved soul . . . *A sin!* And a great one! Precisely *because* it was written well and with feeling."[3]

It is noteworthy that in the passage just quoted Leontiev twice defends *A Husband's Confession* from the point of view of artistic merit while condemning its moral aspect. After the spiritual crisis of 1871 the cult of beauty which had informed his writing up to that time became increasingly incompatible with his newfound religious outlook; the conflict between the two left a void which seemed seriously to inhibit his creative muse, leading to the production after that time of only minor or unfinished works. He himself was well aware of the problem. "When dealing with a man of a broad and manifold fancy," he wrote, "only the poetry of religion can root out refined immorality . . . The poetry of life exerts its fascination, whereas morality is often, alas, tedious and boring . . . Faith, prayer, the Church, the poetry of Orthodoxy with its ritual and the ascetic 'corrective' at its spiritual heart, that's the only means of imbuing conventional morality with lyricism, the best antidote to the subtle poison of heroic or romantic poetry."[4]

Leontiev seriously considered attempting to clothe this "moral lyricism" in literary form. "My ideal is dogmatic and ascetic Orthodoxy," he wrote in1890 to his friend and disciple Anatoly Aleksandrov, "as a bulwark against science and progress. But presenting this ideal in a worthy form would be a huge and complex task (not less than *Anna Karenina* or my *Odysseus*) and you wouldn't believe, being so young, how much the idea scares me!" One senses from this correspondence that Leontiev knew that the task was now beyond his spiritual resources. "The significance and sacredness of the issue inspire me with holy dread," he confessed, "and on the other hand the abundance of materials and the richness and depth of my personal experience, both secular and spiritual, simply weigh me down . . . So it's not likely I'll produce anything first-rate in this area."[5]

In the years immediately before his death Leontiev began projects for several novels, including *Dying Light* and *Girlfriends*, but they remained unfinished. It would seem that the effort of trying to convey his religious and ethical ideas in a form that would satisfy the aesthetic criterion he still held to be the *sine qua non* of any work that claimed the appellation of art was just too difficult and had finally exhausted his creative impulse. This is particularly true of *Girlfriends*, of which several drafts exist. The story centers on the miniature world of a post-emancipation country estate, which it portrays with a Chekhovian level of realism and psychological insight, but unfortunately Leontiev was unable to finish it. "Sinner that I am," he told Aleksandrov, "I love everything that is beautiful in this world, but I have developed to the point where I am not in a position to choose it above the things of the next, where a choice exists."[6]

Leontiev's interest in the fate of Russian letters remained undimmed however and in the last decade of his life he picked up the baton he had put aside on his flight from Petersburg to the Ottoman East almost twenty years before and produced a number of outstanding works of literary criticism which are a key part of his legacy and which shed a unique light on some of the most famous literary figures of the period, notably Gogol, Dostoevsky, and Tolstoy.

To the end of his life Leontiev continued to scorn dry ethicality and to describe himself as an "aesthetic monomaniac" and "artistic psychopath."[7] His view of art remained essentially unchanged from the view he held in the early 1860s, in the formation of which he was indebted to Apollon Grigoriev, who, he declared: "Looked for poetry not in the abstract but in the very midst of Russian life. His ideal was the rich, broad and fiery life of Russia in the furthest extremities of its virtues and its vices."[8] This doctrine had occasioned only incomprehension and ridicule in the ethico-utilitarian atmosphere of 1860s Petersburg; by the 1880s, however, times and attitudes had changed and with them the receptivity of the public to Leontiev's ideas, or at least those sections of the public willing to accept the necessity for art to be artistic.

This view of art as a search for the poetry of life essentially informed Leontiev's lifelong critique of the so-called realist school of Russian literature, from what he described as the "freakish genius" Gogol onward, a school he insisted was not realistic at all. If the Russian novel were to have a future, he argued, "it must throw off the yoke of the Gogolian school (something even Leo Tolstoy has not managed to do)—at least with regard to form and language."[9] In the servile adherence of Russian writers to the "gloomy specter of Gogol"[10] Leontiev identified the root cause of an aesthetic failure which, he believed, Russian literature would one day come to repent.[11] As an antidote to Gogol he suggested a wide range of foreign and Russian writers ranging from George Sand and Byron to Dmitri Rostovsky whose example might stimulate Russian prose to break free from the "gray gloom,"[12] which he felt had come to circumscribe the métier like an iron cage and which he illustrates in the following schema from a letter written in 1888:

	Gogol	
Turgenev	Russian Literature	Dostoevsky
	Tolstoy	

"And I want to smash this cage and tear it down," Leontiev declared, "otherwise there's no point in going into print."[13]

Incidentally, this "gloomy specter" of Gogol may have had a negative influence on Leontiev's muse as a younger man. In his letter of June 1879 to Vsevolod Solovyev Leontiev hints that the real reason he decided to destroy the manuscripts of the story cycle *River of Time* in 1871 was that he felt he had failed to break free of what he regarded as the Gogolian caricature, a contention supported by Marya Vladimirovna in her memoirs.[14] (It is also possible however that Leontiev's discovery of Tolstoy's *War and Peace* in 1867–68 may have made him pessimistic about his ability to produce an epic historical novel of equal worth.)[15]

Leontiev expands on his view of the plight of Russian letters in his three studies of Tolstoy: "Fear of God and Love for Mankind" of 1882; "Two Counts: Aleksei Vronsky and Leo Tolstoy" of 1888; and "Analysis, Style and Tendency" of 1890. These articles, especially the last, show Leontiev at his most brilliant and most paradoxical. His attempts to delineate where Tolstoy is true to the "aesthetic of life" and where he is guilty of excessive "Gogolian realism" and improbable psychological penetration contrive at one and the same time to provide a truly original insight into Tolstoy and to illuminate the conflict between ethics and aesthetics which lay at the heart of Leontiev's creative impulse. The overall conclusion he draws is that Tolstoy succeeds because his artistic integrity ultimately outweighs the tendentious ethical messages with which he attempts to burden his writings. As he famously put it: "Count Vronsky is dearer and more essential to us than Leo Tolstoy himself."[16]

In "Fear of God and Love for Mankind" Leontiev's critique of Tolstoy's ethics takes as its example the latter's moral fable "What Men Live By." In this parable, a poor shoemaker and his wife take in and care for a naked mendicant who turns out to be an angel exiled by God for disobedience, his fault being allowing a woman to live for the sake of her children despite God's command that her time to die had come. The Almighty has now decreed that the angel will be allowed back into heaven only once he has found the answer to the question of what is it that men live by, which the angel finally decides is "love." Leontiev ingeniously turns the fable back on itself to show both that the story adheres despite itself to the principles of true Orthodoxy, at least in part, and that elsewhere the message is self-defeating in its very illogicality.

In Leontiev's analysis the shoemaker's wife is reconciled to taking in the mendicant, not by innate "love for mankind," as Tolstoy suggests, but when her husband reminds her of her immortal soul; likewise a rich man dies, not because he is rich, but for the solidly Orthodox reason that he has no fear of God, and so forth. Besides these particular examples, the central thesis of the story, Leontiev suggests, is faulty: the angel who is exiled to earth for allowing "love" to prevail over faith in God's wisdom then returns to heaven convinced that all men need to live by is this same "love"; in other words having learned nothing.

Thus Leontiev "unmasks" Tolstoy the defective moralist, but without detriment to Tolstoy the artist; he expressly states that the success of the story is due to the fact that "a very *defective* Christian *thinker* was rescued by the storyteller of genius who dwelt inside him."[17] Rescued as an artist perhaps, but behind Tolstoy's fixation on "love" Leontiev detects the sin of spiritual pride. For Leontiev the relationship of man to God must be primarily based on dread, a dread of incurring His wrath, which leads to love as its fruit. So by shifting the emphasis of this equation and advocating first and foremost a love for mankind, which in Leontiev's eyes is "autonomous, ultra-utilitarian, intemperate and haphazard,"[18] Tolstoy is showing a "bias and falsity" which is yet another example of "that ruling notion of our time which is everywhere in the air. They believe in *humanity*, but no longer in *people*."[19]

For Tolstoy the writer Leontiev is generous in his admiration: "Not just an elephant [as Turgenev had described him] but something even more wonderful, a sivatherium!"[20] For Tolstoy the man and the moralist he evinces an equal contempt and disgust. Indeed it is difficult to think of another individual on whom he releases such a storm of invective, calling him an "old madman . . . a godless anathema . . . as a novelist a genius, as a man and a preacher a blackguard" whose doctrine of love without faith in God and the fear of God is both impracticable and revolting, "a heresy of atheist ethicism and implausible universal benevolence."[21] In Leontiev's view this "autonomous love for abstract humanity," besides having little to do with true Christian love, may have dangerous consequences: it may be accompanied by such an extreme desire for the improvement of mankind's material lot on earth that it leads naturally to a "love" of nihilism and revolution. As he told Rozanov: "You're too kind to Leo Tolstoy the *preacher*. He's worse than the nihilist *criminals*. They mount the gallows unbidden; but not him, he's all right, he's like a fish in water . . . To hell with his 'sincerity' that mercilessly and shamelessly crushes the pieties of the poor in spirit!"[22]

Despite finding himself on the receiving end of these tirades, Tolstoy harbored an affection for Leontiev, admiring his way of "smashing windows" and rating him among the five Russians of his day who were "capable of thinking their own thoughts."[23] Leontiev was less indulgent. When the two men met face to face, on the occasion of a visit by Tolstoy to Optina Pustyn in February 1890, Leontiev concluded their discussion of religion by promising to write to his "connections" in Petersburg to get Tolstoy exiled to Tomsk in Siberia. Tolstoy replied that he would be grateful, as he had been doing everything to achieve the same result but in vain![24]

Leontiev's view of Tolstoy's ethical Christianity as the antechamber to Bolshevism may appear extreme, but he was by no means the only one on either the conservative right or revolutionary left to see his teaching in this light. No less a person than Lenin regarded Tolstoy as the "mirror of the revolution,"[25] while the foremost theoretician of anarchism, Peter Kropotkin, recognized a kindred spirit in Tolstoy's principled opposition to the activities of both Church and State.[26] In fact Leontiev approached the question of faith with remorseless logic. Christianity for him was a faith composed of love *and* fear; those like Tolstoy who stressed only the moral and humanitarian faces of faith were for him guilty of a one-sided interpretation which, logically, would lead to the whole emphasis of man's aspirations being placed in this world, in other words, Christianity would become anti-Christian and something very like Marxism. "Whoever writes about supposedly Christian love without acknowledging the other pillars of the creed," Leontiev declared, "is not a Christian writer but an adversary of Christianity."[27] For him, if faith abide in the hearts of men it will show itself eventually in how they act; "works without faith," on the other hand, are the product of spiritual pride (of which Tolstoy's response above is a fairly classic example) and will bring ruin in their train.[28] Christianity, he wrote, has "no worse enemy than ethicism without mysticism."[29]

Of course Leontiev was well aware, had for decades been all too aware, of the seductiveness of what he described as the doctrine of eudaemonism, or the search for the universal welfare of mankind on earth, a doctrine of which Tolstoy's humanitarianism was for him only the latest manifestation. He now believed he had found the idea which might arrest the apparently unstoppable march of eudaemonism: "Orthodoxy, or in other words the culture of Byzantine discipline and secular asceticism, is the only counterweight to the theory of universal secular well-being. And it is the best nourishment and consolation for whoever has lost faith, either in himself or in others, or in the future of his friends and those dear to him, or in the *future* of mankind."[30]

Leontiev had an unusually keen insight into the religious wellsprings of millenarian revolutionary politics, whether these took the form of socialism, anarchism, nihilism, Marxism, or whatever else, and he saw that to oppose these "faiths" something stronger was needed than a vague appeal to love thy neighbor. "Nihilism," he wrote, "how clear and eloquent it is. And to oppose what is forthright and extreme, one needs something equally forthright and extreme. Mystical Christianity (and I *mean mystical*, not just moral), the teachings of asceticism, faith in *my*, in *my very own*, life to come, the credo of the fear of God, fear which will unerringly turn into love in exalted hearts. This too is something forthright, clear and powerful."[31] Lacking this mystical spirit, a spirit based not on humanism but on religious dread, not only Tolstoy but all who followed him in preaching what Leontiev styled sentimental or "rose-tinted Christianity"[32] were for him simply tools of that *"generalized moral principle, a free ethicism* not bound by any orthodoxy . . . the *ethic of the middling bourgeois character* to which the great majority of Europeans aspire in our day," an ethicism which, taken to its logical conclusion, would lead not to Christ, but to Proudhon.[33]

It is easy today to regard Leontiev's postulate of mystical, ascetic Christianity as the antidote to millenarian socialism as simply wishful thinking, building a castle in the air that could not come to fruition in the real world. Easy, until one remembers that a faith in many ways similar to his has stopped Western ideas of "progress," whether of a socialist or capitalist flavor, in their tracks across a large swathe of the world—Islam. We have already seen that considerable similarities exist between Islam and Leontiev's brand of Christianity and in this context it is worth recalling his prophetic words: "Liberalism will find it hard to make inroads in the lands of Islam." Whether liberalism would have found it equally difficult to make inroads in the Christian East and in Russia if the Orthodox Church had adopted Leontiev's prescription is something on which one can only speculate. Given the strength of the current flowing in favor of "progressive" humanitarianism in the late nineteenth century the attempt might well have failed, but that does not mean that it would not, from the conservative viewpoint, have been worth making.

In any event we shall never know now as Leontiev's ideas were never taken seriously by the religious establishment in Russia, which he believed to have taken the exactly opposite path, toward a "Slavic-Anglican Neo-Orthodoxy,"[34] a Bulgar schism writ large, which would bring disaster in its wake. "If new inquisitors should arise," he wrote, "demanding the reinstitution of martyrdom, then in our day they would appear not in the guise of mystical visionaries animated by faith but in that of the most ordinary egalitarian nihilists who had come to power *by the path prepared for them by this same liberal Slavic-Russian Church.*"[35]

Mention of inquisitors reminds us that Tolstoy was not the only icon of Russian letters to attract scathing criticism from Leontiev for what the latter regarded as a flawed interpretation of Christianity. The theological doctrines developed toward the end of his life by his other great contemporary Fyodor Dostoevsky, which found their most developed expression in the latter's masterpiece *The Brothers Karamazov*, also stimulated Leontiev's repugnance. It was essentially the same issue he had with Tolstoy, that the doctrine of "love for mankind" without the fear of God to underpin it amounted to a "rose-tinted" Christianity that would undermine the sacred edifice of Orthodoxy and usher in the era of universal egalitarian dissolution.

Up to a point Leontiev is prepared to accept Dostoevsky's talents as a writer—he told Rozanov that he found the *Legend of the Grand Inquisitor* a "splendid fantasy"—although he finds him all too prone to Gogolian distortion.[36] "Other writers depict normal life," he wrote, "but with Dostoevsky you get only its psychopathic side, its extreme deviations, and maybe (I only say *maybe*) you get the author himself, his ideals, his spiritual convolutions, his private griefs, struggles and fantasies."[37] He has scant regard however for Dostoevsky's religious message. "*The Brothers Karamazov*," he declared, "could be reckoned an Orthodox novel only by those who had little acquaintance with true Orthodoxy, with the Christianity of the Holy Fathers and Elders of Athos and Optina."[38] And he is scathing about Dostoevsky's mouthpiece, the Elder Zosima: "At Optina *they do not accept the Brothers Karamazov as an authentic work of Orthodoxy, or Zosima as being like Father Ambrose, neither as regards teaching nor personal character. Ambrose is first and foremost a strict Church-mystic* and only then a practical moralist. Zosima (through whose lips Fyodor Mikhailovich speaks) is primarily a moralist—the doctrine of love, etc.—and his mysticism is *extremely weak*."[39]

Leontiev's critique of Dostoevsky's religious outlook found its most succinct expression in his 1880 article in the series *Our New Christians* titled "On Universal Love: The Speech of F. M. Dostoevsky given at the Pushkin Festival" (a grand literary jamboree in 1880 marking the dedication in Moscow of the monument to Pushkin). This article was not wholly negative toward *The Brothers Karamazov*. For all that he firmly regarded Dostoevsky's theology as flawed and his lack of mystical feeling as leading him to depart harmfully from reality, he acknowledges here that in this novel Dostoevsky was at least trying to get to grips with the true nature of ascetic Orthodoxy: "He is *attempting more and more* to find the true doctrinal path . . . he is clearly striving at last to clothe the lyricism of his burning but arbitrary and still hazy morality in forms which are defined and sacred to us."[40] Dostoevsky might have ended, Leontiev believed, by writing a "genuinely Orthodox" work had he not, with his "Pushkin" speech, departed once and for all from the basic tenets of that faith. Instead he remained, as Leontiev told his friend Filippov, "searching for Christianity as for a distant planet seen through a telescope."[41]

Leontiev's indignation over the "Pushkin" speech was provoked partly by the implication behind Dostoevsky's vision of universal harmony and reconciliation that a Russian might declare himself the spiritual brother of that "average European" who was busily ushering in the era of "secondary simplification" and cultural dissolution; partly because, in Leontiev's eyes, Dostoevsky's appeal for universal brotherhood here on earth ran directly counter to the words of the Gospel and therefore counter to God's plan. For Leontiev ethical humanism and Orthodox Christianity were like two trains which, although starting from the same place, were now destined, thanks to the branching of their tracks, to meet in headlong collision: "Harmony à la Dostoevsky, universal love, will not come about—for that humans should need to undergo a chemical transformation—and rivers will not flow with milk and honey, it's all rubbish, contrary to common sense, to the Gospels, and even to natural science."[42]

It is worth noting here that, as with his historicism, Leontiev's pessimistic religious outlook has not lacked for critics. In his *A Note in Defense of Dostoevsky against the Accusation of "New" Christianity*, an addendum to his *Three Speeches in Memory of Dostoevsky*, Vladimir Solovyev suggests that Leontiev did not believe in Christ's mission to redeem mankind and accuses him of harboring a de facto and illegitimate dualism by drawing too hard and fast a line between this world and the next, "for such an unconditional border between *here* and *there* is not recognized by the Church." The theologian Konstantin Aggeyev agreed that "Leontiev never crossed the threshold between the Old and New Testaments, he did not know Christ the Savior," accordingly "Christ is not in him, and in this lies the melancholy limit of his worldview." Similar accusations were leveled en masse at the time against Leontiev over his attacks on the Christianity of Dostoevsky and Tolstoy and have continued since. Both Berdyaev and Kologrivov agree with Solovyev that Leontiev's enduringly aesthetic worldview demanded a dualistic approach to the problem of evil which is reflected in an over-rigorous delineation of this world from the next. Berdyaev sees this as stemming from a failure to comprehend "the mystical resolution of dualism in the divine unity," while Kologrivov doubts whether Leontiev ever attained a full understanding of Christ's message, styling him a "Good Friday Christian who never reached Easter Sunday." Even Rozanov believed that his friend and mentor "never found the positive, the good, the holy and blessed aspects of faith, that which turned *Saul* into *Paul*, to which the martyrs made their sacrifice."[43]

Valid though many of these criticisms may be within their own term of reference, which is the compatibility or otherwise of Leontiev's Christianity with Christ's message, they all miss the fundamental point that Leontiev was no more a theologian than he was a philosopher and that in his peculiarly rigorous form of ascetic Christianity he was seeking a mechanism by which human behavior, his own as much as other people's, might be controlled and directed into productive channels. His religious outlook was accordingly intimately connected to his political agenda. And despite his conversion to a rigorously ascetic interpretation of Orthodox dogma, Leontiev remained until the end of his life an aesthete. In the two decades since his conversion he had become ever more convinced of the necessity for what later came to be known as cosmic synergy between the ethical principle and the aesthetic: "There is something enigmatic and mysterious, vexing even, about the manifestations of the aesthetic in this world, for it must be clear to *anyone who is not out to deceive themselves* how frequently aesthetics and morality, aesthetics and what *appears to be human utility,* are destined to fall into antagonism and discord."[44]

For Leontiev "harmony" is an aesthetic concept, the result of tension between opposing forces, whereas Dostoevsky's "pseudo-harmony" would destroy the aesthetic precisely because it seeks to eradicate this essential antagonism: "Harmony is the reconciliation of antitheses, not in the sense of peaceful and fraternal *concord* in the *ethical sense*, but in the sense of a poetic and mutual self-fulfillment in *life itself* and in art . . . The clash of two great armies, taken in the round and stripped of all inessentials, is a manifestation of *genuine aesthetic harmony.*"[45]

In point of fact Leontiev was not alone in his time in regarding true harmony as the product of creative tension between opposites. In 1909 the influential American sociologist Lester Frank Ward declared synergy to be the universal constructive principle of nature. "I have characterized the social struggle as centrifugal and social solidarity as centripetal," Ward wrote. "Either alone is productive of evil consequences. The struggle is essentially destructive of the social order, while communism removes individual initiative. The one leads to disorder, the other to degeneracy. What is not seen—the truth that has no expounders—is that the wholesome, constructive movement consists in the properly ordered combination and interaction of both these principles. This is social synergy, which is a form of cosmic synergy, the universal constructive principle of nature."[46]

Ward did not know it, but "social synergy" had already found its "expounder," in Leontiev. Time and again toward the end of his life, and with increasing vehemence, Leontiev stressed the superiority of the aesthetic standpoint over the ethical and pointed to the danger inherent in the one-sided application of the latter, which he saw ending by placing the individual under the coercive sway of collective morality, an end-state from which there would be no escape: "Some kind of Nirvana. The German thinkers have contended that the attainment of the Absolute will be the termination of history."[47] The aesthetic, he argued, was, like physics, applicable to everything in the universe, unlike mysticism, ethics, politics, and biology, which applied only in their own spheres.[48] The implication is that the aesthetic point of view trumps all the others and is accordingly also the point of view of God. As Leontiev told Rozanov three months before his death: "The aesthetic worldview can *accommodate everything—all religion and all morality.*"[49]

This could have been Milkeyev speaking in *A Place of One's Own* twenty-seven years before. But not quite. Leontiev is now at pains to emphasize that his religious conversion has vanquished his former aesthetic pantheism, a feat that ethics alone never managed: "I venerate the *spiritual* (mystical) consciousness which triumphs over *passionate aesthetics,* I bow before it, I honor and love it; but when utilitarian ethics triumph over this mysterious poetry, which is indispensable to the fullness of life's development, I am outraged, and I expect nothing of a society where this happens too often."[50]

Despite this assertion of the primacy of spiritual Orthodoxy over the aesthetic principle, Leontiev never managed to reconcile these two poles of his existence, which he knew in his heart to be incompatible. Even with regard to the Grand Inquisitor he was in two minds. "I admit," he told Rozanov, "that I am not wholly on the side of the Inquisitor, but of course I am definitely not on the side of that lifeless and all-forgiving Christ Dostoevsky invented for himself."[51] Noting that acceptance of the Christian Gospel and the spread of liberal "progress" both tend toward a reduction in the variety and aesthetic content of life, Leontiev concludes that we must nonetheless help spread the Christian word for reasons of what he calls *transcendental egoism*, in other words for the salvation of our souls; at the same time we must strive to hinder progress, "which is harmful to Christianity and aesthetics alike."[52]

That Leontiev should have arrived at this solution to the conundrum of reconciling ethics and aesthetics at the very end of his life shows a remarkable consistency in his thinking over several decades. Almost thirty years before, in his literary polemics with Chernyshevsky and Dobrolyubov, he appealed to concepts derived from Schelling's *System of Transcendental Idealism.* That was at the time when Chernyshevsky was promoting his idea of "rational egoism" as the ultimate motivation of all human action. It is hard to imagine that Leontiev did not still have both these things in mind when formulating his idea of "transcendental egoism."

There may have been other formative influences. Kologrivov suggests that the thought of the monk Gurias of Optina may have played a role, while Rozanov sees its origins in Leontiev's religious despair (one is tempted to think it might be better located in his despair of his fellow man).[53] Whatever its origin, in his system of transcendental egoism Leontiev comes closest to resolving what was for him the lifelong riddle: how to reconcile the aesthetic impulse which still beat so powerfully inside his breast with the need to discover a reliable basis for ethical action.

The approaches to faith and morals developed by Tolstoy and Dostoevsky were in Leontiev's view inherently flawed as they were based on a demand which he regarded as impossible to meet: that universal love should come to permeate the world and altruism become the key to morality. This world, Leontiev reminds us constantly, is a fallen one, and universal brotherhood and well-being, and therefore genuine altruism, cannot come to pass in it. "Why," he asks, "should I be concerned to save others from damnation? Who can be sure of saving even themselves?"[54] The wellspring of moral action must accordingly lie elsewhere, in the dread of failing to answer for one's life and deeds at the Last Judgement: "Personal Christianity is first and foremost *Transcendental Egoism* (not in this world but in the next). *Altruism* will come of its own accord. The fear of God (for yourself, for your *immortal soul*) is the beginning of *religious* wisdom."[55]

This idea that if you act primarily with your own salvation in mind, altruism will follow—that is, that your apparently self-interested actions will bring in their train benefits to your fellow man—is not confined to Leontiev. It finds an echo in Herzen: "If people concentrated on saving themselves instead of saving the world, and on liberating themselves instead of liberating mankind, what a blow they would strike for the salvation of the world and the liberation of mankind."[56] Leontiev's dismissal of conscious altruism as an unreliable basis for moral action also seems to look forward to its condemnation in the twentieth century by the Russian-American authoress Ayn Rand and to her promotion in its stead of "ethical egoism" in such books as her 1964 collection of essays *The Virtue of Selfishness: A New Concept of Egoism.*[57]

Like Leontiev, Rand is a controversial figure whose extolling of the benefits of selfishness and advocacy of what she described as rational egoism has inspired admiration and revulsion in unequal measure. Rand owed an acknowledged debt to Nietzsche and despite the gulf of sixty years, a revolution, two world wars and the atom bomb which separates her from Leontiev there are intriguing similarities between the heroic individualism of John Galt in her 1957 novel *Atlas Shrugged* and the existential pathos of Vasily Milkeyev in Leontiev's *A Place of One's Own.*

These endorsements notwithstanding, the practical effectiveness of a transcendental egoism based on the fear of God in bringing about the moral regeneration of mankind may well be doubted. As we shall see, Leontiev himself realized that something more might be needed. What is not in doubt is that on a personal level Leontiev felt that he had at last found the answer to the riddle of reconciling one's egoistical impulses with duty to others which had plagued him from his earliest days. In the end it is not so much that Leontiev disagrees with the aspirations of Tolstoy and Dostoevsky, but that he refuses to accept that their humanist prescriptions can ever bring about the desired result. "Fraternity *where possible* and humanity are certainly recommended in the books of the New Testament," he concedes, "but for the salvation of one's soul *after death. Nowhere in scripture does it say that people will achieve peace and contentment by way of philanthropy. Christ did not promise us this. It's a falsehood.* Christ instructs, or recommends, all of us to love our neighbors *in the name of God;* at the same time as he prophesies that many people will not listen to him."[58]

Yet there is undeniably something strained about Leontiev's alternative, about transcendental egoism. One has the feeling that Leontiev is forcing himself to believe against almost every living impulse in his body and that this conscious submission to the dogma of the Orthodox Church, especially in the person of an elder, is truly the last resort of a tortured soul. As Rozanov wrote: "It's impossible not to observe that aestheticism was his *nature* and that he was only baptized into Christianity. It's a question of first order and second order things."[59] Nonetheless, Leontiev's later writings on the relationship between ethics, aesthetics, and religious faith remain a brilliant and disturbing, not to say disquieting, contribution to human thought. As he put it: "What is one to do? Hate the aesthetic? *Pretend* on moral grounds that *you don't notice it?* Despise morality? *Impossible.* Neither the one nor the other nor the third. But here's where positive religion steps in again with its all-conquering truth. It requires no lies or pretenses. Yes, it says, that is graceful, strong, aesthetic—*but it will not redeem your soul.*"[60]

Forced or not, the dread of the wrath of God as the reconciliation of ethics and aesthetics marks Leontiev's nearest approach to the solution of this, his lifelong conundrum.

CHAPTER 11

Reactionary or Revolutionary?

"It was only despair that made Leontiev, the grand aesthete, withdraw into the shell of his rigorous conservatism and hide away from the current of *philistine* ideas and bourgeois certainties of his time and of the approaching future. Accordingly, if something *not conservative, radical* even, had beckoned from afar to his chivalrous soul, as long as it was *not bourgeois, not trite, not vulgar,* then he would have embraced it with the full force of his—I allow myself the word—genius."[1]

Thus wrote Vasily Rozanov in 1905, fourteen years after his friend and mentor's death. As usual, Rozanov gets to the heart of the enigma that was Konstantin Leontiev. For if with the notion of transcendental egoism we may say that Leontiev's struggle to find a synthesis of the conflicting demands of ethics and aesthetics had reached its conclusion, the dread of losing the poetry of the life to come enabling him to some extent to abnegate the poetry of this life when it came into conflict with the demands of faith; yet in the fields of social and political thinking, by contrast, his course was far from run.

In February 1887, thanks to the intervention of his friend Filippov, Leontiev was able to retire from his post as a censor on health grounds with an enhanced pension. He had never really felt comfortable in Moscow, despite the acquisition there of a number of young converts to his views, his "disciples," while his official duties, though hardly onerous, had combined with ill-health to reduce his literary output to a trickle. He now left the city and settled in a small lodge next to the monastery of Optina Pustyn at Kozelsk, which became known as the "Consul's House." He stayed there with Liza Pavlovna until August 1891 when, on the advice of his elder, Father Ambrose, and following his secret ordination as a monk under the name of Brother Kliment, he removed to Sergiev Posad, where he died in November of the same year. The intervening four years, a period he referred to somewhat misleadingly as one of "blessed quietism," were to prove the happiest since his early days in the Ottoman East.[2] The description is misleading because, far from his fading into oblivion, the leisure and freedom from care (and from financial dependency on publishers like Katkov) of his retirement resulted in a remarkable late surge of writing on social and political topics.

The political works of Leontiev's final years are informed by those tendencies toward fatalism and pessimism which were the key elements of his religious outlook.[3] They are also, like his earlier political treatises, strongly deterministic in flavor, predicated on a belief in a "higher, *supra-human* logic of history, her spiritual teleology,"[4] a belief that remained with him until the very end of his days. Leontiev saw this logic working to hidden ends, producing deep impressions on the soul of man the microcosm, who converts them into a psychological whole within himself. The result is to imbue man with the conviction that he is in control of events and the destiny of nations, whereas in reality it is he who is being led by the hand of predetermined fate. "The realization of historical destinies," Leontiev argued, "depends less on the conscious actions of men than on the intervention of *something* higher and more elusive; a conscious goal is indispensable, but it only has a chance of achieving fruition when at least to some extent it coincides with the outline, vague enough in detail, of this design of fate, when it anticipates its general features."[5]

The extent of man's subjection to these cosmic forces varies in Leontiev's writing; most often though he sees statesmen, for example, as simply the helpless tools of the "fateful interplay of mechanical forces in international affairs,"[6] their situation not unlike, in Schopenhauer's phrase, "those wooden figureheads which used to adorn the prows of ships."[7] And Leontiev freely applies this metaphor to even the greatest among his contemporaries. In his late fragmentary story "The Pessimist," the protagonist (who is himself a devotee of Schopenhauer) describes the nation-builder Bismarck as "as much a blind tool of fate as anyone else . . . it might be otherwise if our individual reason and individual will counted for something in history, but they're about as good as nothing . . . Bismarck should realize that there are currents in history against which no-one can prevail."[8]

Informed by this fatalism, Leontiev's later works are in part devoted to seeking a "teleological" explanation for the apparent powerlessness of the forces of conservatism to arrest the unstoppable march of the "proteus of universal European dissolution." Whatever set itself against this tide seemed to him doomed to failure, witness the uprisings in Poland in 1831 and Hungary in 1848 (which he argues failed because they represented a conservative revolt against "liberalism from above"), witness the fall of Napoleon III, the defeat of the Confederacy in America, the humiliations of the Pope at the hands of the Italian bourgeoisie, the hostility of Russia toward conservative Austria.[9] For Leontiev the agents of destruction were everywhere the same, the liberals and revolutionaries, themselves "simply blind tools of that *clandestine will* which is everywhere seeking to democratize, to level, to confuse the social elements, at first across Germano-Roman Europe, then perhaps (who knows) across the whole world."[10]

Alongside the pessimism and fatalism of Leontiev's later articles, his anti-Europeanism persists undiminished, differing from that of the period of *Byzantinism and Slavdom* mainly in its more strident tone. "Oh how we hate you, *contemporary Europe*," he fulminates, "for destroying everything that was great, beautiful and holy in you yourself and through your infectious breath so much that is precious to us, alas."[11] In a series of trenchantly titled articles, including the "Average European as the Ideal and Weapon of Universal Destruction" of 1872, revised in 1884, and "Nationalist Politics as a Weapon of World Revolution" of 1888, Leontiev continued to analyze the genesis and spread of the cult of individualism which he regarded as fatally undermining the conditions for cultural flowering. He now saw no hope that Europe would escape the "new, unexpected coils of the revolutionary serpent, still not sated with destruction;" the key question for him now was whether Russia was doomed through "infection with Western bacteria" or whether she could summon the strength to recover and endure.[12]

Leontiev identified the revolutionary year 1789 as the watershed in European history and was bitter in his condemnation of the revolution in ideas that had led to it. He excoriated the theorists of the Enlightenment for having shattered beyond recall the system of values based on social inequality, absolute monarchy, and the universal Catholic Church—in his eyes the three pillars of the great cultural flowering begun in the Renaissance—and having spawned in place of the cultured state a fragmented and mutually hostile conglomerate of competing individuals. This was for him "the ulcer of Western *individualism*, the worship of the human *individual*, this new form of idolatry."[13] The evident competitiveness of these individuals only served to disguise, thinly, the fact that they all corresponded to the same basic type: "The honest and diligent *average* man, indistinguishable from all the rest, believing in nothing beyond the universal rights of man, and at the same time looking askance at anything more graceful than himself—that is the ideal of the European of today of whatever nationality."[14]

The absolute nadir of this European bourgeois everyman was epitomized for Leontiev in the ubiquitous dress-coat to which all the glorious male attire of past ages had been reduced. "The tail-coat," he observed, "*is the mourning dress which the West has adopted out of grief for her magnificent, religious, aristocratic and artistic past.*"[15] Would it not be unendurable, he asked, would it not be a mockery of history, if all the suffering and striving of humanity had occurred "*so that a French or German or Russian bourgeois in his shapeless and comical dress* should strut about 'individually' or 'collectively' on the ruins of all this past greatness?"[16] This, in Leontiev's eyes, would be the greatest tragedy of all: "Oh, the mighty, blood-soaked yet picturesque mountain of universal history! From the end of the last century you have endured the pangs of new births. And from your suffering womb has crawled a mouse! A self-satisfied caricature of former people has been born . . . *the average rational European.*"[17]

It is consistent with his attack on these tendencies in modern Europe that in this last period of his life Leontiev should return with renewed vigor to his scathing critique of the racial nationalism that was such a hallmark—perhaps *the* defining feature—of his time. "Nationalist politics," he argued, "is one of the strangest *self-delusions of the nineteenth century* . . . *National unity* and *national culture* are two totally different things and in recent times have everywhere shown themselves to be antitheses."[18] The distinction Leontiev makes here is crucial to an understanding of his political outlook, and it was their failure to comprehend it that led many in Russian nationalist circles—most volubly Ivan Aksakov, Aleksandr Kireyev, and Petr Astafyev—to accuse him of treachery to the Russian national idea.[19]

Cultural universality meant for Leontiev not the reduction of cultures to cosmopolitan uniformity but the truly national, the *self-dependent* and individual culture of each nation, "overflowing its national vessel to quench the thirst of other peoples."[20] The racial nationalism of his time he regarded as the inverse of this, "one *of the forms of universal revolution, one* of the most powerful levers *of cosmopolitan cultural fusion.*"[21] Predicated as he saw it on the adoption of the universal pan-European monoculture, nationalism was inherently inimical to the development of individual national culture, serving only toward the destruction of what was good in the old order to pave the way for "the transition to cosmopolitan government, at first pan-European, and then perhaps universal."[22] Under these prevailing conditions, Leontiev viewed undeveloped peoples freeing themselves from foreign oppression, in the way that the Greeks and Slavs strove to throw off the "Turkish Yoke," as in "the position of a man escaping from prison at the time of a raging epidemic."[23]

So how was Russia to escape this epidemic? Leontiev advocated the introduction of an absolute quarantine between Russia and that Western Europe which he saw as in the process of destroying all social and organic differentiation within itself. In his eyes abhorrence of *contemporary* Europe was the only way to preserve the possibility of cultural flowering in Russia. In essence, it was the identical position he had set out twenty years before in a letter to his friend Gubastov of 1868: "Personal and social creativity in Russia is possible only on the basis of this abhorrence. Without it all is dry and dead."[24]

So great is Leontiev's antipathy to Western ideas and their increasing influence in Russia that it is easy to see him as being in a kind of permanent revolt against the whole tendency of nineteenth-century thought. After all, the things he attacks most violently—liberalism, racial nationalism, political emancipation—are what many people would regard as the essential motivating ideas of the period. And he certainly did foresee a different outcome to the "century of progress" to most of his fellows. Contemporary Europe he regarded as having moved definitively into the phase of "secondary simplification" marked by the "fusing" of its various cultural manifestations in the amorphy of cultural death, the essential cause being the "cholera" of political liberalism. The refusal to face up to these unpalatable developments had in his eyes become "Russia's national misfortune."[25]

Leontiev's hatred of liberalism at times drove him to those heights of invective for which he has become notorious: "Oh hateful equality! Oh vile uniformity! Oh accursed progress!"[26] As for the liberals themselves, with their blind faith in progress, they were to him the type of people Lenin would later come to regard as "useful idiots," more dangerous than the open revolutionaries. "Pitiful people," he wrote, "and the more sincere they are, the more honest, the more convinced, the worse they are, the more destructive in their guileless moderation, in their quietly and gently destructive gradualism! It's difficult to pursue them, to bring them to book, to punish them . . . But in their 'legal inviolability' they are more dangerous to our future than open criminals against whom every government has the sword of justice, has penal servitude, has banishment."[27]

For Leontiev the central weakness of liberalism, and the quality that made it most dangerous, was its lack of an underlying and informing "idea," the absence of which rendered it in his eyes pure negation. "With liberals," he wrote, "everything is vague, mixed up, colorless, diffident. The liberal system is, in essence, the absence of all system, it is merely the *negation of all extremes, the fear of everything that is consequent, of everything that is expressive.*"[28] In the last analysis it was all the same to Leontiev whether the liberals should be regarded as malicious or merely deluded, for they remained servants of revolution either way: "The flail of ignorance, the flail of cosmopolitan infection and gradual legalized destruction."[29] He predicted, correctly, that liberalism, which he saw as a wholly negative concept, would in Russia at least ultimately yield to something positive but deeply *illiberal*, and that the nihilists, the convinced revolutionaries, would eventually cast aside their liberal "allies" once the latter had served their purpose.

It is instructive to compare this damning assessment of liberalism to Leontiev's different attitude toward the radical thinker Proudhon (with whom he had an enduring love-hate relationship), who he referred to as "the clearest, most unequivocal and consequential of all the revolutionaries and progressives of the nineteenth century."[30] Leontiev was consistently more antagonistic toward the liberals than toward the nihilists, to whom he at least accorded the compliment of having an "idea" behind their depredations. It is perhaps indicative of this that General Matveyev in *Two Chosen Women*, on being shown a photograph of Sonya Kiseleva's former lover, the nihilist Nesvitsky, admires his "energetic and brooding, though handsome, face."[31]

Leontiev's unrestrained and violent response to the spread of Western liberal values led to him being bracketed among the darkest apostles of reaction under Alexander III, a label that has overshadowed his legacy.[32] And it cannot be denied that many of his later pronouncements have a distinctly reactionary flavor. For example, in the sphere of education and scientific advancement he repeatedly calls for a *"rational, evolutionary obscurantism,"* a slowing down, or if possible reversing, of the spread of knowledge, especially scientific knowledge, among the masses, that being one of the chief sluices through which he believed the "proteus of destruction" spreads through society.[33] In this connection he calls for a wholly new social science that will put an end to the cult of inventions, especially peaceful inventions which, as they threatened the social structure, he regarded as much more dangerous than "dynamite or Krupp cannons."[34] Going one step further Leontiev seems to anticipate the twentieth century by advocating the burning of a great part of "lifeless and unoriginal" contemporary literature and the creation of what he styled a "society for the purification of the intellectual atmosphere."[35]

It is probable that Leontiev saw himself, or at least positioned himself, as a reactionary thinker. He was a warm advocate (though he voiced doubts about their effectiveness and durability) of the reactionary measures introduced after the assassination of Alexander II in 1881 by Konstantin Petrovich Pobedonostsev (1827–1907), imperial adviser and Procurator of the Holy Synod under Alexander III, whose name became a byword for social stagnation and intellectual repression. And his existing antipathy to the Pan-Slavists, whom he styled "moral atheists," was further fueled by their negative reaction to

Pobedonostsev's reforms.[36] His 1891 article "Slavophilism in Theory and Slavophilism in Practice" posed the question: if the Pan-Slavists were as opposed to Western influences as they pretended, why then did they not welcome measures which by increasing the stratification of Russian society might give her the strength to withstand the onslaught of European ideas?[37] Leontiev's answer was that Nicolas I had been right to suspect that "beneath the wide brocaded kaftans in which they parade, unnoticed by themselves, are concealed the narrow and disgusting pantaloons of the ordinary European bourgeois."[38]

Despite this it is probable that in his self-identification with the reactionary party in Russia Leontiev was deluding himself in much the same way he had done when, in the teeth of abundant evidence to the contrary, he saw himself as collaborating with Chernyshevsky to advance the aesthetic ideals of Belinsky; or when he saw himself as allied to Aksakov in furthering the ideals of the Slavophiles of the 1840s. By the time of his retirement he had spent many years in political isolation, as comprehensively ignored by the right as he was roundly vilified by the left. Apart from odd occasions, as when in the winter of 1885–86 Pobedonostsev bought some sixty copies of *The East, Russia and Slavdom*, a collected edition of Leontiev's earlier works on Eastern affairs, for use in seminaries, or when his articles "Nationalist Politics as a Weapon of World Revolution" and "At the Grave of Pazukhin" found their way to the attention of the Czar, the men of power and influence in Saint Petersburg had little time for Leontiev. Why was this?

The simple answer is that they sensed that Leontiev was no more a true reactionary than he was a true Pan-Slavist.[39] His ambiguous attitude to genuine reactionaries like Pobedonostsev and the publisher Katkov betrays this. Publicly, in articles such as "Mr. Katkov and his Enemies at the Pushkin Festival," he was prepared to defend Katkov against his liberal and leftist critics; privately, however, in his autobiographical *My Literary Destiny* and in his letters, he took a much more critical view, scarcely bothering to conceal his antipathy toward this "Public Muscovite"[40] on whom he had depended for employment during the difficult 1870s and who had imposed a humiliating censorship on him over the Eastern question.

Leontiev's relationship with Pobedonostsev was equally problematic. In a letter to Filippov, who was the latter's adversary in government circles, he describes the Procurator of the Holy Synod in lukewarm terms: "He's a very useful fellow, but in what way? He's like the frost, he prevents further decomposition, but nothing will *grow* in his soil. He's not only not an originator, he's not even a reactionary, not a savior, not a restorer, he's just a conservative in the narrowest sense of the word. As I say, frost, a nightwatchman, an airless tomb, a prissy old maid and nothing more!"[41]

Leontiev and Pobedonostsev became indelibly linked in the public mind through one remark of the writer's that was taken up and spread abroad by the statesman: "It is necessary to *freeze* Russia a little, so she does not decay."[42] In making this controversial pronouncement Leontiev may have been thinking back to what he regarded as the beneficial effects of the "Turkish Yoke" in preserving the Christian populations in the Ottoman domains from infection by Western liberalism. "Conquest is hateful," he wrote in the short story "Chrizó" of 1868, "and the Turks are barbaric, no question, but thanks to their bloody yoke the air of Cretan life is filled with the highest lyricism."[43]

At all events the association between Leontiev and Pobedonostsev was only skin deep and masked a gulf of emphasis which separated the two men. For whereas Pobedonostsev was a true reactionary in the sense that he opposed all change and saw salvation only in the preservation of the status quo at any cost, Leontiev was too deep and subtle a thinker to adhere to such a simplistic prescription, which he saw must inevitably fail in the long run. As he was well aware, his own "Triune Theory" of historical development excluded any backward movement in history, any possibility of infinite stagnation, of "freezing," or any return to a former order. We have already seen Leontiev's admonition that conservatives must come to terms with the "unavoidable new." Similarly, with reference to the Byzantine theocracy, he argued that "the triumph of *simple conservatism* was as dangerous to the state as unbridled progress."[44] "The state is its own kind of organism," Leontiev reminded his contemporaries, "and it cannot breathe exclusively either the nitrogen of complete stagnation or the consuming oxygen of continual movement."[45] It followed that "reaction is not a radical cure but only a temporary reprieve for an organism that is *already* affected *by an incurable disorder.*"[46]

"It is time we learned *how to do reaction!*" declared Leontiev.[47] What he may have meant by this is hinted at in the dedication he chose for his seminal work *The East, Russia and Slavdom*, a quotation from his contemporary, the Russian historian and noted authority on Leibniz Vladimir Ivanovich Guerrier, to the effect that: "Not every *reaction* is inimical to progress in the true meaning of that word . . . reaction does not coincide with the notion of regress, on the contrary, *every reaction which corrects and amplifies the contemporary idea of progress reveals itself as a new element of progress.*"[48] When accordingly Leontiev states that the "thawing" of Russia cannot be stopped "by repressive *freezing* alone, without certain retrograde reforms,"[49] then what he means by "retrograde" must be regarded as problematic, as indeed it was by those in positions of influence in Petersburg, to whom he remained a largely incomprehensible and suspicious figure. If true reaction becomes an element of progress, then Leontiev has at least as much claim to be seen as a progressive thinker as a reactionary one. So what were the "progressively reactionary" ideas of Leontiev's late period?

Here one constant theme emerges that may be summed up under the name Czargrad. We have seen already that the annexation of Constantinople by Russia became for Leontiev something of an idée fixe from the late 1870s on, and it remained so until the end of his days. *"We are bound to take her,"* he declared, *"and we will,* for there is no other escape for us from the labyrinth of the Eastern Question or from the mire of our domestic difficulties."[50] For Leontiev it was only through possession of the ancient seat of Byzantine Orthodoxy that Russia and the Christian East could hope for renewal and a new cultural flowering; accordingly, the resolution of the Eastern Question must mean: "1) The joining of Czargrad to Russia with the adjoining areas of Thrace and Asia minor. 2) The creation on the ruins of Turkey of an *Orthodox* (i.e., not *purely Slav*) confederation of the four multi-ethnic Orthodox states: Greece, Serbia, a united Rumania, and Bulgaria. 3) (if possible) the joining of the remnants of Turkey and the whole of Persia to this confederation."[51]

The whole aim of this construct would be to keep open the possibility of cultural renewal in the East by erecting the firmest possible barrier to cultural penetration from the West. The incorporation of Turkey and Persia into an Orthodox confederation might seem surprising, but it is actually consistent with Leontiev's rejection of racial nationalism as the foundation of the cultural state. The purpose of the inclusion of non-Slav, non-Orthodox elements was precisely to achieve: *"The highest degree of Asiatic mysticism and the least possible influence of European rational enlightenment."*[52] In the last year of his life, in a letter to Filippov, Leontiev widened the scope of the federation even further, to include Syria, Palestine, Arabia and Egypt (after the expulsion of the English), a scheme that he urged Filippov to show secretly to the Czar as a blueprint for the salvation of Russia. Such a federation, he argued, would lead to greatness and longevity, whereas a purely Slav confederacy would be the "downfall of Russia."[53]

Apart from all other considerations, a more succinct exemplification than this manifesto of why Leontiev cannot be considered a Slavophile, let alone a Pan-Slavist, it would be hard to imagine. To the end of his days he remained convinced, in opposition to both Slavophiles and Westernizers, that Russia was not a purely Slav nor indeed European nation, but rather Slav-Asiatic. This tendency, often styled "Eurasianism" or "Turanianism," becomes ever more marked in his later writings, where he refers to the Russians as "enigmatic

Slav-Turanians"[54] and asserts that, as well as her Orthodox faith, it is the "fruitful mingling of the Turanian in our Russian blood"[55] that Russia has to thank for whatever creative impulse she may possess. In his advocacy of Russia's Asiatic heritage, Leontiev occasionally goes to extremes—"A pity the Tatars did not stay with us"—but this is an outlook consistent with his pronounced idealism.[56] For Leontiev the Turanian element provided Russia with an ideality he found to be sadly lacking in her European intelligentsia of whatever stripe.

Leontiev was well aware of the potentially centrifugal tendencies of such a multinational, multiethnic, multi-faith community. His answer was the establishment of a cultural and religious epicenter on the seat of the Orthodox faith—"Czargrad-Constantinople"—and a return to something very like the forms of governance of the Byzantine empire: "An *enduring despotism*, acknowledged and accepted more or less by all, freely or under compulsion, from love or from fear, for profit or from self-sacrifice, a *despotism in the highest degree unequal and variegated*, the *constant and habitual coercion of every level of society*."[57] Only under such conditions he felt would the actual idea informing the new confederation—Byzantine Orthodoxy—have a chance to take root in the popular imagination. So "Czargrad must be taken" becomes a constant refrain in Leontiev's later writings, consciously taking its cue from Cato the Elder's "Carthago delenda est."[58] As to the future political capital of the Russian Empire, Leontiev dismisses Westernized Petersburg—which he styled "Russia's ulcer"[59]—out of hand and after considering and rejecting the claims of Moscow, ancient capital of Muscovy, he lights upon a more radical choice, the even older capital of Rurik and Kievan Rus'. "Petersburg is the thesis," he declared, "Moscow the antithesis of the Russian question; Kiev and Czargrad must be the synthesis."[60]

This concept of an Eastern federation predicated on the total eclipse of Saint Petersburg and the relegation of Moscow to secondary status and which included non-Slav, non-Orthodox, and even Asiatic elements encapsulates the chasm which in reality separated Leontiev from Pobedonostsev. It was less of a reactionary blueprint than a revolutionary manifesto and was no more likely to appeal to the brokers of power in Petersburg in the late 1880s than its somewhat less radical pan-Orthodox forerunner had been to Aksakov and the Pan-Slavists in the early 1870s.[61] But Leontiev was exclusively concerned with Russia's cultural development, not with her future as a military and industrial power; he feared Russia might destroy herself by turning into a "new [classical] Macedonia," politically and militarily powerful but culturally barren and doomed to disappear from the face of history.[62] Thus he saw Petrine Russia, the military colossus based upon and symbolized by Petersburg, as having feet of clay, evidenced by the limited success of the reactionary reforms instituted after the assassination of Alexander II, and as sliding unwittingly but inevitably to destruction. *"Petersburg,"* he prophesied, *"her artificially created strength notwithstanding, will not escape her downfall in the wake of the unstoppable, almost involuntary gravitation of our history toward the southeast."*[63]

Thus we see Leontiev advocating a return to first principles: a decisive move away from Peter's "window on Europe" back toward ancient Kievan Rus'; a new conception of Russia as a semi-Asiatic, Byzantine-Orthodox cultural world. At first glance this would seem to be hopelessly romantic and impracticable. So it certainly appeared to those of power and influence in Petersburg and Moscow, where the prescriptions of Leontiev's last years found no more favor, or rather less if that were possible, than had the theories of his maturity in the 1870s. But Leontiev's eyes were set firmly on the future, and the practical side of his prospectus takes as its basis not the medieval world of Rurik and Vladimir but the much more recent period of Catherine the Great, which he regarded as the apex of Russia's most recent cultural renaissance, the key to its success and durability being the firm hand of autocracy supported by a hereditary aristocracy which acted as a buffer between the monarch and society at large.[64]

The importance of the aristocratic caste ranks even higher in Leontiev's pantheon than autocracy itself. "The separation of the various estates," he argued, "inequality between persons and classes, is more important for the state than the monarchy."[65] For Leontiev this was the fundamental feature of the reign of Catherine, a period that provided him with his ultimate blueprint for the social order in the future Eastern Federation: *"A variegation not confused and anarchic but organized and unified; divergences of social position and upbringing* fixed within juridical *boundaries* for the avoidance of *chaotic diversification."*[66] A society thus ordered would also reflect the divine order as expounded in the *Celestial Hierarchy* of the Pseudo-Dionysius, which Leontiev had studied, and chime with God's plan for the ordering of human affairs, a plan which, as we have seen, he regarded as primarily an aesthetic concept. "Organization expresses itself as unity in variety," he wrote, *"even if this sometimes requires coercion, but never as freedom in uniformity,* which is precisely *disorganization."*[67]

The idea of a society based on caste distinctions, which may also owe a debt to his observations of the structure of monastic communities on Athos and at Optina and elsewhere, is central to Leontiev's later thinking. "A system of social hierarchies, inequality of citizens, their division into unequal social strata and groupings," he declares, "is the *normal* condition of mankind."[68] This throws an interesting light on Leontiev's view of history. As we have repeatedly observed, Leontiev was a committed realist and differed from his philanthropically minded contemporaries in refusing to see any "final goal" to human history, indeed in viewing the attainment of such a goal as the end of all history. He is consistently hostile to all such teleological argumentation and concerned only to describe the rise and fall of states and cultures, not to prescribe their final destinations. In so far as he looks at human history as a self-contained process at all, it is to come to quite different conclusions:

> In accordance with real facts, with the examples of nature, which stand outside mankind, with the experiences of contemporary and ancient history, with human psychology, which demands alternation between rest and struggle, which thirsts for variety and change, one cannot but think that endless circles are a better description of the history of this earth than is the blueprint of unbroken utilitarian development by means of scientific progress, put to the service of the equality of persons and the brotherhood of nations.[69]

Leontiev's concept here of history moving in "endless circles" is strongly redolent of Nietzsche's "ewige Wiederkunft des Gleichen" (eternal Recurrence of the Same) under which all ideas of progress and development must be seen as illusory, as the more things appear to change the more they stay the same.[70] The above extract is from the fourth of Leontiev's *Letters from Athos* and can be dated to 1872, ten years before the first mention of eternal recurrence by Nietzsche in aphorism 341 of *Die fröhliche Wissenschaft (The Gay Science)* of 1882. It is another instance of the remarkable convergence in the thinking of two men who lived and worked it total ignorance of each other that we saw in connection with Milkeyev's aestheticism in *A Place of One's Own*. (It also serves to refute the claim by Sidney Monas that Leontiev did not articulate "themes of such resonance as those of the Overman, Eternal Return, or Dionysos, which are central to Nietzsche."[71] Put together with Milkeyev's anticipation of the "Übermensch" in *A Place of One's Own*, Leontiev's discovery of "endless circles" means we have now encountered two-thirds of this triad.)

Leontiev's notion of the cyclical nature of history is based on the belief that there exist "*real social forces* . . . which never disappear but merely fluctuate between the strength and weakness of their temporary appearance at any given moment in human history; regardless of reforms or revolutions everything *remains fundamentally unchanged*, it simply appears in different combinations of strength and preponderance."[72] These "real social forces" or "social psychomechanisms," as Leontiev calls them,[73] include religious institutions, a ruler with army and court, various social institutions including, in one form or another, slavery, ownership of land, movable capital, labor, sciences, and the arts.[74]

For the idea of "real and immutable social forces," Leontiev acknowledges a debt to the German jurist Robert von Mohl (1799–1875).[75] It is possible that he may also have been recalling Herzen's view of: "The endless game of life, pitiless, like death, irrevocable, like birth, *corsi e ricorsi* of history, the *perpetuum mobile* of a pendulum."[76] As his chief authority for the eternal recurrence of these "real social forces" Leontiev turns however to Plato. Leontiev sees a threefold division of society along the lines of Plato's polity of rulers, military guardians, and productive laborers as the basis of all social organization and as natural and inevitable. The flowering of the Russian state under Catherine took place, he argues, against the threefold backdrop of autocracy, Orthodoxy, and serfdom; its recurrence will be the only salvation from anarchy and chaos. "If the whole of contemporary mankind is not to be condemned to *rapid destruction*," he insists, "then Plato's *tripartite division* must reappear *somewhere* in a new and complex guise: priests, warriors and workers; *spiritual discourse, bravery and power, physical labor and obedience.*"[77]

Leontiev frankly admits that this rigid tripartite system is likely to be coercive for many; indeed he welcomes the fact since, as we have repeatedly seen, he views individual liberty as tending to weaken the central "despotic" idea which informs and underpins the social order. The maxim that *"all social organization means compulsion for the majority"* is what he calls his "sociological axiom."[78] In Leontiev's eyes this is particularly true of Russia: "Russians, enough said! Sloth and indiscipline, or else disorder and frivolity! Russians are not made for freedom. Take away fear and punishment and everything goes to the dogs!"[79]

It is worth noting that while Leontiev sees Plato's tripartite system as the blueprint for a stable and productive society, he does not advocate a complete freezing of social mobility. On the contrary, he regards the coercive element in a rigid social hierarchy as being productive of strong and vigorous individuals who can surmount the barriers it puts in the way of the chaotic centrifugalism which he regards as the straight road to social disintegration.[80] For Leontiev, the most significant features of the perceived flowering of Russian culture under Catherine were the "stratifying" measures, such as the Table of Ranks and the Edict of Nobility, which allowed a healthy degree of mobility while preventing it from becoming excessive. "This discipline," he wrote, "accustoming some to power, others to obedience, contributed to the development at all levels and in all segments of society of powerful, passionate and sophisticated characters, whether complex or simple, refined or vigorously earthy . . . thus only the very strongest, in the best and worst senses, the most gifted, the luckiest or the most cunning persons, or the especially original, were able to tear themselves from their social grouping, in their different ways, for good and ill, but by whatever means they employed they managed it."[81]

As we have seen, for Leontiev the basis of right action is that fear of God which induces good behavior in the disciple through *Transcendental Egoism*, the concern for one's immortal soul. Recognizing that his countrymen were unlikely to come quickly to an awareness of this fear and were therefore unlikely to be moved by transcendental considerations, he recommended that the secular authorities should impose a "fear of man" in its place. Society, in short, should be ordered in accord with the divine plan. "Where the unmediated fear of God is lacking, the mediate influence of the *fear of man*, that is the authorities, can be very fruitful."[82] The Czar should exercise his right in Russia as God does in the universe: *"The sacred right of doing violence to our will."*[83]

In the last analysis Leontiev agrees with Plato on the nature of the just society: "Wisdom for some, bravery for others, *obedience for the majority*."[84] If Russia were to have a future, then in Leontiev's eyes it must be based on the strengthening of Byzantine Orthodoxy, the reinforcement of autocracy, maintenance of a hereditary nobility, inalienability of peasant land, and consolidation of the gentry's, independence of thought and artistic creativity, and the preservation of all possible existing Russian forms of life and the creation of new ones. This radical manifesto clearly ran counter to the nineteenth century's prevailing ideas of utilitarian progress and leveling uniformity and in the Russia of the last decades of that century power would be needed to bring it to fruition. The power of the Russian state was unavailable, being directed to other, more mundane goals, not the least of which was the prolongation of its own existence. Where else then was that power to be found?

CHAPTER 12

The Feudalism of the Future

We have now followed the development of Leontiev's thought through to his last years of intellectual and material independence in the blessed seclusion of Optina Pustyn. We should end this journey by examining the ultimate evolution of his socio-political and religious ideas, his remarkable and prophetic legacy to his countrymen and to the world, as it unfolded under the influence of a towering figure in late nineteenth-century Russian thought, the philosopher and theologian Vladimir Solovyev.

Although Leontiev and Solovyev had met as early as February 1878, when the latter was just twenty-four, the first sign of Solovyev exerting a direct influence on Leontiev's ideas comes in the third of the latter's *Letters on Eastern Affairs* of 1882 where Leontiev refers to the young theologian as "someone whose boots I am unworthy to lace when it comes to religious metaphysics or the inner meaning of the general ordinances of the Church."[1] Leontiev's specific debt to Solovyev in this *Letter* is for his support of the necessity of a hierarchy in the church as a reflection of God's heavenly hierarchy, a concept to which, as noted above, Leontiev was naturally drawn. More generally though, in the period up to the mid-1880s Leontiev seems to have been attracted by Solovyev's critique of "abstract" Western philosophical systems and his theoretical subordination of philosophy to theology in such works as his *Critique of Abstract Principles* and *Religious Foundations of Life*. Leontiev's thought too was tending in this direction—he now held ten new mystical sects like the *skoptsy* to be preferable to five new philosophical systems like those of Fichte and Hegel[2]—and he was happy to acknowledge his debt to a fellow thinker who shared his *"pessimistic outlook regarding the feebleness of our spirit and the necessity of bowing to God's power, requiring the subordination of rationalism to mysticism* and of our *crude realism to hidden higher principles* accessible not to reason but to the thirst for faith."[3]

Leontiev's admiration for Solovyev in this early period was at any rate sufficiently strong to survive the publication by the latter in 1883 of *The Great Schism and the Politics of Christianity* which, with its open attack on Russian nationalism and its advocacy of church unification, managed to isolate him from most of the Orthodox-nationalist camp in Russia. In 1885 Leontiev still ranked Solovyev, along with Gubastov and Filippov, as one of his only three "helpers" and remained convinced of his "personal devotion."[4] Slowly though the picture begins to change, and by 1888 a more generalized doubt is beginning to creep into Leontiev's mind. Early in that year he can still "strongly recommend" that his friend Aleksandrov get a copy of Solovyev's *Theocracy* and if possible meet this "most noble fellow, as a thinker more gifted than Tolstoy, as different from him as the sky is from the earth."[5] But by the middle of the year a note of uncertainty is discernible in his reaction to Solovyev's *The National Question in Russia*. He continues to regard Solovyev as an "authentic genius, carrying an exalted mystical sign on his forehead,"[6] but Solovyev's outspoken attack on the Slavophiles generally and, especially in his sister article "Russia and Europe," on Leontiev's long-time mentor Nikolai Danilevsky awoke in Leontiev the consciousness that there might exist between him and the young philosopher a definitive gulf of ideology. In fact the irresistible force of Solovyev's mystical universalism was beginning to come up against the hitherto immovable object of Leontiev's Byzantine Orthodoxy. This divergence of views became clear with the appearance of Leontiev's article "Vladimir Solovyev versus Danilevsky."

The proximate cause of this polemic was Leontiev's need to defend Danilevsky's, and by implication his own, historico-cultural theories against Solovyev's critique. And beneath a veneer of even-handedness it is not difficult to discern Leontiev's growing disillusionment with those tendencies in Solovyev's thinking which he had, perhaps for reasons of personal affection, been somewhat slow, or perhaps reluctant, to appreciate. In essence, Leontiev accuses Solovyev of attempting to undermine the theories of Danilevsky—"the Catechism of Slavophilism"—because they constituted a barrier to his declared aim of the unification of the churches.[7] Possibly as a result of the conflicting emotions in Leontiev's breast, this first public disagreement with a man he wholeheartedly admired is generally unsatisfactory, being overlong and full of digressions and loose argumentation, wholly untypical of Leontiev's normally tight and condensed style. "It's very hard for me," he wrote, "to withstand his spell and not to declare myself openly his disciple. Even when I disagree with him I nonetheless stand in awe."[8] The rift between the two men the article displays was destined only to widen however; before long Leontiev had concluded that Solovyev wanted Russia and the East to be culturally subordinate to the West in order to facilitate his longed-for unification of the Christian world. This made of Solovyev, in Leontiev's eyes, a false prophet, potentially "*a stone on which our already fragile feet may stumble.*"[9] In the autumn of 1888, having read a review of Solovyev's *L'idée russe*, he was moved to declare: "A pity. He's lost to Russia and to Orthodoxy. He's gone beyond the pale."[10]

Indeed, from a reading of *L'idée russe*, and its companion piece *La Russie et l'église universelle*, of which Leontiev obtained a copy in 1889 (they were both published abroad to evade the censorship and accordingly are free of circumlocution), it seems almost incredible that there should have existed such an empathy between the two men. Solovyev's basic thesis contains such a thoroughgoing refutation of Leontiev's most cherished ideas that, although Leontiev is not directly mentioned, the ostensible targets being the Russian nationalists in the figure of Katkov and the "nationalist-Orthodox" hierarchy exemplified by the Metropolitan Philaret, these articles might almost seem to have been written with him in mind.[11]

The introduction to *La Russie* is premised on a convinced "moral interventionism" regarding suffering and injustice here on earth, an explicit desire to see the "City of God" founded in this world, which is overtly at odds with Leontiev's view of the nature of the relationship between God and the created world which we saw in his critique of the "rose-tinted" Christianity of Tolstoy and Dostoevsky.[12] (Solovyev's remark that "the object of international politics must be universal peace" clashes particularly violently with Leontiev's views on the subject.)[13] It is just such a system of morality as Leontiev's transcendental egoism, with its acceptance of an unbridgeable gulf between this world and the next, which Solovyev accuses of Gnosticism or, perhaps more suggestively in the light of the development of Leontiev's religious thinking, of a "Monothelite or Nestorian quietism" (both of which are dualistic interpretations of the God-manhood of Christ, declared heretical by the early Church). This quietism would, on Solovyev's analysis, "give human nature no share in the working out of its own salvation, for it is God alone Who operates and the whole duty of the Christian consists in passive submission to the divine fact which is represented in its spiritual aspect by the unchanging Church and in its temporal aspect by the sacred power of the god Caesar."[14]

Solovyev was unremitting in his attack. "This so-called Orthodoxy of the Byzantines," he continued, "was in fact nothing but ingrown heresy. The dualism of Nestorius, condemned in theology, became the very foundation of Byzantine life."[15] These words are a small part of the sustained assault on Byzantine Orthodoxy which runs like a torrent through the pages of *La Russie*. According to Solovyev, the "pseudo-Christian empire of Byzantium" was an unholy and anti-Christian compromise between an Orthodoxy increasingly reduced to an empty formalism and an essentially pagan state. This arrangement worked to the mutual benefit of a "semi-Orthodox" or "Orthodox anti-Catholic" hierarchy prepared to sacrifice every principle to satisfy its hatred of Rome, and an imperial state-machine concerned above all to keep Christianity firmly out of the secular sphere, a compromise that reached its apogee with the "schism of Photius" which in Solovyev's view was nothing less than "the denial of Christianity as a social force and as the motive principle of historical progress."[16] The Byzantine Empire, he concluded (intriguingly enough in the light of the Islamic element in Leontiev's faith), "deserved to fall before Islam. For Islam is simply sincere and logical Byzantinism, free from all its inner contradiction."[17]

The Photian schism came about when in 857 the Patriarch of Constantinople was forced to resign by the Byzantine emperor Michael III and replaced with Photius, a layman. This led to a dispute between the papacy and the emperor which ended following the accession of Basil I to the Byzantine throne and the deposition of Photius. Solovyev's point is that the "schism" marked a high-water mark in the efforts of "Caesar" to neutralize the secular power of the church. For Solovyev, the only way for the Russian Church now to escape from the power of the "anti-Christian despotism," as he describes the Russian government, was to find for itself a nucleus of Christian unity outside the boundaries of the secular state, that is, to seek union with the Universal Church centered on Rome, a unity that would put it beyond the reach of secular interference.[18]

Solovyev's critique of Orthodoxy here is extreme and one-sided, and it is not difficult to see behind it an attack of the actual state of affairs in Russia under Pobedonostsev. Nonetheless, the net effect of his thesis on Leontiev's concept of history is profound, as effectively the whole history of Eastern Orthodoxy from Photius on is viewed as falling into that very error of "Phyletism," of putting religion to the service of nationalistic aims, which Leontiev had conceived as the unique and original sin of the Bulgar "schismatics." In Solovyev's eyes the separation of Constantinople from Rome came about through the inability of the Greek clergy to accept the primacy of the heirs to Saint Peter, which was Christ's true ordinance; in other words, through adherence to a narrow nationalist viewpoint which was the essence of Phyletism. Indeed for Solovyev the idea of Russo-Greek solidarity, which Leontiev had constantly sought to promote, was just another manifestation of this nationalistic outlook and was only maintained in some quarters to disguise racial preoccupations under the "fiction" of Orthodox ecumenicalism. "This Phyletism, which was heresy among the Bulgarians," declared Solovyev, "was orthodoxy itself among the Greeks."[19]

Russia's Byzantine legacy then, so far from being Leontiev's cherished spiritual or ideal basis for cultural renewal, was for Solovyev nothing but "anti-Christian Caesaropapism."[20] If Russia had a cultural task then for Solovyev it was to put her secular might behind the reunification of the Universal Church under the hegemony of Rome as the "only possible center of Christian unity." As for Leontiev's vision of Constantinople-Czargrad as the mystical focus of Eastern-Orthodox renewal, this was condemned by Solovyev as a "hybrid notion" unworthy of serious consideration. "If we attempt briefly to do justice to these pathetic utopias," he wrote, "it is not because of their intrinsic importance, which is absolutely nil, but simply out of regard for certain estimable writers who in desperation have sought to substitute these imaginary notions for the true ideal of the reunion of the Churches."[21]

Leontiev was in no doubt that he himself was high on this list of "estimable writers."[22] Given his disposition in the 1880s to see treachery in the actions of others, one might have expected his reaction to Solovyev to be furiously hostile. In fact, it was extremely mild. He naturally rejected Solovyev's emphasis on the primacy of Rome, but he was ready to admit that the younger man was "unfortunately only too right about the official Church in Russia."[23] He continued to regard Solovyev as "the most outstanding of contemporary thinkers"[24] and "an Ajax of mystical and philosophical thought,"[25] and rebuked him only gently for "putting his prophetic gifts higher than both Churches."[26]

Perhaps the most revealing picture of Leontiev's relationship to the problematic theologian is given in a letter of January 1891 to Iosif Fudel'. Solovyev's genius, Leontiev declares, lies in the clarity of his message, which will attract to him future Russian generations: "Since the very message 'submit to the Pope' is clear, palpable, practicable and at the same time most idealistic and powerful."[27] He is still, in Leontiev's estimation, "without doubt the most brilliant, deep and lucid philosopher and writer in *contemporary Europe*."[28] At the same time though Leontiev is piqued with Solovyev for his attacks on Russian cultural-nationalism and cannot make up his mind whether the charge of Jesuitry leveled at him by Strakhov and by Fudel' himself is justified, claiming that the ostensibly liberal Solovyev had told him privately that he would be happy to see Russia conquer all of Europe and Asia if that would help bring about the union of the Churches.[29]

The same message comes across in Leontiev's letters to Rozanov in the early part of 1891: affection and admiration for Solovyev despite an acute awareness of the incompatibility of their two worldviews and a conviction, in defiance of Rozanov's hints to the contrary, that the younger man is the more talented of the two as a thinker, the latter's Westernizing sympathies and "progressive Jesuitry" notwithstanding. "I am in love with Solovyev," he writes, "and he—and I have proofs of this—he loves me personally *very much.*"[30] Indeed, the nature of Leontiev's love for Solovyev may have gone beyond the intellectual sphere. Elsewhere he declares that "I love him *very much*, with my heart; *he has an almost physiological attraction for me.*"[31] Yet there is reason to doubt whether these feelings were truly reciprocated. Solovyev long promised to write an article about Leontiev, but this did not materialize during the latter's lifetime. And Solovyev refused to act as a mediator in Leontiev's dispute with Astafyev over his alleged betrayal of Russian nationalism. These are but two instances of a "jesuitical" refusal on Solovyev's part to support Leontiev publicly, despite praising him in private, a stance which caused Leontiev considerable bewilderment and pain, feelings expressed especially poignantly in a letter to Filippov of September 1890 where he complains of Solovyev's public silence even when *"embracing and kissing me"* in private.[32] Whether or not there is an element of homo-eroticism here, it is worth noting that in his relationship to Solovyev we have the supposedly misanthropic Leontiev showing for the sake of friendship every indulgence toward a man who seemed intent on systematically dismantling his most cherished ideals; few indeed of Leontiev's opponents had been prepared to show the same consideration to him.

A definitive rift between Leontiev and Solovyev came about only in the autumn of 1891 after the latter read a paper for the Moscow Psychological Society titled "On the Decline of the Medieval Worldview." In this lecture Solovyev repeated his accusation that medieval Christianity was an "historic compromise between Christianity and paganism," and he had some harsh words to say about those who harbored an "Islamic quietism" and a "blind faith in barren dogma" which was itself a "perversion of Christianity." Such a faith, in Solovyev's estimation, was actually anti-Christian: "You can have the most zealous, burning and orthodox faith and yet not have the Spirit of God in you and be of Satan's party." More uncompromisingly than ever Solovyev emphasized that it was the duty of every "true" Christian to concern himself with the salvation of this world, and he attacked the "pseudo-Christian individualism" of those whose primary concern was personal salvation, which he saw issuing in "a kind of Eastern dualism which rejects the material world as the evil principle." Atheism, Solovyev concluded, was preferable to faith of this stamp for "the Spirit of Christ acts through those who do not believe in him."[33]

If this diatribe was not actually directed at Leontiev, it is difficult to see what other target Solovyev had in mind. Certainly Leontiev believed it to be an attack on him personally and on the conception of Christian faith which he had developed and cherished. In October he declared to his friend Aleksandrov that he was ready to break off relations with the "scoundrel Solovyev" and launched a heated defense of his own system of transcendental egoism as a surer road to genuine altruism toward one's fellow man than the "social progress," in reality "social disintegration," beloved of "Solovyev's atheists," concluding with the declaration that "Solovyev must be expelled, banished from the precincts of the Empire."[34]

This letter is dated 23 October 1891. In the following letter of 31 October, Leontiev was prepared to be indulgent to his old adversary Tolstoy, whom he now found much less dangerous because less coherent "compared to the logical and systematic evangelism of Satan-Solovyev."[35] When considering these statements, however, one must bear in mind that on or about 16 October, before either of these letters was written, Leontiev had contracted the fever which was to bring about his death within three weeks, on 12 November, so it is possible that his mind was already affected by his last illness when he anathematized Solovyev in these terms. In considering Leontiev's debt to the young theologian, it is perhaps more appropriate to recall his estimate of him made two or three years earlier: "Solovyev—the only one among our writers who has to a certain extent been able to dominate my thinking. Not the older Slavophiles (Kireyevsky, Khomyakov, the elder Aksakov), nor Danilevsky himself, nor Katkov were able to gain ascendancy over my mind . . . Solovyev is the first and only person (or writer) who from the time I matured has been able to shake my convictions and force my thinking into a new direction."[36] Indeed, Leontiev's disciple Iosif Fudel' recalled that his master "in all seriousness dreamt of seeing his beloved Vladimir Sergeyevich Solovyev installed in the chair of the Universal Patriarch in Czargrad."[37]

Ironically, "On the Decline of the Medieval Worldview" marked a turning point in Solovyev's own outlook. With this lecture his disillusion with the established Churches reached its zenith, and he began to move away from ecumenicalism and the desire to found the "City of God" on this earth. As noted by Kologrivov, by the time of his *Three Conversations* of 1900 Solovyev had reached a view not dissimilar to Leontiev's that the world will remain steeped in evil until Christ comes again to redeem it. Indeed in his *Short Story about*

Antichrist of the same year he assigns the role of the interventionist social reformer precisely to the Antichrist.[38]

Of the convictions shaken by his acquaintance with Solovyev the most profoundly affected was Leontiev's belief in Russia's future, which had been hitherto an *"unconditional concept, shared with Danilevsky, of the ideal."*[39] He now came to fear that Russia's calling might be solely religious, that its future civilization would inevitably be a European one. Indeed Iosif Fudel' cites a letter from Leontiev to Strakhov in which he admits that the first time he heard that Solovyev had declared that Russian civilization was a European civilization, he tore up a newly presented photograph of the theologian "because I knew how close to the truth it was."[40]

The "new direction" Leontiev mentions was a branching of his thinking into two channels which at first might appear contradictory but which are in reality closely linked. The first of these was a change in his attitude to Catholicism. In Leontiev's eyes any religious faith was better than no faith at all or, worse, faith in the new religion of "progress" and "eudaemonism," and as far back as the 1870s, before he had come under the direct influence of Solovyev, he had defended Catholicism, for example in his *Father Kliment Zedergolm*, where he declared "a certain passion for Catholicism . . . the most powerful, the most expressive of the bulwarks of the social edifice."[41] Leontiev's sympathies for Catholicism had in the intervening period been limited by his strict devotion to Orthodox dogma, but toward the end of his life, under the influence of Solovyev, his inclinations became more overt. "Fear of sinning against dogma prevents me from submitting completely to Solovyev's Roman sympathies," he wrote, "although I am very drawn to them."[42]

At this time Leontiev also began to see the force of Solovyev's arguments in favor of ecumenicalism. Although the dangers foreseen by the two men were not identical—Leontiev dreaded the infection of Russia by Western liberalism and nihilism, whereas Solovyev feared the ossification of Russia under the dead hand of a formal Orthodoxy subject to state control—Leontiev now joined Solovyev in viewing a strengthening of true religion through the unification of the Churches as a key element in the struggle for the preservation of culture, whether in Russia or more widely in Europe and beyond. "The unification of the Churches," he declared, "is of paramount importance in the coming struggle against Antichrist."[43] This goal was all the more achievable in that the differences between Orthodoxy and Catholicism were in Leontiev's eyes chiefly points of detail regarding dogma and ceremony: he now found Solovyev's advocacy of Rome "a splendid counterweight to the moralizing Protestant leanings of the Slavophiles."[44] As for the Pope, "I'm personally *enormously* attracted to papal infallibility," he wrote, "The elder of elders! If I were in Rome I wouldn't hesitate to kiss Leo the Thirteenth's shoe, never mind his hand . . . Quite apart from the fact that Roman Catholicism accords with my avowedly authoritarian tastes and my inclination toward spiritual submission, it speaks to my mind and my heart in many other ways too."[45]

It is impossible to know whether, had he lived another ten or twenty years, Leontiev would have ended his life as a Catholic. He prophesied a great future for Solovyev's ideas in Russia, and he seems to have come to view Catholicism as a stronger bulwark against Western secular liberalism than the state-regulated Orthodoxy of his motherland, seeing in it the "clear and eloquent" message needed to oppose to the clarity and eloquence of nihilism. Thus he can foresee the day when: "The Russians, at one and the same time so inclined to *mystical submission* and yet so unbridled in destruction once enflamed, so fanatical when aroused . . . these Russian Papists will not only not be meek, as Solovyev vainly advises them to be, but they will *cudgel* the whole of liberal Europe to kneel before the Papal throne, they will arrive at its steps through rivers of European blood."[46]

When we recall the strength of Leontiev's conviction that "Czargrad" should form a new nexus for Russian and Eastern religious and cultural renewal beyond the reach of Western liberal ideas, or the vehemence of his condemnation of the Bulgar "schism" as tending to detract from the authority of the Orthodox Patriarch, the full import of this late conversion to Rome and to the Pope as the more reliable guarantor of his most cherished beliefs becomes startlingly clear. As radical as this change in his religious outlook may have been, however, the second of the new channels into which Leontiev's thinking was directed by the influence of Solovyev betrays an even more surprising change of heart in the political sphere, nothing less than a conversion to *socialism*, an idiosyncratic and original brand of socialism perhaps, but socialism nonetheless. This extraordinary seeming conversion took many years to complete and constitutes the very last word he had to say on the future of Russia and of mankind in general.

In *La Russie* Solovyev had enquired rhetorically whether "there is in the Christian world a power capable of taking up the work of Constantine and Charlemagne with better hope of success." His answer was that "it is the historical destiny of Russia to provide the Universal Church with the political power which it requires for the salvation and regeneration of Europe and of the World."[47] Such an appeal to the Russian Czar to put himself as the service of the Pope may have been a utopian dream: Leo XIII is said to have commented:" Bella idea, ma fuor d'un miracolo, e cosa impossibile" ("A nice idea, but short of a miracle it's impossible").[48] Yet it appealed so greatly to Leontiev that he urged the Czar to make the attempt, adapting lines from Tyutchev to the purpose: "Kneel before him (the Pope), Oh Russian Czar! And rise, as Czar of all the Slavs." (In his poem "Prophecy" Tyutchev had urged the Czar to kneel not before the Pope but at the altar he hoped to see placed in Saint Sofia in Constantinople once that cathedral was restored to Orthodoxy.)[49]

Solovyev's suggestion that the Czar might become a second Constantine the Great ruling over a reunited Christendom appears to have fired Leontiev's imagination. Although in his final year he could still speak of the "horrors of socialist anarchy" and describe communism as the "servant of Antichrist,"[50] there were strands in Leontiev's thinking that had predisposed him toward a socialistic political philosophy well before the appearance of *La Russie*. One such was his attachment to the monastic life of Athos and the Russian Orthodox monasteries, which was strongly socialistic in structure. As far back as 1872 in his *Four Letters from Athos*, Leontiev had noted the similarity between the monastic rule and the manifestos of the socialists. "The communistic monasteries on Athos," he wrote, "might serve as a useful pattern for the communists themselves. An examination of the life of the communistic monastery might show that communism is possible, not as a general rule but as a *particular manifestation* of social life, but only under the condition of maximum discipline and, if you will, dread."[51]

By 1878 we can find Leontiev rating socialism higher than "vague" liberalism for its "seriousness, nourishment and vigor, unlike the doctrine of personal liberty."[52] And as his acceptance grew of the logic of Proudhon's analysis— *"that revolution is the inevitable synthesis of all foregoing movements in religion, philosophy, politics, political economy etc., etc."*[53]—as he became ever more convinced of the inevitability of the triumph of socialism, and especially as he came to understand ever more clearly its inherently *illiberal* tendencies, Leontiev's interest in the phenomenon began to gather pace. A diary entry from January 1879 shows this development clearly. Socialism, he reflects, is in reality a "disguised form of reaction, unaware of its true self . . . it will embrace any religion and any monarchy, provided it is allowed to contrive in the economic sphere, in the relations of capital and labor, as great an upheaval as Christianity once did in the realm of faith . . . and in so doing it will again destroy equality of rights and freedom."[54]

By 1880, in his article on Dostoevsky's "Pushkin" speech, Leontiev is already considering the possibility that, while socialism *might* mean the dissolution of society into anarchy, it might conversely also be the means of inaugurating the new despotism of the central idea over the centrifugal parts, which he saw as the essential building block of social cohesion and cultural flowering. As the 1880s progressed, he began to equate socialism less with anarchy and chaos than with "new forms of political inequality and conscious submission to the *chronic despotism* of the new order" that he believed would be necessary if human civilization were to survive at all.[55] And here he received support from an unexpected quarter. *"Socialism,"* he wrote, "is ever more clearly, in theory and in practice, revealing its despotic character. As I write, the liberal Spencer is disseminating his book against socialism—*The Coming Slavery*. He prophesies that socialism can only be realized on the basis of *slavish* subordination to the collective and to government. And I believe he is right."[56]

We have earlier regarded Leontiev and Nietzsche as an example of "convergent evolution," where two thinkers confronting the same issues at the same moment in time have reached remarkably similar conclusions entirely independently of one another. The same phenomenon applies to Leontiev and Herbert Spencer. It is all but certain that Spencer knew nothing of Leontiev, while Leontiev only got to know of Spencer late in life. And how much Leontiev was directly influenced by Spencer is difficult to say. The name Spencer does not bulk large in his works, the main direct reference to him appearing in the unfinished and unpublished *Average European as the Ideal and Weapon of Universal Destruction*.[57] It is more probably a late case of his method, which we observed earlier, of "flitting," of taking corroborating evidence from authors whose views seemed to confirm a thesis he had himself already developed in principle. Certainly Spencer's forecast that liberalism would issue in universal slavery was precious grist to Leontiev's mill as it seemed to give the influential Englishman's endorsement to his central thesis about the destructiveness of liberal tendencies in the West.

What is for us the truly striking thing about the two men (and was so apparently for Leontiev) is the congruity of their conclusions on certain points, starting as they did from widely different orientations. At first sight Spencer, the great Victorian optimist and laissez-faire individualist, and Leontiev, the advocate par excellence of the corporate state and coiner of the slogan "individualism destroys individuality," would seem to have little to say to one another. What both had in common though is that they were products of that peculiarly nineteenth-century obsession with natural sciences which led to the near universal dominance of "Darwinian" theories of evolution and determinism. Both Leontiev and Spencer refer constantly to "social organisms" and draw on openly biological metaphors to describe social change; both indeed arrived entirely independently at strikingly similar theories of historical evolution based upon the growth, flourishing, and decay of natural organisms.

"This is the history of all organisms whatever," wrote Spencer. "It is settled beyond dispute that organic progress consists in a change from the homogeneous to the heterogeneous."[58] Like Leontiev, Spencer saw this organic

theory as applicable to the social organism as well, although there are important differences of emphasis, particularly Spencer's relentless optimism. For
Spencer "progress" works in only one direction, and his analysis lacks Leontiev's third phase of "decay into uniformity." Consequently, Spencer's view of
the respective roles of the state and the citizens, the whole and the parts, is
the exact reverse of that held by Leontiev. "This is one everlasting reason,"
wrote Spencer, "why the welfare of the citizen cannot rightly be sacrificed to
some supposed benefit of the state . . . the state is to be maintained solely for
the benefit of the citizens. The corporate life must here be subservient to the
lives of the parts; instead of the lives of the parts being subservient to the corporate life."[59] Of course for Leontiev this was the high road to secondary
simplification and social dissolution, so he regarded Spencer's analysis as correct but his conclusions as wrong-headed, calling him "Spencer the liberal (in
his inane *conclusions*, not in his *premises*, which are completely right)."[60]

Among Spencer's "inane conclusions" however, one in particular made a
strong impression on Leontiev. That was the thesis in *The Man versus the State*
of 1884 that the interventionist policies of liberal governments in England were
likely to lead to socialism and a new bondage under which the individual would
lose all freedom of action and become the mere slave of the all-powerful state-
machine. It is utterly logical, given their respective ideologies, yet also peculiarly ironic, that the thought which filled the Englishman with foreboding
should have inspired the Russian with enthusiasm; for it was exactly the laissez-
faire individualism so cherished by Spencer that Leontiev regarded as the
chief principle of social pathology that would inevitably lead: "either to universal catastrophe, or to *a slower but more certain transformation of human societies on entirely new and not at all liberal principles, on the contrary, on principles
which are highly coercive and constrictive. It may be that a new slavery will emerge,
slavery in a new guise, that of the most brutal subordination of the individual to
smaller or larger collectives, and of those to the state. This will be a new* feudalism,
the feudalism of collectives, which will have varied and unequal relations *between
themselves and with the state power.*"[61]

Leontiev claimed not to have known of Spencer's work until 1885 (*The Man
versus the State* was published in translation in Petersburg in 1884).[62] If so, the
degree of convergence between the two men is truly striking.[63] For the foregoing quotation is from an article written in 1880, while in a letter of September 1882, again some years before he admits to having become acquainted with
Spencer, Leontiev unveiled "his version" of socialism to Filippov: "Socialism
is working toward the rejection of the old European revolution, it is the *profound, enduring, gradually unfolding reaction of the future* (and it's not too far off
either, the XIX century is drawing to its close)."[64]

He continued in truly prophetic vein: "Socialism will soon drop its *insurrectionist* ways and become the tool of a new state *structure* which will be corporatist, *caste-based, stratified* and neither liberal nor egalitarian. It will have one way or another to come to terms with *historical, traditionalist and conservative principles,* transmuting both them and itself, and *liberalism, individualism, mercantilism and all such stuff* will be crushed between the *remnants of the past and the oncoming economic whirlwind.* Great will be the state or the race which takes control of this gigantic movement of *neo-feudalism."*[65]

Building on this prognosis, Leontiev argued that the way forward for Russia was to aim for a uniquely Russian synthesis of the two opposing forces which seemed most to threaten her from without: Western communism on the one hand and an awakened Orient on the other. "If we could unite Chinese statecraft with Hindu religiosity," he declared, "and *bring European socialism under their sway,* might we not soon create *new and durable social groupings* and *recast society into new horizontal strata?"*[66] In such a manner socialism might come to resemble the "new feudalism," which was Spencer's nightmare and in many ways Leontiev's aspiration: "*Socialism, properly understood, is nothing less than the new feudalism* of the not too distant future," wrote Leontiev, "understood in the broadest sense, that is, in the sense of a profound inequality of classes and groupings, in the sense of a variegated decentralization and consolidation of social forces, subject to one or another form of active religious or governmental nucleus, in the sense of a *new subjection,* of individuals to other individuals and to institutions, of collectives to other collectives."[67]

It is suggestive of the direction in which Leontiev's assessment of socialism was tending that he explicitly links Plato, whose tripartite order, as we have seen, he predicted would recur in every historical age and who is commonly regarded as a precursor of fascistic philosophies,[68] with *socialist* theoreticians such as Proudhon, Cabet and Fourier.[69] For in practice the above blueprint sounds less like socialism than like the corporatist arrangement of economic activity in fascist Italy under Mussolini. The Russian historian Alexander Repnikov indeed cites Soviet researchers who consider Leontiev to be the precursor not just of Hitlerite fascism but also that of Mussolini and quotes Yuri Ivask's view that his theories could be prayed in aid by apologists for corporatist Spain and Portugal.[70]

In point of fact Leontiev had as early as 1881 come to see the absolute necessity of ending the destructive conflict of capital and labor and to believe that only autocracy could achieve it, not as a "nihilistic chaos" but "as the legal organization of labor and capital, as a *new corporative thralldom of human societies."*[71] Concomitant to this, a certain amount of Marxian jargon creeps into Leontiev's later writing, although his personal knowledge of Marx's work was probably slight. In a letter to Gubastov of June 1889 he speaks of the ideas "of that ponderous Karl Marx, with whom I am somewhat acquainted as the last word in contemporary socialism."[72] He goes on to say that he found Marx such heavy going, and in German to boot, that he took fright and that the books had remained on his shelf untouched ever since. To compensate, Leontiev was of course acquainted with a range of other socialist writers from Proudhon and Saint-Simon to Lassalle and Louis Blanc.

Over the next two years, Leontiev developed this system, which he referred to as "monarchical socialism" and which he believed would lead inevitably to "a new *horizontal stratification* and new *vertical associations of collectives, reconciled to each other in the higher unity of the untrammeled monarchical power.*"[73] In the Russian "folk" he believed he had found the ideal people for this project, accustomed as they were to the "obshchina" system and feeling themselves to be, at bottom, *"peaceful, moderate and monarchical socialists."*[74]

A further, and crucially important, aspect of socialism, of which Leontiev was acutely aware, was the role of the religious or mystical element in the "faith" of the nihilist and other revolutionary groups (we may recall, for example, that the ex-nihilist Sonya Kiseleva in *Two Chosen Women* explicitly compared her revolutionary views with her "former faith" in God). In a letter of March 1889 he enlarges on this "religious destiny" of socialism: "I am of the opinion that socialism in the twentieth and twenty-first centuries will start to play that role in the sphere of *government and economics* which Christianity used to play in the sphere of *government and religion* in the days when she began to triumph . . . Men will never consent to live without religion. Socialism by no means equates to atheism."[75] And in Leontiev's eyes there is a further parallel between the rise of socialism and the rise of Christianity: "Socialism is now *in the stage of martyrdom and its earliest congregations*, scattered here and there, but it will find *its Constantine* . . . What is now the doctrine of *revolution* will then be the apparatus of repression, the instrument of extreme compulsion, discipline, perhaps even of *slavery . . . Socialism is the feudalism of the future.*"[76]

As the 1880s drew to a close Leontiev's acquaintance with Solovyev and Spencer had prepared the way for him to achieve the final synthesis of his vision of Russia's future: "Reconciliation of the Churches, Primacy of the Pope, the power, limited only by the Church, of the Russian Czar who seeks the best possible material conditions of life (conservative socialism)."[77] The shifts in Leontiev's thinking under the influence especially of Solovyev were by now profound. Gone was the emphasis on transcendental egoism as the driver of human regeneration. Gone was the obsessive concern with the erection of an Eastern Federation in opposition to the Romano-German West. The significance of Constantinople-Czargrad as the future cultural nucleus was much reduced. In their place we have ecumenicalism, the primacy of the Roman Pontiff, a vision of Europe's future as a fruitful interaction between the Western tradition and native Russian autocracy, and above all a version of socialism, that most materialistic of all social philosophies, previously anathematized as the final stage in Western liberal dissolution and the end of culture.

In a letter of August 1889 to his friend and disciple Anatoly Aleksandrov, Leontiev was able to crystallize his new outlook. "My feelings tell me," he wrote, "that an Orthodox Czar of the Slavs will one day take the reins of a socialist movement (just as Constantine of Byzantium took the reins of a religious one) and with the blessing of the Church establish a socialist form of life in place of the liberal-bourgeois one. And this socialism will be a new and rigorous triple slavery: to the commune, to the Church, and to the Czar."[78]

Such was Leontiev's final legacy to his countrymen: a vision of an "autocratic socialism" that might secure for Russia a cultural future in the teeth of all the indications to the contrary with which Leontiev had battled for a quarter of a century. In the last year of his life he wrote to Rozanov: "*A union of socialism* (the coming slavery in Spencer's opinion) with *Russian autocracy and fiery mysticism* (which philosophy will serve as a faithful hound), this is not impossible, though *it may be painful* for many. And then the Grand Inquisitor can rise from the grave and stick his tongue out at Fyodor Mikhailovich Dostoevsky. If not, we are looking at insipidness or anarchy."[79]

It remains for us to consider how far this vision became a reality in the turbulent century that followed Leontiev's death in November 1891.

CHAPTER 13

The Red Czar

"I have been reading Konstantin Leontiev," wrote the writer Mikhail Prishvin in 1930 in his *very* private diary. "His worst foreboding has come to pass, his darkest prophecies have been realized. This is our actual reality: 'They didn't want to revere the Czar, now they revere Stalin. The royal mantle is cast aside, the throne destroyed, the Czar himself is shot, but the need for a czar remains: so stuff a bung in the hole and the boat, though it sails badly, will somehow stay afloat.'"[1]

Leontiev himself was anything but sanguine about the efficacy of his prophecies. By the time his life was drawing to its close, he had become fully convinced that he had the power of vision but not of persuasion. "A meteorologist may accurately *predict* the weather," he wrote to his friend Vasily Rozanov, "but does that mean he can *influence it?*"[2] And indeed Leontiev found few followers in his day, at least few prepared openly to acknowledge their indebtedness.[3] In the early 1880s his ideas had attracted a number of young disciples—Leontiev himself suggests there may have been up to fifteen during his time as a censor in Moscow—but after his retirement to Optina he believed only Ivan Kristi, Iosif Fudel', and Anatoly Aleksandrov remained true to him. So it is not in the foundation of a school of thought or of a political or philosophical doctrine that Leontiev's significance for us lies; rather it must lie in what Leontiev's writings tell us about the history of the violent century which followed his death, and indeed about our own times. For despite the obvious defects of the "scientific" approach to history and sociology which, following his mentor Danilevsky, he espoused, he achieved a keener awareness of, and deeper insights into, the coming age of totalitarianism and global wars than most of his contemporaries, not excluding the likes of Dostoevsky and Solovyev. This may have been the easier for him because, unlike most liberal Europeans of his day, he viewed these things as not wholly bad but as phenomena which, under the right combination of circumstances, could become possible roads to the salvation of his native land and its culture.

Reading Leontiev's later writings one gets a definite feel of the quickening pace of history as the nineteenth century approached its close. This was no doubt partly the effect of his gathering preoccupation with his approaching death, yet he had a dark foreboding that the development of science might lead to not very beneficial ends in the coming twentieth century, and certainly would not achieve those *"delightful* results expected by the leading persons of the eighteenth century and the first half of this one."[4] The very words "twentieth century" take on an ominous aspect in Leontiev's later work, his vision of the near future being a kind of wave-diagram for the end of the world, as a cultural whimper, be it said, taking as its leitmotif the famous text from Paul: "For when they shall say, peace and safety; then sudden destruction cometh upon them, as travail upon a woman with child; and they shall not escape."[5]

Leontiev's power of prophecy is sometimes uncanny. "Let's imagine," he wrote in 1888 to Fudel', "that in about fifty years [i.e., around 1938] Europe is racked by new wars and eventually unites in a single liberal and nihilistic republic along the lines of modern France. Even if this form of society has no long-term future, such temporary but sharply defined movements may find inspirational leaders and for twenty to twenty-five years the outbursts of this universal-federal republic may be horrific." This could have particularly dire consequences for Russia. "And should the Slavs not want to unite with this Europe," his letter continues, "then republican Pan-Europe may come to Petersburg, or Kiev, or Czargrad, as the case may be, and demand: 'renounce your dynasty or we will not leave one stone standing on another and will lay waste to the land.'"

Leontiev then sees two possible ways of meeting this threat: either the Romanovs must renounce the throne to save the land from destruction, or: "We *will be true to ourselves.* In which case in defiance we will unleash on them the *whole of Asia,* even the Muslims and the Pagans, and then there will be nothing for us to do but salvage their *monuments of art.*"[6] (Leontiev was not wrong in his prediction that Asia would be a powerful weapon in Russian hands; it has been estimated that during the Great Patriotic War the Red Army contained as many as eight million non-Slav soldiers out of a total of thirty-four million mobilized.)[7]

This vision of the events of 1941–45 has a horrifying prescience about it. Leontiev's hope for the twentieth century was that it should abandon the prevailing doctrine of rational utilitarianism and find salvation in a new mysticism, but he remained to the end a pessimist on this score, and his sense of the precariousness and instability of nineteenth-century industrial civilization led naturally to the prediction that it would perish in the conflagration of a general war fought with the weapons of modern science. His *Letters of an Anchorite* set out a chillingly detailed and prescient scenario for the outbreak of such a conflict, beginning in the Balkans and involving Austria, Germany, Russia, and France, a vision that closely anticipated the actual events of 1914.[8]

Austria and Turkey were for Leontiev a useful though temporary barrier to the expansion of political Pan-Slavism, but in the long run, when Russia should have matured sufficiently to assume their mantle, he felt they had no future. As to Germany, a more vigorous and potentially dangerous power, Leontiev had much to say that would prove both accurate and prophetic. For one thing he put his finger on the essential weaknesses of the German Reich: for all its post-1870 industrial might it was both geographically vulnerable to attack on two fronts and politically overdependent on the great man who had created it. "For a long time," he wrote, "the towering figure of Bismarck obscured the weaknesses of the edifice he had created, but the giant has gone now and Germany is slowly ceasing to inspire apprehension."[9] Behind the facade of power the German was, in Leontiev's eyes, basically a petty-bourgeois, as the departure of the Iron Chancellor would reveal: "Bismarck is a colossus, but Germany has become petty; after the death of this great but fateful figure the triviality of a German society, which has already been subject to *excessive leveling and amalgamation*, will become clear—once it is no longer gripped in his iron fist."[10] For Leontiev, Wilhelmine Germany was fundamentally show and offered the world nothing new or significant: "Conquest for the sake of conquest, nothing more."[11]

Leontiev's attitude to Germany was typically paradoxical. As long as Bismarck remained at the helm, he believed that Germany and Russia should be natural allies, as his the *Letters of an Anchorite* demonstrate vividly in their enduring polemic with the Francophile Katkov over the issue of Russia's long-term strategic interests. Yet he had little doubt about the outcome of the reign of the new German sovereign: "The reckless Wilhelm II, who you can see at a glance will lead us to war, a war for which I long as the resolution of the Eastern Question."[12] This assessment of the new Kaiser would prove all too accurate, even if the eventual outcome was not such as Leontiev hoped for. By 1891, after the lapsing of the Reinsurance Treaty between Germany and Russia, he apparently felt that war with Germany had become inevitable, and he welcomed the prospect, largely because of his fatalistic conviction that Russia must ultimately prevail in any conflict which involved the Eastern Question and the fate of Czargrad; if Germany opposed Russia's historical destiny in the East then, with France implacably at her back, she would sooner or later be drawn into a war on two fronts and crushed.[13]

"Bismarck is between a rock and a hard place," he reasoned. "If he gets in Russia's way he may come to grief, but likewise if he doesn't. Either way he won't be able to rescue Germany."[14] From this perspective Leontiev wondered whether Bismarck was Germany's Napoleon I, come to lead her to glory, or Napoleon III, representative of her final exhaustion. If the latter, which he believed probable (and which in 1873 he believed would reveal itself within a quarter of a century, by about 1900), he foretold with uncanny accuracy that the Hohenzollern dynasty would be relegated to a footnote in history and that a defeated Germany would reject Prussian militarism in favor of a bourgeois republic.[15] He also warned that the cultural homogeneity which was the inevitable result of Bismarck's policy of unification would not necessarily bear wholesome fruit: "The fragmentation of Germany hindered, it is true, the development of a unified social order, but at the same time it also hindered the coalescing of anarchic elements. Similar temperaments, related organisms are more easily infected with identical epidemics!"[16]

Prophetic as many of his utterances on Germany were, however, Leontiev's main preoccupation was always with the future of his homeland. We have seen how late in life he came to believe in the inevitability of a socialist revolution, for which contemporary laissez-faire liberalism was in his eyes but paving the way. For Leontiev it was essential that something occur quickly to stop the march of liberalism in Russia if she was not to be the vehicle for the end of the world: *"Having put an end to history,* having *destroyed* humanity; she is to make human life on this earth utterly insupportable through the spread of universal liberty and a flood of universal equality."[17] Liberalism in Russia must therefore succumb either to the forces of revolution or to those of reaction: *"Ground into dust between two extremely illiberal forces,* between a frenzied nihilist storm and the firm and unshakeable bulwark of our great historical principles."[18]

We noted above that Leontiev took leave to doubt Dostoevsky's vision of the Russian people as "God-bearing," fearing that they might all too easily bring forth Antichrist instead. They must therefore be *"restricted, confined, paternally and diligently coerced . . .* otherwise in about a half-century, no more, from being a God-bearing people they will become, bit by bit and not noticing it themselves, God-persecutors, faster than any other people perhaps, for in reality they are capable of taking everything to extremes."[19] When the inevitable revolution came therefore—and Leontiev had no real doubt that the extremists would win—the victorious nihilists would have no choice but to return to time-honored forms of coercion in order to establish and maintain their authority.

"However much these people condemn the *current conservatives* and the forms and practices of conservatism which they find unacceptable," he warned, "nonetheless *they themselves will find they need all the practical aspects of the reactionary code. They will require dread, they will require discipline*, they will require *the tradition of obedience*, they will require *the habit of submission*. The people, having by then (we suppose) transformed the economic conditions of life, but *on no account to be satisfied with anything belonging to this world*, will be inflamed by a new *craving for mystical doctrine*."[20] Whatever form the future government of Russia might take, the very nature of the Russian people meant that it would have to be essentially despotic: "The historical development of the people has meant that *without the intervention of the state* they have been unable to achieve worthwhile results . . . everything that is great and enduring in the life of the Russian folk has been achieved in a sense *artificially* and more or less *forcibly*, on the initiative of the rulers."[21]

As Prishvin was later ruefully to acknowledge, the ring of prophecy in these later musings by Leontiev about the future of his homeland is unmistakable and even eerie. It is difficult not to conclude that among historicist thinkers it was Leontiev who came closest to proving that it is indeed possible to predict future events by extrapolating from the past, via "common-historical induction." As a contemporary Russian commentator observes: "Leontiev was mistaken in some things, though not more than other people, but almost all of his prophecies came to pass. That's something to ponder for anyone who comes into contact with him."[22]

The late nineteenth century was still the era of optimism, and that held true whether one's instincts were liberal or nihilistic, revolutionary or reactionary. And although others too questioned whether the blind pursuit of individual liberty through the overthrow of existing values might not end in universal slavery—Dostoevsky did for one, and Spencer, whose voice is very clear here, was another—they were in the minority, and there were few writers who expounded the problem so consequentially and with such fearless clarity as Leontiev. And few indeed whose soothsaying bore such uncanny fruit.

"I sometimes think," wrote Leontiev, "that a Russian czar, perhaps not far into the future, will stand at the head of a socialist movement (as Constantine once stood at the head of a religious one—'in this sign you thou shalt conquer') and will *organize it* in the way that Constantine facilitated the organization of Christianity." He then asked: "But what do we mean by 'organization'? Organization means *compulsion*, it means benevolent *despotism*, it means the *enshrinement in law* of a permanent, unremitting, imaginatively and wisely regulated *coercion of the individual wills of the citizens.*"[23]

It is virtually impossible for the modern reader not to identify this "socialist Constantine" with Stalin and the "feudalism of the future" with the brutal totalitarian state over which he presided. There is a paradox here however. Despite his sometimes extreme rhetoric, it is universally attested by those who knew him at all well that Leontiev was personally a kind-hearted and compassionate individual, far removed from the paranoid psychopathy of a Stalin, while as an aesthete he would have detested the bleak reality of Stalin's Russia.[24] Yet in Leontiev's vision his homeland stood face to face with the apocalypse. "*Universal constraint* will be necessary," he wrote, "if we are not to give way to *dissolution* and decay."[25] That Stalin would have wholeheartedly agreed with this proposition is hardly in doubt. But how could two such different men have come to the same extreme conclusion? Should we file it as another case, as with Spencer and Nietzsche, of "convergent evolution"?

Perhaps. But again, perhaps not altogether. We have noted that in the winter of 1885–86 the Procurator of the Holy Synod, Pobedonostsev, bought some sixty copies of Leontiev's *The East, Russia and Slavdom* for use in seminaries.[26] This compendium contains all of Leontiev's major works on Eastern affairs, including his masterpiece *Byzantinism and Slavdom*, and it is not beyond the bounds of possibility that a copy found its way into the spiritual seminary of Tiflis, modern Tbilisi, in Georgia, where the fifteen-year-old Stalin enrolled in 1894 and in which he remained for the next five years. The teachers in the Georgian seminary were apparently mostly reactionary and of an extreme Russian nationalist persuasion,[27] and it is not improbable that one or other of them would have promoted Leontiev's ideas among the students, especially if, like many other people, he mistakenly believed him to be an arch-Slavophile.

Beyond this circumstance there is no direct evidence that Stalin was exposed as a young man to Leontiev's ideas. For example no copy of Leontiev's works was found in Stalin's extensive private library when it was opened after his death. This need not surprise us however. It is unlikely that a youthful revolutionary activist would leave evidence to suggest he had come under the influence of a man considered by most people at the time, not least through his association with such as Pobedonostsev, to be one of the darkest reactionary thinkers of the late nineteenth century. As Robert Service observes: "As a revolutionary and militant atheist [Stalin] disdained to acknowledge the contribution made by the Imperial regime and the Orthodox Church to his personal development."[28] And as Geoffrey Roberts points out, Stalin did not begin assembling his collection until he was firmly established in power, and it is overwhelmingly a Soviet library, a collection of largely post-1917 texts published in Soviet Russia with comparatively few examples from earlier periods.[29]

Any connection between Stalin and Leontiev must rest accordingly on two things: the possibility that Stalin may have come into contact with Leontiev's ideas during his time at the Tiflis seminary; and an examination of how far these ideas appear to resurface in Stalin's own writing, particularly in the period before the revolution when his ideas were still in the formative stage and when one might expect his experiences in the seminary to have been still vivid in his mind.

Many of Stalin's biographers have remarked on the fact that alone among the major figures in the pre-1917 revolutionary movements he had a thoroughgoing religious upbringing, first in the spiritual school in his hometown of Gori and afterward in the Tiflis seminary. Service notes that Stalin got top marks at Gori in, among other subjects, the Old and New Testaments, Orthodox catechism and liturgy, and Russian and Church Slavonic, a trend which continued once he entered the Tiflis seminary, where he again received top marks in Scripture and Russian literature and history.[30]

What Stalin actually read during his time in the seminary is not fully documented. His biographers and their primary sources, the memoirs of contemporaries, naturally tend to concentrate on the literature that the aspiring revolutionist, like many of his fellow-seminarians, read clandestinely away from the eyes of the teachers. In Stalin's case this was most notably Karl Marx, but he also devoured a broad spectrum of mainstream European writers, including Shakespeare, Cervantes, Schiller, Heine, Hugo, Thackeray, and Balzac, as well as Russians (many of whose works were, bizarrely, banned within the seminary precincts) including Gogol, Chernyshevsky, Tolstoy, Dostoevsky, and Chekhov.[31] What he made of the works on the prescribed seminary syllabus is less well documented, or rather largely undocumented, but the marks he received show that he was a more than able student (especially in his early years before his attention became distracted by revolutionary activity). In addition Stalin was an enthusiastic autodidact who claimed to be capable of reading up to 500 pages a day[32] and it is beyond doubt that through his official and unofficial studies he left the Tiflis seminary with a thorough grounding in Russian history and Orthodox theology as well as a broad overview of the currents of contemporary European thought and literature.

This overview appears to have embraced the enduring tendency among nineteenth-century thinkers to view the development of human societies through comparisons with organic nature. In his *Stalin and the National Question*, Erik van Ree discusses at some length the presence of "organicism" in

Stalin's writing. He notes that the concept was central to a number of strands of Russian thought in the nineteenth and early twentieth centuries, notably among thinkers of Orthodox persuasion, and cites in particular Leontiev and Danilevsky as two writers who applied biological concepts to the life of nations, states and cultures. Van Ree gives primacy to Danilevsky as the most influential of the two (which in general terms he was) and as the chief theorist of Pan-Slavism and concludes that Stalin's concept of nations shows "interesting similarities to the theory of cultural types which Danilevsky's book contains."[33] There are grounds to suppose however that if Stalin was influenced by either Danilevsky or Leontiev, then of the two it was more likely to have been the latter.

Van Ree rehearses a very condensed version of Danilevsky's theory of the organic development of "cultural types" from birth through flowering to death to illustrate the similarity with Stalin's own conception of nations as integrated organic wholes. But we have seen that a key aspect of Leontiev's concept of society and the historical development of culture, perhaps *the* key aspect, was just this view of human society as an *organism*, and as an organism subject like every other to the processes of birth, maturity, and decay. We have earlier discussed Leontiev's debt to Danilevsky in this area and noted a high degree of similarity between their respective theories; indeed we suggested that the similarity was so close as potentially to expose Leontiev to a charge of plagiarism. This means however that if there is cogency in Van Ree's postulation that Stalin's view of the nation follows, directly or indirectly, Danilevsky's organic view of society and historical development, then that thesis is equally applicable to Leontiev, indeed more so, for while there is *no* direct evidence that Stalin knew Danilevsky, we at least have an indication that Stalin *may* have been exposed to Leontiev through the distribution in seminaries of *The East, Russia and Slavdom*.

Perhaps the most compelling similarity in this regard is the use by all three men of organic metaphors to describe the development and organization of human society. Stalin's use of such imagery is well documented. In his 1913 article "Marxism and the National Question," Stalin refers to nations specifically as "national organisms"[34] and goes on to describe their basic characteristics as follows: "A nation is a historically constituted, stable community of people, formed on the basis of a common language, territory, economic life, and psychological make-up manifested in a common culture . . . It goes without saying that a nation, like every historical phenomenon, is subject to the law of change, has its history, its beginning and end."[35]

The second part of this statement is redolent both of Danilevsky's theory of historical development and Leontiev's similar "Triune Theory," according to which all organisms are subject to the three phases of original simplicity, flowering complexity, and finally secondary simplification, decay, and replacement. And of course Leontiev regards states and cultures as organic entities like any other: "On further reflection we find that this triune process is not confined solely to that world which is usually regarded as organic, but is possibly applicable to everything which exists in time and space . . . last but not least, *the life of peoples, state organisms and whole cultural worlds.*"[36]

The youthful Iosif Dzhugashvili agreed: "The history of science shows that the dialectical method is a truly scientific method: from astronomy to sociology, in every field we find confirmation of the idea that nothing is eternal in the universe, everything changes, everything develops. Consequently, everything in nature must be regarded from the point of view of movement, development. And this means that the spirit of dialectics permeates the whole of present-day science."[37] This quotation is taken from Stalin's earlier pamphlet, his *Anarchism or Socialism* of 1907, in which the organic component of his writing receives perhaps its clearest exposition. "It is said," he writes, "that social life is in continual motion and development. And that is true: life must not be regarded as something immutable and static; it never remains at one level, it is in eternal motion, in an eternal process of destruction and creation. Therefore, life always contains the *new* and the old, the *growing* and the *dying*, the revolutionary and the counter-revolutionary."[38]

Stalin's organicism thus far recalls that of Danilevsky and Leontiev in fairly equal measure. Yet there are two key areas where both Stalin and Leontiev depart radically from Danilevsky. One is their deep-rooted aversion to racial nationalism. Danilevsky consistently argued, as we have seen, that the only reliable basis on which a distinctive historically determined culture may develop is that of racial and linguistic affinity, calling it "the highest political principle" and "the root principle on which the state must be founded." For Danilevsky, it is a cardinal principle that "by this formative, unifying, life-giving and life-saving idea of the state we can have only nationality in mind," for it is "the ethnographic principle which is really the only lasting foundation of the state system; it alone gives it true meaning and significance."[39]

Stalin disagreed utterly with this. He may have seen the nation as "primarily a community, a definite community of people," but he was emphatic that "this community is not racial, nor is it tribal."[40] Indeed he regarded racial or tribal nationalism as one of the greatest dangers to class solidarity: "When the workers are organized according to nationality they isolate themselves within their national shells, fenced off from each other by organizational barriers." For Stalin, rather than commonality of peoples, the emphasis of nationalism is "on what distinguishes them from each other. In this type of organization the worker is primarily a member of his nation: a Jew, a Pole, and so on. It is not surprising that national federalism in organization inculcates in the workers a spirit of national seclusion. Therefore, the national type of organization is a school of national narrow-mindedness and stagnation."[41] Referring to the rise in nationalist sentiment in the period immediately after the 1905 revolution, he wrote that: "At this difficult time Social-Democracy had a high mission—to resist nationalism and to protect the masses from the general 'epidemic.'"[42]

Stalin's use of the word "epidemic" here is suggestive. We have seen that Leontiev used the same word to describe people in the Balkans seeking liberation from the "Turkish Yoke" through nationalist agitation as being in "the position of a man escaping from prison at the time of a raging epidemic."[43] Leontiev was of course one of the chief critics of racial nationalism, calling it "one of the strangest *self-delusions* of the nineteenth century."[44] And his excoriation of nationalism based on racial affinity does seem to prefigure Stalin's. "The idea of purely racial nationalism in the form in which it appears in the nineteenth century," wrote Leontiev, "is in essence a fully cosmopolitan idea, inimical to the state, inimical to religion, possessing considerable destructive and no creative power, incapable of forming a *cultural* nation, for culture is nothing other than individuality and individuality is today everywhere dying pre-eminently from political freedom. *Individualism* is killing *individuality*, of people, of regions, of nations."[45]

Like Leontiev, Stalin was inclined to see "unity in variety" as the highest goal for cultural development and regarded national exclusivity as its deadly enemy. Being founded on racial separatism, *national* autonomy was for him inherently inimical to cultural flowering, but *regional* autonomy, whereby the disparate parts would be able to flower in their own fashion but always subject to the controlling force of the center, was acceptable and even helpful. In "Marxism and the National Question" Stalin argued, with reference to the Caucasus, that: "Regional autonomy . . . is acceptable because it would draw the belated nations into the common cultural development; it would help them to cast off the shell of small nation insularity; it would impel them forward and facilitate access to the benefits of higher culture." National autonomy, however, acted in Stalin's eyes in a diametrically opposite direction since it "shuts up the nations within their old shells, binds them to the lower stages of cultural development and prevents them from rising to the higher stages of culture. In this way national autonomy counteracts the beneficial aspects of regional autonomy and nullifies it."[46]

The second area in which Leontiev and Stalin depart radically from Danilevsky is in their attitude toward the historical significance of Byzantium. Leontiev was in no doubt about Russia's debt to the culture he regarded as her spiritual forerunner. In his *Byzantinism and Slavdom* he wrote that: "The Byzantine spirit, Byzantine principles and influences, like the complex web of a nervous system, permeate the whole of the Great-Russian social organism."[47] (It is interesting, though possibly coincidental, that in *Anarchism or Socialism*, Stalin uses a similar metaphor, asserting that "the development of consciousness needs a particular structure of the organism and development of its nervous system . . . The same thing must be said about the history of the development of human society.") Danilevsky, by contrast, treats Byzantium only in passing, believing that, like ancient Rome, it had "exhausted its creative force," and he did not include it among the ten cultural types which he identified as constituting the core of world history.

Stalin seems to have taken Leontiev's side in this argument. He is said to have retained through much of his life a penchant for historical studies, keeping up with debates in the study of Russian, Mesopotamian, ancient Roman, and, most interestingly in this context, Byzantine history.[48] And there is some evidence that the last left a particularly strong impression. Sergo Beria, son of the notorious Lavrenti, recalled that some forty years after Stalin left the Tiflis seminary: "One day he gave Svetlana [Alliluyeva] and me a regular course in the history of Byzantium."[49]

It is not altogether surprising that Byzantine history should have exercised a fascination over Stalin, for the structures of Byzantine state power held considerable appeal for an aspiring despot. Once he had established himself in absolute authority, and especially after his rehabilitation of the Orthodox Church (which began during the war but continued until his death), his rule increasingly assumed the aspect of that of the Byzantine emperors - he even described himself as the executor on earth of God's will.[50]

It is intriguing in the context of this remark that Leontiev sympathized with the ostensible goal of Vladimir Solovyev's desire for Church unification, the idea (stemming from the view of humanity as an organic whole espoused by the mystical philosopher Nikolai Fyodorov) of the salvation of the maximum number of souls in preparation for the coming of Antichrist and the Last Judgement.[51] By 1891 though Leontiev had transferred the role of a redeemer to the czar, whose task it was to restrain the "folk" from atheism with the aim of saving the souls of the greatest number of his subjects. Accordingly, whoever served the autocrat in this task was doing God's work at the same time.[52] Thus the threefold division of society—autocracy, Orthodoxy, and the commune— which had in Leontiev's estimation allowed Russia to achieve her period of flowering complexity under Catherine, and which he saw as rooted in the spirit of Byzantium, was reconstituted under the Red Czar. Socialism had indeed "found its Constantine."[53]

Van Ree concludes his assessment of the possible influence on Stalin of Russian organicism by reiterating that there is no indication that Stalin read Danilevsky, and that if he did the impression it made on him was not enough for him to include a copy in the personal library which he collected after the revolution. He notes however that "the idea of the 'organic unity' of human collectives was part and parcel of Russian thinking and as such naturally 'available' to Stalin. His 1913 definition of the nation deserves to be treated as part of that same tradition of Russian organicism to which Leontev's and Danilevsky's thinking belonged."[54] Indeed it does. But it may be that, thanks to the intervention of the arch-reactionary Pobedonostsev, the Russian organicist who was most readily "available" to Stalin was, ironically enough, not Danilevsky but Leontiev. At the very least it is plausible to surmise that in Leontiev Stalin found a theoretical corrective to Danilevsky's emphasis on racial nationalism and to his underplaying of the historical significance, to Russia in particular, of the Byzantine inheritance.

Since perestroika one senses there has been a certain reluctance in Russian academic circles to delve too deeply into whether and to what extent Leontiev can be seen as a precursor of Bolshevism and, in particular, of Stalin. A desire to tread carefully becomes the more understandable when one considers that Leontiev has even been posited as a formative influence on Nikolai Ustryalov, the founder of the fascistic "National Bolshevism" faction, by the historian of that movement, Mikhail Agursky.[55] Nevertheless the historian Aleksandr Repnikov, for one, has found the comparative silence on this issue surprising. "It is odd," he writes, "that among all the comparisons that have been made between Danilevsky and Stalin over the years nobody has made a serious effort to draw a parallel between Stalin's rule and the prognoses of Leontiev. There are issues here which are in need of thoroughgoing analysis and specialist investigation."[56]

For all his fiery and apocalyptic rhetoric, one is drawn to think that the kindly and humane Leontiev would have balked at implementing measures that led to misery, hardship, and death for millions. Stalin of course had no such qualms; he may or may not have declared that *"one death is a tragedy, a million deaths a statistic,"* but the remark seems entirely in character.[57] It is clear nonetheless that Leontiev's vision of an omnipotent autocrat presiding as a coercive and unifying force over an acutely despotic form of socialistic order closely modeled on the closed ascetic monasticism of Mount Athos corresponds, as Prishvin and Repnikov have noted, uncannily closely to the actuality of Stalin's Russia.[58] (The one component his regime lacked was the hereditary aristocracy positioned between monarch and people which was a key moderating influence in Leontiev's vision of the ideal state-form, possibly a fatal defect, as in Leontiev's prophetic view: "The life of a state without a social hierarchy will be a short one.")[59]

In any comparison of Leontiev and Stalin it is also worth noting that Rozanov, who in a short year of correspondence came to understand Leontiev better than perhaps anyone else, was in no doubt that a mailed fist lay not too far beneath the velvet glove. Observing Leontiev's powerlessness and isolation, he styled him a "dictator without a dictatura," a "Cromwell without a sword, but a Cromwell entire." And comparing him favorably to Nietzsche in terms of intellectual consistency, Rozanov opined that: "Given the power and the opportunity (with which Nietzsche would have done nothing), Leontiev would have drowned Europe in fire and blood in a spectacular metamorphosis of politics."[60]

As we have seen, Leontiev's thought was full of paradoxes. He opposed liberalism, even though he predicted time and again that liberalism would issue in its exact opposite, something deeply illiberal. But why then, given that his own prescriptions for Russia's future were themselves equally illiberal, was he not content to wait for the liberal experiment to end in disaster and be replaced by its illiberal Janus face? The answer must be that he was primarily concerned with preserving the conditions for Russia's future cultural flowering and he saw, correctly, that both liberalism and the illiberal regime which was likely to, and did, replace it would both of them annihilate any possibility of a cultural renaissance in his homeland. Hence his construction of a Byzantine "culturophile" manifesto to offer his countrymen a third way between these two anti-cultural extremes. Hence his adoption of socialism once he perceived that his manifesto would, yet again, be ignored by those with the power to make a change. His hope was that socialism, if it remained an economic movement and allied itself spiritually to Orthodoxy and Autocracy, could provide the illiberal bedrock on which the future edifice of the Russian renaissance might be erected.

Leontiev was deceived in this, as history shows. Or rather, he deceived himself. It is peculiarly ironic that while, with the possible exception of Dostoevsky, he acquired a more acute perception of the quasi-religious nature of the revolutionary mindset than almost anyone else of his time, he failed to foresee that the religious impulse would find its adequate outlet in Marxist-Leninist dogma and that the post-revolutionary order would have no use for the old religion (until of course changed geopolitical circumstances demanded its reinstatement as a matter of national survival). In 1917 though Bolshevism had no need of Byzantine Orthodoxy, it had its own orthodoxy; just as ten years later Stalin had no need of Autocracy, he *was* the autocrat.

Leontiev had predicted as long ago as 1880 that the "feudalism of the future" would be predicated on "constant refined dread, constant unrelieved pressure of conscience, discipline and the will of the superiors."[61] And there is no room for doubt that when he wrote these words he was not just describing, he was *prescribing*, for he worked actively for the next eleven years until his death, both through his published articles and via his circle of "disciples," to get his prescriptions accepted more widely in those circles of society that were in a position to give them effect. Even if we are prepared then to acknowledge the moral gulf that separates Leontiev from Stalin, it is difficult to exonerate the former from to some extent at least paving the way for the latter, for those who play with edged tools are likely to end up bleeding. It is true of course that Leontiev believed firmly that he was living in the last days before Armageddon, that European civilization in the twentieth century would collapse in economic and political chaos, and that people would renounce the liberal ideals which had led them into catastrophe and seek security at any price, in which case the sufferings of the Russian people would be justified.

"Happy and powerful in those days," Leontiev declared, "will be that people whose faith and habit of obedience will be stronger than the rest."[62] But Leontiev's unqualified conviction that Russia could only achieve cultural flowering by rejecting utterly the values of Western liberalism led him, not for the first time, into extremes and to argue that to this end any price would be worth paying. "If cultural independence must be bought at the price of a degree of organized violence, of harsh despotism, even at the price of an internal *slavery* in a new form," he wrote, "there would be no harm in that and we need to accustom our minds to it. I even suppose that *it is by some such price that our spiritual originality* will be purchased in the twentieth century."[63]

Aleksandr Repnikov is in no doubt about the import of those words. "In the lifetime of the thinker," he writes, "the idea of *socialist autocracy* was not understood, but after 1917 it assumed the dimensions of genuine prophecy."[64] A political manifesto on these lines would naturally require a highly centralized, despotic power to carry it through. In fact, it would require a Stalin. It seems improbable now that new evidence will emerge proving or disproving a direct link between Stalin and Leontiev and in its absence any connection must remain speculative and circumstantial. What is not in doubt though is that Iosif Vissarionovich Dzhugashvili could hardly have summarized his political philosophy better than did Konstantin Nikolaevich Leontiev. "By the fundamental law of our Empire," declared Leontiev, "by the essential spirit of our nation, everything that proceeds from the Highest Power is lawful and good . . . The will of the Sovereign is sacred *in all circumstances,* even when the wrath of God seems to be upon us, as in the time of Ivan the Terrible."[65]

Epilogue

"Storms. The forest is crashing down. Our beloved motherland has fallen. Weeping, weeping and sighs. Everything that Leontiev foresaw has come to pass. Come to pass more horribly than he prophesied. Russia is a toothless hag. Oh, how frightful you are, witch, harridan with tangled hair. And then the furies of retribution, of execution. A Cassandra, Leontiev, Cassandra wandering through Troy and prophesying, and like her, no-one listened to him."[1]

The writer and philosopher Vasily Rozanov wrote these words on 4 November 1918 (new style), three months before his death from hunger and neglect at the age of sixty-three. His friend and mentor Konstantin Nikolaevich Leontiev had died of pneumonia twenty-seven years earlier on 12 November 1891 at the age of sixty. Both men died at the Holy Trinity Lavra of Saint Sergius in Sergiev Posad outside Moscow and are buried side by side in the nearby Chernigovsky-Gethsemane Hermitage.

Without directly mentioning her, by the time of his death Leontiev had come to be convinced that he was destined to play the role of a Cassandra.[2] Until the outbreak of the First World War his memory endured, for good or ill, in the minds of those who had known the man himself and his writings. His devoted niece Marya Vladimirovna and his "disciples," chief among them Anatoly Aleksandrov, Iosif Fudel' and Ivan Kristi, did what they could to preserve the memory of the man and his ideas, and were instrumental in putting together the first edition of his collected works, published in nine volumes in 1912–13 by V. M. Sablin.[3]

For much of the century that followed Leontiev, the "lonely dreamer" as Fudel' described him, was a largely forgotten figure in Russian letters.[4] This is not altogether surprising. A bare quarter of a century after his death came the Revolution, the cataclysm of whose advent he had so often warned in vain, after which he came to be regarded, insofar as he was regarded at all, as something in the nature of an antediluvian curiosity. And Leontiev had no defense against this relegation to the status of a nonperson; he left behind no enduring masterpiece of fiction which might have guaranteed him an afterlife despite official disapproval, no *Dead Souls*, no *Anna Karenina*, and no *Brothers Karamazov*. He had held no prominent position in Russian academic or political life, he founded no school of philosophy or social science, and he exerted a direct influence on only two followers who were to leave their own marks on Russian letters. One was Rozanov. The other was the repentant revolutionary Lev Tikhomirov (1852–1923), a one-time leading member of the "People's Will" group that had assassinated Alexander II in 1881.

Leontiev's relationship with Rozanov was not an easy one and is full of enigmas. They differed widely on social and religious questions, Rozanov's Christ of the meek and oppressed clashing head-on with Leontiev's God the aesthete and hierarch. And at times a certain impatience with Leontiev's paradoxical thought processes is detectable in Rozanov's writing. At one point he describes him as a "black hole for ideas, there's no way in to him and no way out."[5] And elsewhere: "His thoughts? They cross each other out. His whole *opera omnia* is a series of works each struck through with a blue pencil. They make splendid *reading*. But there's nothing there to *ponder* about. There's no *guidance* in them, no *wisdom*."[6] Yet less than six months before his death, when the two men had been corresponding for only three months, Leontiev was moved to exclaim: "*At last*, after waiting almost twenty years, I've found someone who understands my work in *just the way I wanted it to be understood*."[7]

Despite occasional outbursts of frustration, Rozanov in his turn fully realized the debt he owed to the man who was in many ways his mentor and at the end of his life requested that he be buried near him. In his memoir *Opavshie list'ia (Fallen Leaves)* Rozanov provides a generous eulogy: "What was Leontiev then? Not a difficult question. He was an unusually fine Russian man with a pure and candid soul, one whose tongue never knew duplicity. And in this respect he was almost *unicum* in the sufficiently false, artificial, and dishonest world of Russian letters. In his person the good Russian God gave *good* Russian literature a *good* writer."[8] For Rozanov, "the whole man was there in his words, like Adam without clothes."[9] In years to come, he predicted, academic

FIGURE 10. The Holy Trinity Lavra at Sergiev Posad near Moscow, where Leontiev died in November 1891.

researchers would scour Leontiev's papers to elucidate his thoughts, and "everything would be done for his posterity, just as nothing was done for him alive."[10]

By the time Tikhomirov met Leontiev in 1890 he had abjured revolution and become a staunch defender of autocracy. During Leontiev's final years the two men corresponded regularly, and Tikhomirov's essays such as "Contemporary Social Mirages" (1891) and "Contemporary Echoes of Slavophiles and Westernizers" (1892) are heavily influenced by Leontiev's later works, notably his views on the need for a conservative "idea" based on autocracy, Orthodoxy, and the separation of social groupings as an alternative to revolutionary socialism. Tikhomirov later defended Leontiev against his detractors in essays such as "The Ideals of Russia and K. N. Leontiev" (1894) and "Shades of the Late K. N. Leontiev" (1905). During their brief acquaintance, which was cut short by Leontiev's untimely death, Tikhomirov became an ardent admirer of the older man, describing him (accurately, but with unconscious irony) as the "prophet of our future."[11] At the same time it did not take the perspicacious Tikhomirov long to penetrate the essential riddle of Leontiev's fate. "What is one to make of Leontiev?" he wrote in his diary. "No influence, no posterity. Yet as regards talent and vitality I am not worth the soles of his shoes."[12]

Leontiev's rapport with Tikhomirov appears to have been yet another case of "convergent evolution," with both men having reached their final positions through repentance of their former lives, Tikhomirov as revolutionist, Leontiev as radical aesthete. Leontiev himself appears to have felt this, telling Tikhomirov that it was "nice to see someone else coming by a different path to much the same things we have been thinking for a long while."[13] If we may view both men as repentant sinners, then it is interesting that Leontiev's interpretation of Orthodoxy, especially the institution of elders, also resonated with Tikhomirov. "It is the greatest pity," wrote Tikhomirov, "that you are so little read by those who would most benefit from your teaching of Orthodoxy and who, forgive the strangeness of the idea, might be your likeliest converts."[14]

Despite repenting his former role as a revolutionary terrorist, Tikhomirov seems never to have lost his penchant for conspiracy, and he expended a great deal of energy trying to convince Leontiev that a more active proselytizing approach than writing articles for little-read journals was needed if the latter's ideas were ever to gain traction. He wrote at length on the need for Leontiev to engage personally in "missionary work" with his potential audience, to reach out in particular to the young, and most especially (and tellingly) in "those circles where revolutionaries are recruited," and even went so far as to propose the creation of a secret, which meant illegal, organization to that end.

By this time however, little over a year before his death, Leontiev was too exhausted, emotionally and physically, to contemplate a strenuous program of proselytizing, let alone indulge in illegal activity, and he confined himself to his literary output and to working through his small band of "disciples." (He jokingly suggested that Tikhomirov was encouraging him to establish a kind of "Jesuit Order.") Leontiev did apparently suggest that they might cooperate on a work on the future of socialism as the despotic organizing principle of the future, but death intervened before anything could come of the proposal. In any event Tikhomirov did not share Leontiev's view that the development of socialism along these lines would be beneficial, viewing it instead as an anti-Christian and destructive tendency.[15] In the end Tikhomirov's ideas for their future collaboration, in his own words, "died in the seed, the title of an unwritten novel."[16]

Leontiev spent his life rowing "against the current" of ideas in his homeland.[17] First came the almost inevitable failure of his overambitious attempt to rally his countrymen to the standard of aesthetics and to row back the powerful bias toward ethical denunciation in the Petersburg literary world of the early 1860s. Thirteen years later he would return to a capital, Moscow this time, after a lengthy absence believing that he was destined to rescue those members of the intelligentsia he believed to be his natural allies, the Pan-Slavists, from the errors into which they had fallen, or been led. And once again he was to find only incomprehension, disbelief, and ostracism. As it was with Chernyshevsky and Dobrolyubov in 1861, so it would be with Aksakov and Katkov in 1874. Finally, in his declining years, his prophecies regarding the impending fate of the motherland and of civilization fell on the deaf ears of those with the power and position to effect political change in Russia and who preferred "freezing" to any attempt at positive reform.

In later years Leontiev came to believe that he was haunted by a "fatum" determined to prevent him at all costs from achieving recognition. Partly this was true—Leontiev suffered the customary fate of a prophet in his own land—but to some degree his own inflexibility and inexplicable failure to sense which way the cards were stacked must bear part of the responsibility.

Was Leontiev a good writer? Emphatically yes. Was he a good novelist? No, or at best only intermittently. He had talent, without a doubt. His writing is often fluent, his descriptive power self-evident, his dialogue natural and unaffected and at times strikingly modern in feel, reminiscent perhaps of Chekhov, but he lacked restraint, he lacked self-discipline, he lacked discrimination. His masterpiece, in his own estimation, was the story from Greek life *Odysseus Polichroniades*, which he rated as on a par with Ivan Goncharov's *Oblomov*.[18] Obviously posterity has disagreed with this assessment, yet Leontiev himself seems to have been unable to recognize the obvious fact that, regardless of its intrinsic artistic merits, a novel 800 pages in length recounting the growing pains of the son of a Greek merchant in European Turkey whose chief ambition at the end is to become a shopkeeper would test the stamina of even the most sympathetic Russian reader (he did though entitle the fourth part of the novel, which appeared in 1877, "The Rock of Sisyphus," which may be a cryptic acknowledgment of his manifold difficulties in getting his ideas across to the reading public). In addition to this blindness to the needs of his prospective readership, Leontiev could never resist the temptation to use his stories as vehicles for the promulgation of his socio-political manifesto—however much he may have condemned this tendency in others. The story from contemporary Russian life *Two Chosen Women*, a tightly drawn account of a ménage between three very different individuals, might well have become his literary memorial, had he found the staying power to finish it without introducing political messages extraneous to the plot that are psychologically unconvincing and only serve to divert attention from the interplay between the characters.[19]

As with his novels, so with his political, ethical, and social writing. For despite his service in the diplomatic corps, he seems never to have acquired the people skills necessary to gain a wide audience for his undoubtedly groundbreaking, not to say revolutionary, ideas and his uncannily accurate predictions. Yet if it was his misfortune to live and die a voice crying in the wilderness, it has at least been to the benefit of posterity, for the bold ideas of this remarkable man have been handed down to us unsullied and undiluted by any vain attempts on his part to trim his sails according to the prevailing winds.

"A great man strode through Russia," wrote Rozanov, "and laid himself down to die. His going had no accompaniment but the cawing of the rooks. He lay down and he died, for all his remarkable abilities, in despair . . . like Jacob he wrestled with God and was made lame, but he was a powerful antagonist."[20]

Leontiev was, as we have seen and as he was always ready to admit, but an indifferent scholar. His erudition was broad but not deep and his methodology, if it may be called such, was to "flit" through the works of others in search of passages to support theories he had devised in his own head. Rozanov surely gets close to the heart of the matter when he says that Leontiev's thoughts make "splendid reading." For if Leontiev has a claim to greatness, and he surely has, it lies in his ability to clothe his radical ideas about the direction of travel of nineteenth-century civilization, and his apocalyptic yet accurate prophecies about the future of Europe and of Russia, in language worthy of the Old Testament. His works, for all they are deeply concerned with the vital social, political, and religious questions of his day, and ours, are primarily literature, and literature of a high order, dramatic episodes for our own time as well as his which, whatever narrow technical shortcomings they may contain, deserve to be read and appreciated as such. As do his letters, a voluminous correspondence, particularly of his later years of peace and seclusion when he had the leisure to condense and summarize for the benefit of new friends and disciples a lifetime's reflection on the nature of man and his place in the world and in the cosmos. They merit detailed study in their own right, for in them we see the man entire, as Rozanov puts it, "an Adam without clothes."

Leontiev's life was one of struggle, a ceaseless attempt to reconcile the ultimately unreconcilable. This shows clearly in his efforts to square the circle of ethics and aesthetics in the human psyche. His solution, transcendental egoism, is flawed as a standard of human conduct, at once demanding too blind a faith in dogma and ignoring that inherent weakness in human nature which seeks forgiveness in Christ. Similarly, his political testament, socialist autocracy, may be seen as either unrealizable or, if realized under Stalin, as opening the door to what was in effect the very antithesis of his cherished ideal of cultural flowering.

Yet it is not by the practical nature of his conclusions that Leontiev must be appraised; few of the great system builders could withstand so rigorous a yardstick. The enduring importance of Leontiev as a thinker lies in his having dared, like Nietzsche, to ask questions and reach conclusions about the nature of man and the human condition which his optimistic contemporaries would much rather have left undisturbed. To the end Leontiev took his cue from the words of his hero Milkeyev in *A Place of One's Own*: "If Lady Macbeth is the price we pay for Cordelia, bring her on, but spare us from debility, slumber, indifference, meanness and mercantile caution."

Perhaps the last word should be left to Lev Tikhomirov, the person who, though he knew Leontiev for only eighteen months, came to understand him better, with the possible exception of Rozanov, than any other of his contemporaries. On 21 September 1891 Tikhomirov wrote about him to Olga Novikova, the lady of Slavophile inclinations whom Leontiev had met and possibly pursued in Petersburg twenty years before:

> I've been corresponding with Leontiev. I'm very taken with him. His personality is quite unique: immoral, crippled, yet with a great resource of goodness in him. He's very intelligent and I would really like him to live another ten years as he might become a very useful, even indispensable fellow . . . But he's one of those who are half angel, half devil, the two forever grappling in a desperate struggle for supremacy. His angel has not been banished though, it will not capitulate. He attracts me deeply through mixed feelings of admiration and pity.[21]

Alas, Leontiev did not have another ten years to live; he had but a brief nine weeks. He ended his life believing, as cited in the epigraph to this book, that he was "a man who tried his hand at everything and brought no benefit to anyone, aside from three or four people." And certainly his warnings about his country's future were disregarded by his countrymen, to their cost. Yet what Richard Hare called the "chronic ethical itch," the compulsion to sacrifice all other considerations to the overriding ideal of egalitarian leveling, which so obsessed the Russian intelligentsia from the mid-nineteenth century, and which brought catastrophe in its train, this preoccupation with equality at all costs has come to exercise a similar dominance in Western intellectual circles today. So it may pay us to ponder Leontiev's chilling insight into the banality of evil, his prophecy that future inquisitors would arise "not in the guise of mystical visionaries animated by faith but in that of the most ordinary egalitarian nihilists."[22] If this apocalyptic vision gives us at least some pause for thought about our own direction of travel and the possible nature of our destination, then it may be that, a hundred and more years later, it will bring benefit to considerably more people than merely "three or four."

NOTES

Abbreviations

LCW	*Polnoe sobranie sochinenii i pisem v dvenadsati tomakh* (*Complete Collected Works and Letters in 12 Volumes*), SPB, Vladimir Dal', 2000.
EdCom	Editorial commentaries in the collected works.
Leontiev Letters	*Konstantin Nikolaevich Leontiev: izbrannye pis'ma (1854–1891)*, SPB, Pushkinskii Fond, 1993.
Aleksandrov Letters	*Pamiati Konstantina Nikolaevicha Leontieva i pis'ma k Anatoliiu Aleksandrovu*, Sergiev Posad, 1915.
Filippov Letters	*Proroki Vizantizma*, SPB, Pushkinsky Dom, 2012.
Rozanov Letters	*Konstantin Leontiev: pis'ma k Vasiliiu Rozanovu*, London, Nina Karsov, 1981.
SPB	Saint Petersburg

Introduction

1. Letter of 14 August 1891 in *Konstantin Leontiev: pis'ma k Vasiliyu Rozanovu* (*Letters to Vasily Rozanov*), London, Nina Karsov, 1981, 110–11.

2. *Rozanov Letters*, 111.

3. Only one story fragment survives, titled *From Autumn to Autumn* (*Ot oseni do oseni*), in Vol. 5 of K. N. Leontiev, *Polnoe sobranie sochinenii i pisem v dvenadsati tomakh* (*Complete Collected Works and Letters in 12 Volumes*) (LCW), SPB, Vladimir Dal', 2000. Leontiev's niece Marya Vladimirovna, who was staying with him at the time, stated that the destruction of the manuscripts took her by surprise. See the Editorial Commentary (*EdCom*) in LCW, Vol. 5, 785.

4. Article of 16 January 1880 from *Leading Articles of the Warsaw Diary*, LCW, Vol. 7.2, 25.

5. Quoted in F. M. Dostoevsky, *Polnoe sobranie sochinenii v 30 tomakh* (*Complete Collected Works in 30 Volumes*) (PSS), Nauka, Leningradskoe Otdelenie, 1972–88, 26:142.

6. Article of 7 February 1880 from *Leading Articles of the Warsaw Diary*, LCW, Vol. 7.2, 53.

7. See A. M. Konoplyantsev, *Pamiati Konstantina Nikolaevicha Leontieva 1891 goda* (*To the Memory of Konstantin Nikolaevich Leontiev 1891—a Literary Compilation*), SPB, Sirius, 1911,114.

8. Letter to K. A. Gubastov of 13 September 1880, LCW, Vol. 11.2, 386–87. On Leontiev's depression after the demise of the *Warsaw Diary*, see also his letter of 10 October 1880 to T. I. Filippov in *Proroki Vizantizma*, SPB, Pushkinskii Dom, 2012 (*Filippov Letters*), 160ff.

9. R. G. Hare, *Pioneers in Russian Thought: Studies in Non-Marxian Formation in 19th Century Russia and Its Partial Revival in the Soviet Union*, Oxford University Press, 1951, 36.

10. The bibliography in Olga Volkogonova's recent biography of Leontiev lists some forty-two books and articles about or referencing Leontiev which have appeared in Russian since 1990. See her *Konstantin Leontiev*, Moscow, 2013, 449–452. An exhaustive bibliography would be considerably larger.

11. By the historian A. E. Kotov, quoted by Olga Fetisenko, *"Geptastilisty": Konstantin Leont'ev, ego sobesedniki i ucheniki: idei russkogo konservatizma v literaturno-khudozhestvennykh i publit̆sisticheskikh praktikakh vtoroi poloviny XIX–pervoĭ chetverti XX veka*, SPB, Pushkinskiy Dom, 2012, 14n.

12. Michel Eltchaninoff, *Inside the Mind of Vladimir Putin*, London, Hurst & Co, 2018, 72. Quoted from the speech by Putin at the meeting of the Valdai International Discussion Club, Novgorod region, 19 September 2013.

13. From the article "The Russian Jupiter" by Stanislav Khatuntsev, cited by Eltchaninoff, 69, available online: https://politconservatism.ru/thinking/russkiy-yupiter.

14. See Eltchaninoff, especially the chapters "The Conservative Turn" and "The Russian Way."

15. B. Adrianov writing in *K. Leontiev, Nash sovremennik*, SPB, Izdatel'stvo Chernysheva, 1993, 9.

16. Quoted from *Leading Articles of the Warsaw Diary*, LCW, Vol. 7.2, 43. The belief is not confined to ultranationalists; as astute a commentator as Edward Thaden mistakenly attributes "national egoism and exclusiveness" to Leontiev. See his *Conservative Nationalism in Nineteenth Century Russia*, University of Washington, Seattle, 1964, 127.

17. By Yuri Pushchaev in his "Otnoshenie K. N. Leontieva k kommunizmy," avaliable online at https://cyberleninka.ru/article/n/otnoshenie-k-n-leontieva-k-kommunizmu-sotsializmu-o-nesostoyavshemsya-soyuze-sotsializma-s-russkim-samoderzhaviem-i-plamennoy-mistikoy.

18. Repnikov, "Ot Leontieva do Stalina: konservatizm, sotsializm i liberalizm," *Nash Sovremennik*, No. 10, 2005, online at: http://nash-sovremennik.ru/p.php?y=2005&n=10&id=10. Nikolai Yakovlevich Danilevsky (1822–85), Slavophile, author of the influential *Russia and Europe* of 1869.

19. Lev Gumilev, "Seek Out What Is True," interview, *Soviet Literature*, 1990, Vol. 1, 72–76. Referenced in Mark Bassin's *The Gumilev Mystique: Biopolitics, Eurasianism, and the Construction of Community in Modern Russia (Culture and Society after Socialism)*, Cornell University, Ithaca, 2016.

20. See the essay titled "Aristocracy and the Kallipolis: Konstantin Leontiev and the Politics of 'Flourishing Complexity,'" in *Aristocratic Souls in Democratic Times*, edited by Richard Avramenko and Ethan Alexander-Davey, Lexington Books, Lanham, Boulder, New York & London, 2018.

21. Further details on these and other studies are given in the bibliography.

22. Alexander-Davey, in "Aristocracy and the Kallipolis," concedes in one or two places that Leontiev's critique of utilitarian liberalism has application to globalization, but he does not develop the point.

1. The Divided Self

1. *A Story of My Mother's about the Empress Maria Fedorovna*, LCW, Vol. 6.1, 561, 552.

2. *A Smolensk Deacon's Tale of the Invasion of 1812*, LCW, Vol. 6.1, 364. Nikolay Alekseyevich Nekrasov, 1821–77, poet, writer, and critic, whose poems about the condition of the peasants made him a hero of Russian liberalism. His poem "The Troika" was published in 1847. Nikolai Platonovich Ogarev, 1813–77, Russian poet and political activist, friend of Herzen, and fellow exile after 1856.

3. *My Literary Destiny*, LCW, Vol. 6.1, 30.

4. LCW, Vol. 6.1, 35, 52.

5. LCW, Vol. 6.1, 52.

6. "Some Reminiscences on the Late Apollon Grigoriev," LCW, Vol. 6.1, 15.

7. Letter to V. G. Avseyenko of 24 October 1883 in *Konstantin Nikolaevich Leontiev: izbrannye pis'ma (1854–1891)*, SPB, Pushkinskii fond, 1993 (*Leontiev Letters*), 277.

8. *My Literary Destiny*, LCW, Vol. 6.1, 30–31. After his war experiences Leontiev came to view this relationship as a relic from a former life, as exemplified by the petrified remains of love depicted in Ogarev's poem "An Everyday Story," LCW, Vol. 6.1, 70.

9. *Turgenev in Moscow: From M y Recollections*, LCW, Vol. 6.1, 743.

10. In the novel *Two Chosen Women of 1870*, LCW, Vol. 5, 78.

11. Due to problems with the censorship, "Nationalist Politics as a Weapon of World Revolution" was published only in 1854 under the title *Gratitude*.

12. *My Literary Destiny*, LCW, Vol. 6.1, 37–38.

13. Iosif Fudel', *K Leontiev*, LCW, Annex 1, 388.

14. *My Literary Destiny*, LCW, Vol. 6.1, 40. There is an oblique hint in Konoplyantsev, Leontiev's earliest biographer, that Turgenev may have used Rudnev as a model for Bazarov in *Fathers and Sons* (Konoplyantsev, *Pamiati 1891 goda*, 20). Leontiev believed that with Bazarov Turgenev had acted on his suggestion that he produce a "Russian Insarov" (the hero of "On the Eve"). See his *For the Biography of K N Leontiev*, LCW, Vol. 6.2, 8.

15. *Turgenev in Moscow (Continuation)*, LCW, Vol. 6.2, 69.

16. *My Literary Destiny*, LCW, Vol. 6.1, 57–58.

17. *The Surrender of Kerch in 1855*, LCW, Vol. 6.1, 647.

18. LCW, Vol. 6.1, 665.

19. From *A Story of My Mother's about the Empress Maria Fedorovna*, LCW, Vol. 6.1, 560–61.

20. Letter of 25 August 1856, LCW, Vol. 11.1, 173. In 1925 the literary historian S. N. Durylin recorded the words of Leontiev's niece, Marya Vladimirovna: "His mother adored K. N. It was the strongest, the most exclusive love and devotion." Cited in *EdCom* in LCW, Vol. 6.2, 292.

21. Letter of 1 May 1857, LCW, Vol. 11.1, 213. Pierre-Jean de Béranger, 1780–1857, French poet, songwriter, and anti-establishment icon.

22. *Turgenev in Moscow*, LCW, Vol. 6.1, 727.

23. In 1999 only ruins remained of Kudinovo. D. M. Volodikhin includes some photographs of these in his *Vysokomernyi strannik: filosofiia i zhizn' Konstantina Leontieva*, Moscow, Manufaktura, 2000.

24. See *The Chronology of My Life*, LCW, Vol. 6.2, 28. In 1925 Marya Vladimirovna confirmed to Durylin that there was a "great deal" of Durnovo in her uncle's character. Cited in *EdCom* in LCW, Vol. 6.2, 641. See also Vasily Rozanov, *Opavshie list'ia (Fallen Leaves)*, in *Izbrannoe*, A. Neimanis, Munich, 1970, 203.

25. Letter of 7 October 1855, LCW, Vol. 11.1, 121.

26. Letter of 25 August 1856, LCW, Vol. 11.1, 172.

27. *My Literary Destiny*, LCW, Vol. 6.1, 56.

28. LCW, Vol. 6.1, 68. Georges Cuvier, 1769–1832, French naturalist and zoologist; Alexander von Humboldt, 1769–1859, German naturalist and explorer.

29. "Second Marriage," LCW, Vol. 1, 345.

30. Chernyshevsky, *Esteticheskie otnosheniia iskusstva k deistvitel'nosti (The Aesthetic Relationship of Art to Reality)*, in his *Polnoe sobranie sochinenii v 15 tomakh*, Moscow, Goslitizdat, 1939–1953 (*PSS*), Vol. 2, 83.

31. *Podlipki* translates roughly as *Under the Lime Trees*, but as it is a proper name I have left the original in the text. Leontiev wrote the first chapter of this novel, conceived as a stand-alone piece "A Winter's Morning on a Deserted Country Estate," in 1853 or 1854 and read it aloud the same evening at the salon of Evgeniya Tur, Countess Salias. The countess was delighted, calling it a "magnifique tableau de genre." She took to Leontiev and was instrumental in getting "The Germans" finally published in 1854. See *My Literary Destiny*, LCW Vol. 6.1, 47; also *EdCom* in LCW, Vol. 1, 665.

32. Vsevolod Solovyev, cited in *EdCom* in LCW, Vol. 4, 961n24. Turgenev too counseled Leontiev to aim for greater conciseness of style and to concentrate on essentials rather than burdening his work with a confusion of minor details. See his letter of 11 February 1855 in I. S. Turgenev, *Polnoe sobranie sochinenii i pisem v 30 tomakh (Complete Collected Works and Letters in 30 Volumes)*, Moscow, Nauka, 1978 (*PSS*), Letters, Vol. 3, 14–15. The literary critic of *Otechestvennye Zapiski*, S. S. Dudyshkin, was of the same opinion (see *EdCom* in LCW, Vol. 1, 665–66) as was (among others) the critic of *Sankt-Peterburgskie Vedomosti*, V. V. Markov, in his reviews of Leontiev's longest novel, *Odysseus Polichroniades*, and his fable *Child of the Soul* (*EdCom* in LCW, Vol. 4, 957).

33. *Podlipki*, LCW, Vol. 1, 590.

34. LCW, Vol. 1, 596.

35. *The Egyptian Dove*, LCW, Vol. 5, 295.

36. *Podlipki*, LCW, Vol. 1, 551–52.

37. LCW, Vol. 1, 549.

38. For a perceptive discussion of these articles, and Leontiev's later writing on Tolstoy and Dostoevsky, see S. G. Bocharov, "Esteticheskoe okhranenie v literaturnoi kritike (Konstantin Leontiev v russkoi literature)," *Kontekst*, 1977, 152–63.

39. Letter from Turgenev to Leontiev of 16 February 1860. Leontiev actually sent the manuscript of the *Letter from a Provincial* to Turgenev, presumably at the latter's invitation, to use his influence with the publishers. On this episode, see *EdCom* in LCW, Vol. 9, 575–77.

40. *Letter of a Provincial to Turgenev*, LCW, Vol. 9, 8. A decade later Leontiev came to see the "objective, featureless, ubiquitous realism of contemporary letters" as a

sign of the "secondary simplification" to which, according to his view of history, all culture is reduced in its final phases. See *Byzantinism and Slavdom*, LCW, Vol. 7.1, 381.

41. Leontiev was later to deprecate Belinsky's reproach to Gogol. In his article "Literacy and National Character" of 1868–69, he refers to Belinsky as "nothing but a talented applier to our literature of European ideas" and *"an extreme example of Europeanism and positivism*—thus he was in the pages of *Sovremennik*, especially in the revolting letter to Gogol which is known to all Russia." LCW, Vol. 7.1, 102.

42. Taken from Chernyshevsky's *Ocherki gogolevskogo perioda russkoy literatury* (*Outlines of the Gogolian Period of Russian Literature*), 1855, in *PSS*, Vol. 3, 259.

43. Chernyshevsky, *PSS*, Vol. 2, 51.

44. Chernyshevsky, *PSS*, Vol. 2, 13, 138, 239–40, 292.

45. M. I. Daragan, literary critic of *Russkaia Beseda* and *Nashe Vremya* during the 1860s.

46. *Letter of a Provincial to Turgenev*, LCW, Vol. 9, 7.

47. See Schelling, *Werke*, edited by M Schröter, Munich, C. H. Beck, 1927, Vol. 2, 349, 614, 619.

48. Cited in *EdCom* in LCW, Vol. 9, 577.

49. *Letter of a Provincial to Turgenev*, LCW, Vol. 9, 8.

50. LCW, Vol. 9, 10.

51. LCW, Vol. 9, 14.

52. *My Literary Destiny*, LCW, Vol. 6.1, 127, 56; see also letter to Filippov of 3 March 1876 in *Filippov Letters*, 92.

53. N. A. Dobrolyubov, 1836–61, left-wing activist, influential literary critic, and collaborator with Chernyshevsky on *Sovremennik* until his death of tuberculosis at the age of twenty-five.

54. Dobrolyubov, *Sobranie sochinenii v 9 tomakh* (*Collected Works in 9 Volumes*) (*SS*), Moscow, Gosudarstvennoe izdatel'stvo khudozhestvennoi literatury, 1963, Vol. 6, 96.

55. Dobrolyubov, *SS*, Vol. 6, 286–87.

56. Dobrolyubov, *SS*, Vol. 6, 223–24.

57. Cited in *Edcom* in LCW, Vol. 9, 595–96.

58. "Regarding the Stories of Marko Vovchok," LCW, Vol. 9, 19. F. K. A. Schwegler, 1819–57, author of the popular *Geschichte der Philosophie im Umriss*, 1848, subsequently translated into Russian.

59. *Who Is More in the Right? Letters to Vladimir Sergeyevich Solovyev*, LCW, Vol. 8.2, 136.

60. See letter 35 of 12 September 1889 in A. Aleksandrov, *Pamiati Konstantina Nikolaevicha Leontieva i pis'ma k Anatoliiu Aleksandrovu*, Sergiev Posad, 1915. The article and letters are available separately online: http://az.lib.ru/a/aleksandrow_a_a/text _1915_leontiev.shtml.

61. "Regarding the Stories of Marko Vovchok," LCW, Vol. 9, 25–26.

62. LCW, Vol. 9, 30–31. The question of whether a "bad" person can be a good artist is of course very much alive in our own time. In his third essay of literary criticism, "Our Society and Our Belles Lettres," Leontiev took issue with Dobrolyubov on this point with regard to Pushkin, whom the latter had found "insufficiently humane" as a poet. LCW, Vol. 9, 71.

63. Turgenev, *PSS, Letters*, Vol. 4, 162, 185, 242–23.

64. Turgenev, *PSS, Letters*, Vol. 9, 144–5; Vol. 15.1, 94.

65. Turgenev, *PSS, Letters*, Vol. 3, 47.

66. *My Literary Destiny*, LCW Vol. 6.1, 120.

67. Leontiev was personally well-disposed toward Dobrolyubov, despite the fundamental antagonism of their views, and was typically honest enough to say so publicly. In his 1869 article "Some Reminiscences on the Late Apollon Grigoriev" he declares, with reference to Dobrolyubov: "A sparrow hawk doesn't stop being a bold and nimble bird just because it lays grotesque eggs" (LCW, Vol. 6.1, 16). Some rancor seems to have persisted however: Dobrolyubov appears in Leontiev's later novel *Two Chosen Women* thinly disguised as the "notorious anarchist" Dobromyslov (LCW, Vol. 5, 83).

68. *My Literary Destiny*, LCW Vol. 6.1, 120.

69. "Our Society and Our Belles Lettres," LCW, Vol. 9, 67. Dobrolyubov, looking through the opposite end of the telescope, had blamed the "lifelessness" of Insarov and Yelena in "On the Eve" on Russian social conditions, which in his view had failed to produce real life prototypes on which Turgenev could have based his characters. Dobrolyubov, *SS*, Vol. 6, 123.

70. "Our Society and Our Belles Lettres," LCW, Vol. 9, 69.

71. LCW, Vol. 9, 70–71.

72. *From Autumn to Autumn*, LCW, Vol. 5, 41.

73. Hare, *Pioneers in Russian Thought*, 34–35, 184–85. Conversely, Ivan von Kologrivov makes the telling point that Leontiev may have failed to arrive at a true appreciation of Gogol because, like all his generation, he was a realist with regard to fiction, whereas Gogol was not. See his *Von Hellas zum Mönchtum*, Regensburg, Gregorius, 1948, 80n. Interestingly, Kologrivov's point is foreshadowed by Filippov in his letter to Leontiev of 22 February 1888 (*Filippov Letters*, 492–93).

74. ~~Rozanov Letters~~, 104–5n (I paraphrase slightly).

75. Taken from the Tate Gallery London: https://www.tate.org.uk/art/art-terms/a/aesthetic-movement.

76. *The Chronology of My Life*, LCW, Vol. 6.2, 30–31.

2. The Best of All Possible Worlds

1. *V svoem kraiu*, literally "In a place of one's own." The novel may have been work in progress since 1858; see *EdCom* in LCW, Vol. 2, 426–28.

2. Letter of 20 May 1863, LCW, Vol. 11.1, 236.

3. By Henrietta Mondry and Sally Thompson in *Konstantin Leont'ev: An Examination of His Major Fiction*, 1993. See especially chapter 2, "In My Own Land: As a Political Pamphlet of the 1860s." Chernyshevsky's novel inspired imitation in Tolstoy and Lenin but drew mockery from Dostoevsky in *Notes from Underground*.

4. *A Place of One's Own*, LCW, Vol. 2, 27.

5. LCW, Vol. 2, 92.

6. LCW, Vol. 2, 90.

7. LCW, Vol. 2, 158. Milkeyev is another thinly disguised version of Leontiev, who recalled living with the Rozens on much the same terms as his hero lives with Novosilskaya in the novel. See *My Literary Destiny*, LCW, Vol. 6.1, 124n.

8. *A Place of One's Own*, LCW, Vol. 2, 23. The figure of the Athenian general and adventurer Alcibiades remained strongly symbolic for Leontiev throughout his life as

representing strength and beauty beyond good and evil. His niece Marya Vladimirovna said many times that Leontiev was Alcibiades, "a Hellene by blood." See *EdCom* in LCW, Vol. 6.2, 650.

9. *A Place of One's Own*, LCW, Vol. 2, 35.

10. LCW, Vol. 2, 45. In 401 BC Xenophon, the Greek statesman and general, commanded the "Ten Thousand" Greek mercenaries in support of Cyrus the Younger's unsuccessful attempt to claim the throne of Persia from his brother Artaxerxes II.

11. Letter of 13 August 1891 in *Rozanov Letters*, 102.

12. *A Place of One's Own*, LCW, Vol. 2, 45–46. Cordelia is King Lear's third daughter and the only one to remain true to him.

13. *A Place of One's Own*, LCW, Vol. 2, 152.

14. It is not possible now to know what Welles actually had in mind, though it is worth noting that Milkeyev's speech is both closer to Lime's and precedes Whistler by two decades.

15. Letter of 6 July 1888, LCW, Annex 1, 82. Mikhail Dmitrievich Skobelev, Russian general, hero of the Russo-Turkish War of 1877.

16. M. E. Saltykov-Shchedrin, *Sobranie sochinenii v 20 tomakh* (*SS*), Moscow, Gosudarstvennoe izdatel'stvo khudozhestvennoi literatury, 1965–77, Vol. 5, 454. Leontiev's mother, Feodosia Petrovna, foresaw the negative reception the novel was likely to receive in the atmosphere of the day, comparing Milkeyev to a second Icarus and hoping that his creator would not meet the same fate. See extract from her letter to Leontiev's niece Marya Vladimirovna in *EdCom*, LCW, Vol. 2, 428.

17. Noted by Joseph Frank in *Dostoevsky: A Writer in His Time*, Princeton University Press, 2010, 569.

18. Saltykov-Shchedrin, *SS*, Vol. 9, 413. For an overview of the critical response to *The Idiot*, see Victor Terras, *The Idiot: An Interpretation*, Boston, Twayne Publishers, 1990, chapter 3, "Critical Reception."

19. Dostoevsky, *The Devils*, PSS, Vol. 10, 372–73.

20. *Reminiscences of F. I. Inozemtsov and Other Moscow Doctors of the Fifties*, LCW, Vol. 6.1, 358.

21. "Some Reminiscences on the Late Apollon Grigoriev," LCW, Vol. 6.1, 13.

22. *A Place of One's Own*, LCW, Vol. 2, 267. Leontiev was not alone in associating woodlice with Petersburg. The anarchist Dudkin in Andrei Bely's 1913 novel *Petersburg* goes insane watching woodlice crawl up the walls of his tenement.

23. "The Average European as the Ideal and Weapon of Universal Destruction," LCW, Vol. 8.1, 222–23.

24. *Our New Christians: On Universal Love*, LCW, Vol. 9, 197.

25. "Grundlinien der Philosophie des Rechts (Vorrede)" in G. W. F. Hegel, *Werke*, Berlin, Duncker und Humblot, 1832–45, Vol. 8, 17, 19. Hegel is perhaps best known in Russia for his radicalizing effect on the intellectuals of the 1830s and for thereby spawning, directly and indirectly, the whole tribe of the nihilists from Bakunin onward. The other strand of Hegelianism, conservative quietism, also had its impact in Russia however. On Belinsky's period of "reconciliation with reality," see Dmitro Chizhevsky, *Hegel in Russia*, Paris, 1939, 134–42; Boris Jakowenko, *Geschichte des Hegelianismus in Rußland*, Buchdruckerei Josef Bartl, Prague, 1938, 52–56, 85. Bakunin's dictum that: "Nothing is evil, everything is good, only restraint is bad" is quoted by Jakowenko, 21. On Bakunin, see also Chizhevsky, 91ff.

26. *A Place of One's Own*, LCW, Vol. 2, 276.

27. See G. W. Leibniz, *Monadology*, sections 87–90, in *Philosophical Papers and Letters*, ed. L. E. Loemker, Dordrecht, Reidel, 1972, 652; see also *Theodicy*, ed. A. Farrer, trans. E. M. Huggard, London, Routledge & Kegan Paul, 1952, 128–29. The notion stuck with Leontiev through his many vicissitudes: one of the "enlightened" Turks in his long novel *Odysseus Polichroniades* (1873–78) declares that: "Tout est pour le mieux dans le meilleur des mondes possibles." LCW, Vol. 4, 116.

28. Leibniz, *Monadology*, sections 58, 648.

29. *A Place of One's Own*, LCW, Vol. 2, 72.

30. LCW, Vol. 2, 46.

31. Leibniz, *Theodicy*, passim.

32. *Four Letters from Athos*, "Letter 2," LCW, Vol. 7.1, 140 (emphasis added).

33. *Our New Christians: On Universal Love*, LCW, Vol. 9, 204.

34. "Analysis, Style and Tendency: On the Novels of Count L. N. Tolstoy," LCW, Vol. 9, 320.

35. *Odysseus Polichroniades*, LCW, Vol. 4, 44.

36. *Why and How Our Liberalism Is Harmful*, LCW, Vol. 7.2, 141.

37. *Two Representatives of Industry*, LCW, Vol. 8.1, 140.

38. Letter of 26 January 1891 to Iosif Fudel', LCW, Annex I, 267.

39. Letter to Fudel' of 28 January 1891, LCW, Annex I, 278.

40. Christopher Dawson, "Karl Marx and the Dialectic of History," in *The Dynamics of World History*, New York, Sheed and Ward, 1957, Nabu Public Domain Reprint, 361.

41. An accusation leveled by the Pan-Slavist Ivan Aksakov.

42. Kologrivov is eloquent in his defense of Leontiev as a moral thinker. As he notes in connection with Leontiev's later polemic with Tolstoy, Leontiev's morality is "not philanthropic but heroic, the morality of supra-human values, not that of mundane contentment." *Von Hellas zum Mönchtum*, 181, 185. For all the divergences between them, Nikolai Berdyaev also stresses the fundamentally ethical nature of Leontiev's strivings. See his *Konstantin Leontiev: ocherk iz istorii russkoi religioznoi mysli*, YMCA Press, Paris 1926, 100ff., 109ff., 146.

43. VasilyRozanov, *Neuznannyi fenomen* (*Unrecognized Phenomenon*), in *Pamiati 1891 goda*, 182; *Rozanov Letters*, 34–35, 40n2.

44. See, among others, Berdyaev, *Ocherk*, chapter 1, part 6; Simon Frank, *Konstantin Leontiev: ein russischer Nietzsche*, Hochland, 1928–29, Vol. 2, 613–32; B. Glatzer Rosenthal, ed., *Nietzsche in Russia*, Princeton University Press, 1986.

45. *A Place of One's Own*, LCW, Vol. 2, 89.

46. LCW, Vol. 2, 152–53. The "underdeveloped man" in *A Place of One's Own* is represented by the left-Hegelian rationalist Bogoyavlensky, "a seminarist and a boor," who orients his actions according to a statistical barometer of happiness and unhappiness and ends up in Petersburg thriving among the woodlice. Mondry and Thompson detect in Bogoyavlensky'sappearance and attitudes a deliberate parody of Chernyshevsky. *Konstantin Leont'ev: An Examination of His Major Fiction*, 44ff.

47. *A Place of One's Own*, LCW, Vol. 2, 152. Alexander Herzen harbored similar reservations about utilitarian ethics, declaring that: "The truly free man creates his own morality." *From the Other Shore*, in Herzen, *Sobranie sochinenii v 30*

tomakh (*Complete Collected Works in 30 Volumes*) (*SS*), Moscow, Nauka, 1954–65, Vol. 6, 131.

48. Friedrich Nietzsche, *Also sprach Zarathustra*, first published 1885. Available in English online as *Thus Spake Zarathustra*: http://www.gutenberg.org/files/1998/1998 -h/1998-h.htm#link2H_4_0002.

49. *A Place of One's Own*, LCW, Vol. 2, 134–35.

50. See, for example, Volodikhin, *Vysokomerny strannik*; Aleksandr Zakrzhevsky, *Odinokii myslitel'* in *Khristianskaia Mysl'*, Kiev, 1916.

3. The Gathering Storm

1. *A Place of One's Own*, LCW, Vol. 2, 114.

2. Jürgen Lehmann, *Der Einfluß der Philosophie des deutschen Idealismus in der russischen Literaturkritik des 19. Jahrhunderts*, Heidelberg, Winter, 1975, 171–72.

3. *A Place of One's Own*, LCW, Vol. 2, 327.

4. *My Memories of Thrace*, LCW, Vol. 6.1, 143.

5. LCW, Vol. 6.1, 164.

6. *Sketches of Crete*, LCW, Vol. 3, 24. These "sketches" form an introduction to the story cycle *Scenes from the Life of Christians in Turkey*.

7. *My Memories of Thrace*, LCW, Vol. 6.1, 208.

8. *Odysseus Polichroniades*, LCW, Vol. 4, 405.

9. LCW, Vol. 4, 309.

10. LCW, Vol. 4, 534.

11. *My Memories of Thrace*, LCW, Vol. 6.1, 159–60.

12. *Two Chosen Women*, LCW, Vol. 5, 171. Elsewhere in the same novel Matveyev laments that "even in Samarkand you can't get away from liberal phrase mongering nowadays." LCW, Vol. 5, 149.

13. *My Memories of Thrace*, LCW, Vol. 6.1, 189.

14. "Two Counts: Aleksei Vronsky and Leo Tolstoy," LCW, Vol. 8.1, 299.

15. Letter to Gubastov of 29 February 1868, LCW, Vol. 11.1, 258.

16. Rozanov, *Literaturnye izgnanniki* (*Literary Exiles*), SPB, Novoye Vremya, 1913, 324n.

17. *Rozanov Letters*, 33.

18. Letter of 22 April 1892 cited by Rozanov in *Literaturnye izgnanniki*, 324, 28.

19. *Rozanov Letters*, 33.

20. Letter of 24 May 1891 in *Rozanov Letters*, 58, 67n7.

21. *The Brigand Sotiri*, LCW, Vol. 6.1, 432.

22. Letter to Gubastov of 12 August 1875, LCW, Vol. 11.1, 453.

23. See letter to Vsevolod Solovyev of 18 June 1879, LCW, Vol. 11.2, 336. A. A. Fet (1820–92), Russian poet, regarded as the finest exponent of lyric verse in Russian literature.

24. *My Memories of Thrace*, LCW, Vol. 6.1, 164.

25. Leontiev had great sympathy for the Cretan patriots and donated his earnings from "Chrizó" to the relief of their families. See his letter to Gubastov of 29 February 1868, LCW, Vol. 11.1, 259.

26. *Sketches of Crete*, LCW, Vol. 3, 16.

27. See *EdCom* in LCW, Vol. 4, 960–62.

28. See *EdCom* in LCW, Vol. 3, 711–12.

29. From the foreword to *Scenes from the Life of Christians in Turkey*, LCW, Vol. 3, 7.

30. For example, from the critic V. G. Avseyenko, writing in *Russkii Mir* in 1875, who rated them "extremely highly." See *EdCom* in LCW, Vol. 3, 714–15 and LCW, Vol. 4, 956.

31. *EdCom* in LCW, Vol. 3, 716.

32. The stories were well-grounded in the life of the Ottoman domains. Leontiev's friend T. I. Filippov reported the opinion of the senior Russian diplomat Baron A. G. Zhomini that for gauging the mood of Greek affairs in the 1870s *Aspazia Lampridi* was worth more than any 200 consular reports (*EdCom* in LCW, Vol. 3, 744). And in 1890 Leontiev negotiated for a translation into Greek of two of the shorter stories, "Chrizó" and "Captain Ilia," and for translation into Greek and Turkish of *Odysseus Polichroniades* (*EdCom* in LCW, Vol. 3, 716; letter to Filippov of 10 January 1890 in *Filippov Letters*, 572). The idea of translation may have been in Leontiev's mind from the outset, for he mentions the possibility in the letter to his friend Gubastov of 29 February 1868 (LCW, Vol. 11.1, 259). "Pembé" was published in Serbo-Croat in 1883 and in Czech in 1903 (*EdCom* in LCW, Vol. 3, 733).

33. Letter to Gubastov of 29 February 1868, LCW, Vol. 11.1, 258. We can only speculate on what lay behind this enigmatic confession.

34. *A Husband's Confession (Ispoved' muzha)*, LCW, Vol. 2, 385.

35. LCW, Vol. 2, 339, 329.

36. LCW, Vol. 2, 331.

37. Reported by Anatoly Aleksandrov in *Pamiati Konstantina Nikolaevicha Leontieva i pisma k Anatoliiu Aleksandrovu*.

38. *A Husband's Confession*, LCW, Vol. 2, 329.

39. LCW, Vol. 2, 369.

40. Schelling, *Werke*, Vol. 3, 406: "The Universe exists in God in unending beauty as the supreme work of art."

41. *A Husband's Confession*, LCW, Vol. 2, 339.

42. LCW, Vol. 2, 349.

43. LCW, Vol. 2, 362–63.

44. LCW, Vol. 2, 363. Compare Herzen: "They turn out the French by thousands from the same pattern" (*My Past and Thoughts, SS*, Vol. 10, 70).

45. *A Husband's Confession*, LCW, Vol. 2, 371.

46. LCW, Vol. 2, 373.

47. LCW, Vol. 2, 389

48. LCW, Vol. 2, 396.

49. LCW, Vol. 2, 396. Strakhov told Rozanov that in his view Leontiev, whom he described as a "great philanderer," was "incapable of being unhappy." See letter from Strakhov to Rozanov of 12 December 1890 in Rozanov, *Literaturnye izgnanniki*, 261. The tragic denouement of *A Husband's Confession* suggests that this was a superficial estimate. Strakhov was anything but an impartial observer.

4. Desperate Times

1. Letter to Gubastov of 23 August 1867, LCW, Vol. 11.1, 253.

2. *My Literary Destiny*, LCW, Vol. 6.1, 93.

3. Letter to Gubastov of 23 August 1867, LCW, Vol. 11.1, 253.

4. *My Arrival in Tulcea*, LCW, Vol. 6.1, 453–44. The neighboring Russified town of Izmail also held a great appeal for Leontiev, see LCW, Vol. 6.1, 455ff.

5. Letter of 15 October 1869, LCW, Vol. 11.1, 274. The name "Czargrad" or "City of Caesar," a Russianized form of Constantinople, was commonly used by writers of a Slavophile persuasion. The name goes back at least to the late fifteenth century and Nestor Iskander's *Tale on the Taking of Czargrad*, which describes the fall of the city to the Turks in 1453.

6. Gubastov in *Pamiati 1891 goda*, 209.

7. "In Ioannina," LCW, Vol. 3, 661.

8. *Autumn to Autumn*, LCW, Vol. 5, 17. Compare her letter to Leontiev's niece Marya Vladimirovna of 28 April 1864: "I am not the first mother, and probably won't be the last, who has no children by her side in her declining years. The times are not what they were" (*EdCom* in LCW, Vol. 6.2, 703).

9. See *My Literary Destiny*, LCW, Vol. 6.1, 74. Leontiev recalled reading the novel in Moscow in 1874 on three successive evenings to the publicist F. N. Berg who he recalled was delighted with it and believed that, with a few revisions, it would become a classic of its kind (LCW, Vol. 6.1, 119). It is a shame it remained unfinished, although it has to be said that the second and third (unpublished) parts fall below the standard set by the first.

10. Until 1882 the novel was titled *General Matveyev.*

11. *Two Chosen Women*, LCW, Vol. 5, 77–78. In this clash of duty and poetry we have Leontiev's divided self distilled to its essence. In *Odysseus Polichroniades* the Russian consul Blagov declares that a relationship soon becomes base and contemptible if the woman's husband is indifferent and compliant "like ours in Russia" (LCW, Vol. 4, 560).

12. *Two Chosen Women*, LCW, Vol.5, 79.

13. LCW, Vol. 5, 112.

14. LCW, Vol. 5, 112.

15. LCW, Vol. 5, 78.

16. *Girlfriends*, LCW, Vol. 5, 543.

17. *Two Chosen Women*, LCW, Vol. 5, 66.

18. LCW, Vol. 5, 68.

19. LCW, Vol. 5, 69. Charles Fourier, 1772–1837, French radical thinker, theorist of utopian socialism.

20. LCW, Vol. 5, 118.

21. Sonya's character may also contain elements taken from Marya Vladimirovna and her friend Sofia Maikova. See *EdCom* in LCW, Vol. 5, 814. George Ivask suggests *Marina from Aly Rog* by B. M. Markevich as a prototype for Sonya. See his *Konstantin Leontiev: zhizn' i tvorchestvo*, Bern, Herbert and Peter Lang, 1974, 155. Markevich became a favorite of Leontiev's in the 1870s and 1880s, but the suggestion is anachronistic as Markevich's novel was not published until 1873.

22. *Two Chosen Women*, LCW, Vol. 5, 67.

23. LCW, Vol. 5, 125.

24. LCW, Vol. 5, 84, 129.

25. "Analysis, Style and Tendency," LCW Vol. 9, 276.

26. Hegel, *Grundlinien der Philosophie des Rechts*, section 324, in *Werke*, Vol. 8, 417–18.

27. "Literacy and National Character," LCW, Vol. 7.1, 98. Pierre-Joseph Proudhon (1809–65), French socialist theoretician and "father of anarchism."

28. *Two Chosen Women*, LCW, Vol. 5, 84.

29. LCW, Vol. 5, 82.

30. Letter of 23 April 1878 to Ekaterina Sergeyevna Kartsova, LCW, Vol. 11.2, 217.

31. *Leading Articles of the Warsaw Diary*, LCW, Vol. 7.2, 65.

32. *Two Chosen Women*, LCW, Vol. 5, 89, 125. Mikhail Lermontov (1814–41), regarded as the leading writer of Russian romanticism, his best-known work being *A Hero of Our Time*.

33. *Two Chosen Women*, LCW, Vol. 5, 119.

34. LCW, Vol. 5, 120.

35. LCW, Vol. 5, 98–99.

36. Described in *EdCom* to *Two Chosen Women* in LCW, Vol. 5, 816–20.

37. *Chronology of My Life*, LCW, Vol. 6.2, 31. A similar marriage between a sophisticated man and an "empty-headed but good-natured" peasant girl occurs in the novel fragment *From Autumn to Autumn* (LCW, Vol. 5, 24–52).

38. *Two Chosen Women*, LCW, Vol. 5, 98.

39. LCW, Vol. 5, 78.

40. LCW, Vol. 5, 127–28.

41. *The Egyptian Dove*, LCW, Vol. 5, 198.

42. *My Literary Destiny*, LCW, Vol. 6.1, 39.

43. Letter of 26 April 1868, LCW, Vol. 11.1, 261. In her interview with the literary historian S. N. Durylin in 1925, Marya Vladimirovna strenuously denied that Liza Pavlovna's mental condition had been affected by her husband's unfaithfulness. See *EdCom* in LCW, Vol. 6.2, 300.

44. This seems to have been the opinion of Leontiev's first biographer, Konoplyantsev. See his somewhat guarded comments in *Pamiati 1891 goda*, 46–47.

45. *The Egyptian Dove*, LCW, Vol. 5, 277.

46. *Two Chosen Women*, LCW, Vol. 5, 91.

47. Letter of 15 November 1868, LCW, Vol. 11.1, 267. The lady in question was possibly the society lady, Slavophile, and friend of Gladstone Olga Novikova. Marya Vladimirovna remembers their meeting in 1869 and declares that there was considerable empathy between them. See *EdCom* to *Two Chosen Women* in LCW, Vol. 5, 820; also in LCW, Vol. 8.2, 841.

48. *Two Chosen Women*, LCW, Vol. 5, 109, 137. Elsewhere Matveyev seeks to draw a distinction between "fidelity of the flesh and fidelity of the spirit" (LCW, Vol. 5, 170).

49. LCW, Vol. 5, 78, 140.

50. LCW, Vol. 5, 138. Matveyev's views on marriage here closely parallel Leontiev's own. The notion of the transfiguring power of the sacrament of marriage (as opposed to strict adherence to its vows) clearly had significance for him. In the third of his *Four Letters from Athos* of 1872, he refers to a "stern, religious, ethical marriage" being like a "gentler form of monkhood" (LCW, Vol. 7.1 163).

51. *Two Chosen Women*, LCW, Vol. 5, 141.

52. LCW, Vol. 5, 142.

53. LCW, Vol. 5, 160 and 161. When Matveyev goes on to declare that "it is essential for me to be at peace with myself" and "one has to know how to be happy" (LCW, Vol. 5, 161), we seem to hear an echo of Ladnev in *Podlipki*, written over ten

years earlier. Appeasing an often guilty conscience was an abiding issue for Leontiev and a key ingredient of his religious crisis.

54. LCW, Vol. 5, 194.

55. LCW, Vol. 5, 184. Leontiev seems to have consistently failed to heed Turgenev's admonishment to keep the psychologist firmly in the background. There is a similarly rapid and complete "conversion" in the novel fragment *From Autumn to Autumn* where Olga Frantsovna seemingly out of nowhere begins to address her lover Nikolai Obleskov as "my czar, my deity, my master" (LCW, Vol. 5, 57).

56. *Two Chosen Women*, LCW, Vol. 5, 181. Marya Vladimirovna annotated the manuscript of *Two Chosen Women* at various points with remarks like "this is L speaking," "sounds completely like L," "so like L," and so on. See *EdCom* to *Two Chosen Women* at LCW, Vol. 5, 814.

57. *My Literary Destiny*, LCW, Vol.6.1, 122. In his *My Arrival in Tulcea* of 1883 Leontiev again refers to his mother being "abandoned" in Kudinovo while he served in the East (LCW, Vol. 6.1, 457).

58. *Two Chosen Women*, LCW, Vol. 5, 167.

59. For details of Leontiev's experiences on Athos and on the nature of Eastern Orthodox mysticism generally, see Ivan von Kologrivov, *Von Hellas zum Mönchtum*, chapter 4, 95–125.

60. *Podlipki*, LCW, Vol. 1, 590.

61. "There's a monastery not far from here, in the hills, only seven or eight monks . . . shouldn't I conceal myself there and leave my estate to them?" *A Husband's Confession*, LCW, Vol. 2, 380.

62. *My Conversion and Life on the Holy Mountain of Athos*, LCW, Vol. 6.1, 797. Leontiev's fourth *Letter from Athos* of 1873 hints that he may have been considering finishing his life in an Orthodox monastery seven years before, circa 1865 (LCW, Vol. 7.1, 168).

63. *My Conversion and Life on the Holy Mountain of Athos*, LCW, Vol. 6.1, 797. Leontiev could not remember this incident. To his knowledge, this conversation with Marya Vladimirovna was the first time his mother had mentioned it to anyone.

64. Letter of 14 August 1891 in *Rozanov letters*, 110.

65. As suggested by Stephen Lukashevich in his *Konstantin Leontiev: A Study in Russian "Heroic Vitalism,"* Pageant-Poseidon, New York, 1967, 72–77.

66. A theory advanced by Olga Fetisenko, deputy editor in chief of Leontiev's *Collected Works*, in her *Geptastilisty*, 14.

67. *Janina*, LCW, Vol. 6.2, 92–93.

68. LCW, Vol. 6.2, 85.

69. *K. Leontiev in Turkey*, LCW, Vol. 6.2, 108ff.

70. *EdCom* in LCW, Vol. 6.2, 649.

71. In *Geptastilisty* Fetisenko describes them as both praying to the Virgin, presumably for forgiveness, though she does not reference this.

72. See Durylin's commentary to Leontiev's *My Literary Destiny* in *Literaturnoe Nasledstvo*, Moscow, Zhurnal'no-gazetnoe Ob'edinenie, 1935, Vols. 22/24, 476.

73. S. N. Durylin, *V rodnom uglu (In One's Own Corner)*, Moscow, Moskovskiy Rabochiy, 1991, 280.

74. Durylin, *Literaturnoe Nasledstvo*, 482

75. *EdCom* in LCW, Vol. 5, 792.

76. *EdCom* in LCW, Vol. 5, 922.

77. *Good News*, LCW, Vol. 8.1, 430.

78. Konoplyantsev in *Pamiati 1891 goda*, 44.

79. Letter of 30 April 1865 cited in *EdCom* in LCW, Vol. 5, 897.

80. *EdCom* in LCW, Vol. 5, 923.

81. *EdCom* in LCW, Vol. 5, 926.

82. *EdCom* in LCW, Vol. 9, 709.

83. Archive material cited in *EdCom* in in LCW, Vol. 5, 923.

84. *EdCom* in LCW, Vol. 5, 924.

85. *EdCom* in LCW, Vol. 5, 924–25.

86. *EdCom* in LCW, Vol. 5, 925.

87. *EdCom* in LCW, Vol. 5, 925.

88. *EdCom* in LCW, Vol. 6.2, 691.

89. *Girlfriends*, LCW, Vol. 5, 478.

90. LCW, Vol. 5, 492.

91. In his *Chronology of My Life* Leontiev recalls the "first signs of love on the part of Masha" appearing in the summer of 1863. (LCW, Vol. 6.2, 31.)

92. *Two Chosen Women*, LCW, Vol. 5, 142.

93. *EdCom* in LCW, Vol. 6.2, 687.

94. Letter of 24 October 1883, cited in *EdCom* in LCW, Vol. 5, 802–3.

95. "A Few Words about Three Characters from the Gospels," LCW, Vol. 1, 604.

5. Russians, Greeks, and Slavs

1. *My Conversion and Life on the Holy Mountain of Athos*, LCW, Vol. 6.1, 782; letter of 14 August 1891 in *Rozanov Letters*, 110.

2. Described in *EdCom* in LCW, Vol. 7.2, 636.

3. Recalled by Leontiev in a letter of 12/13 November 1878 to Olga Sergeyevna Kartsova, LCW, Vol. 11.2, 270.

4. *My Literary Destiny*, LCW, Vol. 6.1, 130. See also Konoplyantsev, *Pamiati 1891 goda*, 84–85.

5. Letter of 1 October 1875, LCW, Vol. 11.1, 470.

6. For an account of this journey, see his *Sotiri the Brigand* in LCW, Vol. 6.1, 404–43.

7. *A Place of One's Own*, LCW, Vol. 2, 155.

8. LCW, Vol. 2, 157.

9. LCW, Vol. 2, 157–58.

10. On Leontiev's relationship to the Pochvenniki see E. C. Thaden, *Conservative Nationalism in Nineteenth Century Russia*, University of Washington Press, Seattle, 1964, 164–66.

11. This incident was related by Konoplyantsev in *Pamiati 1891 goda*, 53–54. See also A. Aleksandrov, "Konstantin Nikolaevich Leontiev" in *Russkii Vestnik*, 1892, Vol. 4, 265–68.

12. "Two Counts: Aleksei Vronsky and Leo Tolstoy," LCW, Vol. 8.1, 299.

13. "Some Reminiscences on the Late Apollon Grigoriev," LCW, Vol. 6.1, 11.

14. LCW, Vol. 6.1, 17.

15. LCW, Vol. 6.1, 12.

16. "Vladimir Solovyev versus Danilevsky," LCW, Vol. 8.1, 350.

17. *My Literary Destiny*, LCW, Vol. 6.1, 130–31.

18. "Some Reminiscences on the Late Apollon Grigoriev," LCW, Vol. 6.1, 25. See also "From the Danube," LCW, Vol. 7.1, 58: "I don't believe in the decay of the West, I believe in its ossification."

19. "Some Reminiscences on the Late Apollon Grigoriev," LCW, Vol. 6.1, 17–19. A. N. Ostrovsky, Russian playwright, generally considered the greatest representative of the Russian realistic period.

20. "Where to Seek Out My Works after My Death," LCW, Vol. 6.2, 20.

21. See letter of 26th October 1869, LCW, Vol. 11.1, 275ff.; see also *EdCom* in LCW, Vol. 7.2, 553–55.

22. Dostoevsky, *PSS*, Vol. 29.1, 179–80.

23. "Literacy and National Character," LCW, Vol. 7.1, 90. The phrase appears to have been coined by John Stuart Mill with reference to the necessity of continuing British rule in India. On the difficulties of publication of this article, see *EdCom* in LCW, Vol. 7.2, 555ff.

24. "Literacy and National Character," LCW, Vol. 7.1, 98.

25. LCW, Vol. 7.1, 129.

26. LCW, Vol. 7.1, 100.

27. LCW, Vol. 7.1, 118, 130. The metaphor from nature is quintessentially Leontiev.

28. "Some Reminiscences on the Late Apollon Grigoriev," LCW, Vol. 6.1, 9–10.

29. I use the terms "Slavists" and "Slavism" to indicate Russians with pro-Slav sympathies where it is not necessary to distinguish between cultural Slavophilism and racial Pan-Slavism. For a useful guide to the issues see Andrzey Walicki, *The Slavophile Controversy*, Oxford University Press, 1975.

30. *My Literary Destiny*, LCW, Vol. 6.1, 114–15.

31. "Pan-Slavism and the Greeks," LCW, Vol. 7.1, 187.

32. *Aspazia Lampridi*, LCW, Vol. 3, 261, 277–78.

33. "Pan-Slavism and the Greeks," LCW, Vol. 7.1, 177n; see also 234n.

34. LCW, Vol. 7.1, 184.

35. LCW, Vol. 7.1, 204.

36. *Grundlinien der Philosophie des Rechts*, sections 259, 269, 337, in Hegel, *Werke*, Vol. 8, 320, 331, 428.

37. "Pan-Slavism and the Greeks," LCW, Vol. 7.1, 204.

38. LCW, Vol. 7.1, 178–79. Leontiev made the same differentiation between Germany and the Slav states in the autumn of 1867 in a report to Ignatiev of a conversation with an ostensibly pro-Russian Polish merchant whom he suspected of being an agent provocateur working for the Austrians or the Turks (LCW, Vol. 10.1, 613).

39. "Pan-Slavism and the Greeks," LCW, Vol. 7.1, 182.

40. LCW, Vol. 7.1, 181.

41. LCW, Vol. 7.1, 199.

42. "Pan-Slavism on Athos," LCW, Vol. 7.1, 231.

43. LCW, Vol. 7.1, 266–67. In his *More on the Greco-Bulgar Dispute* of 1875 Leontiev reiterates his belief that the maintenance of Turkish power is beneficial both to Russian policy in the Balkans and to Orthodoxy (LCW, Vol. 7.2, 274).

44. "Pan-Slavism on Athos," LCW, Vol. 7.1, 267.

45. *Aspazia Lampridi*, LCW, Vol. 3, 306.

46. *Odysseus Polichroniades*, LCW, Vol. 4, 393. This is a view of Russia's destiny which recalls the sweeping vision of the poet Fyodor Tyutchev in his poem "Russian Geography." Although Leontiev does not mention Tyutchev often, he was undoubtedly influenced by his messianism, especially in connection with the destiny of Constantinople, which became for him, as we shall see, a key pillar of his vision for the future of Russia and of the Christian East.

47. "Pan-Slavism and the Greeks," LCW, Vol. 7.1, 204.

48. LCW, Vol. 7.1, 209.

49. *AspaziaLampridi*, LCW, Vol. 3, 223. In his *A Short History of Modern Greece*, Richard Clogg remarks on the persistent myth that Greece would one day be liberated by "a fair-headed people from the North," generally taken to mean Russia (Oxford University Press, Oxford, 1979, 25–26).

6. The Social Organism

1. Alexander Herzen, *From the Other Shore*, SS, Vol. 6, 67.

2. Letter to Fudel' of 6 July 1888, LCW, Annex 1, 83–84. For Herzen's antagonism toward the European bourgeois, see *My Past and Thoughts*, in SS, Vol. 10, 124ff. For his critique of Proudhon, see *My Past and Thoughts*, part 5, chapter 41, SS, Vol. 10, esp. 196–8.

3. *Four Letters from Athos*, LCW, Vol. 7.1, 132. French liberal and socialist thinkers were to become a particular bête noire with Leontiev. In addition to Proudhon, we have here François Pierre Guillaume Guizot (1787–1874), historian and liberal statesman, a dominant figure in French politics prior to the Revolution of 1848; Augustin Thierry (1795–1856), liberal historian; François Marie Charles Fourier (1772–1837), influential early socialist thinker and one of the founders of utopian socialism; Étienne Cabet (1788–1856), philosopher and utopian socialist.

4. Letter of 12 May 1888, XIV in *Aleksandrov Letters*.

5. Letter to Rozanov of 24 May 1891 (postscript of 25 May) in *Rozanov Letters*, 60–61.

6. Gubastov in *Pamiati 1891 goda*, 226.

7. Letter of 20 February 1892 in Rozanov, *Literaturnye izgnanniki*, 320.

8. E.g., from Schwegler's *Geschichte der Philosophie im Umriss*.

9. See Strakhov's letter to Rozanov of 21 May 1891 in *Pis'ma k V. V. Rozanovu*, Moscow, Direkt-Media, 2010, available at http://az.lib.ru/s/strahow_n_n/text_1896_pisma_k_rozanovy.shtml.

Also in Rozanov, *Literaturnye izgnanniki*, 288. In this letter Strakhov describes Leontiev's tastes as "perverse" and denies that he had any original ideas.

10. Described in *Polish Emigration on the Lower Danube*, LCW, Vol. 6.1, 459.

11. One outcome of this time was a proposal Leontiev put to the Ministry of Education that a scientific institute be established on the southern shore of the Crimea for the study of botany and zoology. The Ministry thanked him for the proposal but regarded it as too ambitious to take forward. See his *For the Biography of K. N. Leontiev*, LCW, Vol. 6.2, 8. Leontiev's scientific studies are collected in LCW, Vol. 7.2.

12. *My Memories of Thrace*, LCW, Vol. 6.1, 184. Paraphrasing Matthew 10:16.

13. "From the Danube," LCW, Vol. 7.1, 59.

14. On Mill see especially "The Average European as the Ideal and Weapon of Universal Destruction," LCW, Vol. 8.1, 184ff. Despite these criticisms Leontiev was greatly

impressed by Mill and considered writing an article about him provisionally titled *J. S. Mill in Russia*. This never came to fruition, though Leontiev did make an abridged translation of two chapters of Mill's *On Liberty*, which was published in 1862 in the journal *Russkii Invalid*. It appears in LCW, Vol. 7.1, under the title *John Stuart Mill's View of Individuality*. For the provenance of this article and its publication, see *EdCom* in LCW, Vol. 7.2, 529ff.

15. Herzen, *From the Other Shore*, SS, Vol. 6, 135. On Leontiev's debt to Herzen, see S Durylin's note to Leontiev's *My Literary Destiny* in *Literary Inheritance*, 22–24, 479–80, n28. See also P. Preobrazhensky, *Gertsen i Konstantin Leontiev* in *Pechat'irevoliutsiia*, 1922, Vol. 2, No 2, 78–88.

16. Letter to Fudel' of 6 July 1888, LCW, Annex 1, 83–84.

17. "Mr. Katkov and his Enemies at the Pushkin Festival," LCW, Vol. 7.2, 206.

18. Herzen, *From the Other Shore*, SS, Vol. 6, 84.

19. *From the Other Shore*, SS, 60, 97, 94.

20. *My Literary Destiny*, LCW, Vol. 6.1, 129–30.

21. *Chronology of My Life*, LCW, Vol. 6.2, 33. Gubastov recalled him reading extracts aloud to his embassy acquaintances in Constantinople in 1873. *Pamiati 1891 goda*, 213–14.

22. As reported in *EdCom* in LCW, Vol. 7.2, 607.

23. See *My Literary Destiny*, LCW, Vol. 6.1, 96; *Edcom* in LCW, Vol. 7.2, 665.

24. The campaign was orchestrated by Terty Ivanovich Filippov (1825–99), a senior government official and writer on church history and social affairs who had long been a supporter of Leontiev's work. In gratitude Leontiev dedicated to him the first part of his compendium *The East, Russia and Slavdom*. The two kept up a regular correspondence from the mid-1870s until Leontiev's death. The letters of the 1870s, in particular, provide a vivid narrative of Leontiev's financial, health, and other difficulties during this period. They are collected in *Proroki Vizantizma*, referenced in this work as *Filippov Letters*.

25. See *List of Works by Leontiev with Descriptions*, LCW, Vol. 6.2, 25.

26. See *My Literary Destiny*, LCW, Vol. 6.1, 95–6; also *EdCom* in LCW, Vol. 7.2, 665.

27. *Byzantinism and Slavdom*, LCW, Vol. 7.1, 374.

28. LCW, Vol. 7.1, 374.

29. LCW, Vol. 7.1, 374.

30. LCW, Vol. 7.1, 375.

31. LCW, Vol. 7.1, 375ff.

32. LCW, Vol. 7.1, 377–78.

33. LCW, Vol. 7.1, 413.

34. LCW, Vol. 7.1, 379.

35. LCW, Vol. 7.1, 379–80.

36. LCW, Vol. 7.1, 379.

37. LCW, Vol. 7.1, 395.

38. Quoted by Konoplyantsev in *Pamiati 1891 goda*, 54. This is the conclusion of the "Piotrovsky" incident noted above.

39. *Byzantinism and Slavdom*, LCW, Vol. 7.1, 383.

40. LCW, Vol. 7.1, 384.

41. LCW, Vol. 7.1, 430.

42. LCW, Vol. 7.1, 386.

43. LCW, Vol. 7.1, 389.

44. LCW, Vol. 7.1, 385, 387.

45. LCW, Vol. 7.1, 392

46. LCW, Vol. 7.1, 394–95.

47. LCW, Vol. 7.1, 392–93.

48. Hegel, *Werke*, Vol. 8, *Grundlinien der Philosophie des Rechts*, sections 139, 140.

49. *Byzantinism and Slavdom*, LCW, Vol. 7.1, 393–94.

7. Blood Is Not Enough

1. Auguste Comte (1798–1857), French philosopher and writer who formulated the doctrine of positivism and is regarded as a founder of modern sociology. He developed the "Law of Three Stages," according to which every society passes successively through three different conditions: the theological, the metaphysical, and finally the scientific or positive.

2. Fetisenko, *Geptastilisty*, 61.

3. S. V. Khatuntsev, "The Socio-Political Views and Intellectual Evolution of K. N. Leont'ev in the 1860s and early 1870s," *Russian Studies in Philosophy*, Spring 2008, Vol. 46, No. 4, 24–25.

4. N. N. Strakhov, *Pis'ma k V V Rozanovu*; also in Rozanov, *Literaturnye izgnanniki*, 288.

5. Khatuntsev, 24–25.

6. Letter of 12 March 1870, LCW, Vol. 11.1, 284.

7. Danilevsky had studied physics and especially botany at University and spent many years in the Russian Ministry of Agriculture organizing and participating in numerous expeditions to study fishery conditions in various parts of Russia, an activity which gave him ample time to develop his "scientific" view of social development.

8. Fetisenko, *Geptastilisty*, 61.

9. N. Ia. Danilevsky, *Rossiia i Evropa (Russia and Europe)*, SPB, Obshchestvennaya Pol'za, 1871, 74.

10. Danilevsky, 384.

11. Danilevsky, 165.

12. Danilevsky, 52.

13. Danilevsky, 30. This preference for expediency over morality in politics, especially foreign policy, is common to Danilevsky and Leontiev. For a discussion, see Walicki, 506f.

14. *Letters of an Anchorite*, LCW, Vol. 7.1, 557.

15. Friedrich Nietzsche, *Beyond Good and Evil*, section 44.

16. *Janina*, LCW, Vol. 6.2, 88. Leontiev himself said he read it three times without pausing, which would be a heroic effort indeed. See letter to Strakhov of 12 March 1870, LCW, Vol. 11.1, 284.

17. "Mr. Katkov and his Enemies at the Pushkin Festival," LCW, Vol. 7.2, 204.

18. Danilevsky, 247, 251.

19. Danilevsky, 353, 354.

20. Danilevsky, 385, 395.

21. Danilevsky, 66.

22. Danilevsky, 127. Danilevsky was unsure about the Poles following their nationalist uprising of 1863–64.

23. *Byzantinism and Slavdom*, LCW, Vol. 7.1, 300.

24. LCW, Vol. 7.1, 302.

25. LCW, Vol. 7.1, 303.

26. LCW, Vol. 7.1, 304.

27. LCW, Vol. 7.1, 307–8.

28. LCW, Vol. 7.1, 323.

29. LCW, Vol. 7.1, 326.

30. Danilevsky, 308, 322.

31. Danilevsky, 160.

32. Danilevsky, 126.

33. Danilevsky, 492.

34. Danilevsky, 493.

35. Danilevsky, 427.

36. *Byzantinism and Slavdom*, LCW, Vol. 7.1, 333.

37. LCW, Vol. 7.1, 333.

38. LCW, Vol. 7.1, 333.

39. LCW, Vol. 7.1, 300.

40. LCW, Vol. 7.1, 334.

41. LCW, Vol. 7.1, 443. On the meeting with Aksakov, see *My Literary Destiny*, LCW, Vol. 6.1, 114.

42. *Byzantinism and Slavdom*, LCW, Vol. 7.1, 351.

43. LCW, Vol. 7.1, 367n.

44. LCW, Vol. 7.1, 436.

45. LCW, Vol. 7.1, 372.

46. LCW, Vol. 7.1, 442–43.

47. "Vladimir Solovyev versus Danilevsky," LCW, Vol. 8.1, 357.

48. LCW, Vol. 8.1, 316ff.

8. The Tide of History

1. For a critique of the historicist theories of Hegel and Marx and their debt to Plato, see Karl Popper, *The Open Society and Its Enemies*, London, Routledge, 1945; also his *The Poverty of Historicism*, London, Routledge, 1957; and Isaiah Berlin's 1953 lecture *Historical Inevitability*, Oxford University Press, 1955.

2. Letter to Gubastov of 30 May 1888, in *Russkoe Obozrenie*, 1897, Vol. 3, 447; "Vladimir Solovyev versus Danilevsky," LCW, Vol. 8.1, 357. Whatever question marks surround Leontiev's methodology, as a prophet he was uncannily accurate, as will appear later on.

3. For a forensic, and often amusing, deconstruction of once fashionable historicist theories, especially those of an organicist tendency, see Pitirim Sorokin, *Social Philosophies of an Age of Crisis*, Boston, The Beacon Press, 1950, especially chapter 12, "Critical Examination of the Theories of Danilevsky, Spengler and Toynbee." Sorokin's critique is all the more devastating coming from a fellow historicist, albeit his approach is radically different to that of the aforementioned writers, whom he describes as the "undertakers of civilizations."

4. See Berdyaev, *Konstantin Leontiev, filosof reaktsionnoi romantiki*, 1904, also in English in *Sub specie aeternitatis*, 1907; P. E. Astafyev, *Natsional'noe samosoznanie v obshchechelovecheskie zadachi* in *Russkoe Obozrenie*, 1890, Vol. 3; P. N. Milyukov, *Samorazlozhenie slavianofilstva*, in *Voprosi filosofii i psikhologii*, 1893, Vol. 5; V. S. Solovyev, *Pamiati K. N. Leontieva*; S. Trubetskoy, *Razocharovannyi slavianofil*, in *Vestnik Evropy*, 1892, Vol. 10.

5. Berdyaev, *Ocherki iz storii russkoy religioznoy mysli*, YMCA Press, Paris, 1926.

6. Letter of 28 January 1879 to Olga Sergeyevna Kartsova, LCW, Vol. 11.2, 296.

7. *Byzantinism and Slavdom*, LCW, Vol. 7.1, 406

8. LCW, Vol. 7.1, 408.

9. LCW, Vol. 7.1, 410.

10. LCW, Vol. 7.1, 411.

11. LCW, Vol. 7.1, 419.

12. LCW, Vol. 7.1, 437.

13. *My Literary Destiny*, LCW, Vol. 6.1, 81.

14. "Vladimir Solovyev versus Danilevsky," LCW, Vol. 8.2, 222.

15. *My Literary Destiny*, LCW, Vol. 6.1, 94.

16. "Some Reminiscences on the Late Apollon Grigoriev," LCW, Vol. 6.1, 14.

17. *My Literary Destiny*, LCW, Vol. 6.1, 106.

18. *Dedication to Ignatiev*, LCW, Vol. 7.1, 298–99; *EdCom* in LCW, Vol. 7.2, 352–53. The draft was apparently written in 1874 while Leontiev was still in Constantinople. Fortunately, possibly after his meeting with Aksakov, he had second thoughts and the dedication did not get into print.

19. *My Literary Destiny*, LCW, Vol. 6.1, 94.

20. Walicki, 495ff., 504–5.

21. *My Literary Destiny*, LCW, Vol. 6.1, 94–95.

22. Reported by Leontiev in *My Literary Destiny*, LCW, Vol. 6.1, 113, 115.

23. LCW, Vol. 6.1, 103ff.; Fetisenko, *Geptastilisty*, 162.

24. "Phanariot" was used as a term of abuse by many Greeks from Hellas at the time because of the Phanariots' close links with the Ottoman Porte. Aksakov is also referring to Leontiev's support for the Moscow Metropolitan Philaret, a pillar of the Orthodox Church anathematized by the liberal tendency among the Slavophiles. Aksakov's remarks cited by Fetisenko in *Geptastilisty*, 172–73.

25. "A voluptuous cult of the rod" to be exact. Unbelievably, Solovyev later included this allegation in his article on Leontiev in the Brockhaus and Efron Encyclopedia, 1896.

26. *My Literary Destiny*, LCW, Vol. 6.1, 117.

27. M. B. Petrovich, *The Emergence of Russian Pan-Slavism, 1856–1870*, New York, Columbia University Press, 1956, 11.

28. Kologrivov, 174; see comments by Gubastov in *Pamiati 1891 goda*, 230f.

29. LCW, Vol. 6.1, 97–98.

30. LCW, Vol. 6.1, 106.

31. "Nationalist Politics as a Weapon of World Revolution," LCW, Vol. 8.1, 538.

32. Letter of 14 August 1876, LCW, Vol. 11.2, 49.

33. Letter to Gubastov of 5 December 1876, LCW, Vol. 11.2, 54.

34. Letter of 2 August 1877, LCW, Vol. 11.2, 84.

35. "Mosque and Church," LCW, Vol. 7.1, 509.

48. Leontiev sets this out schematically in his letter to Fudel' of 6 July 1888, LCW, Annex 1, 76.

49. Letter of 13 August 1891 in *Rozanov Letters*, 103.

50. Letter to Aleksandrov of 7 October 1888, letter XIX in *Aleksandrov Letters*; letter to Fudel' of 6 July 1888, LCW, Annex 1, 79.

51. Letter of 24 May 1891 (postscript of 25 May) in *Rozanov Letters*, 59.

52. Letter of 13 August 1891 in *Rozanov Letters*, 104.

53. Kologrivov, 246n; *Rozanov Letters*, 40n5.

54. Letter to Aleksandrov of 11 June 1890, letter XLVII in *Aleksandrov Letters*.

55. Letter to Rozanov of 13 April 1891 in *Rozanov Letters*, 39.

56. Herzen, *From the Other Shore*, SS, Vol. 6, 119.

57. On Ayn Rand's ethics, see, for example, N. K. Badhwar and R. T. Long, "Ayn Rand," Chapter 2 "Ethics," in *The Stanford Encyclopedia of Philosophy*, edited by E. N. Zalta, Fall 2020 edition. Available online at https://plato.stanford.edu/entries/ayn-rand/#Ethi

58. *Our New Christians: On Universal Love*, LCW, Vol. 9, 212–13.

59. *Rozanov Letters*, 107.

60. Letter to Fudel'' of 6 July 1888, LCW, Annex 1, 78–79.

11. Reactionary or Revolutionary?

1. Rozanov, *Iz starykh pisem: pis'ma Vlad. Serg. Solovyeva*, in his *Polnoe sobranie sochinenii v 35 tomakh (Collected Works in 35 Volumes)*, SPB, Rostok, 2014, Vol. 3, 454.

2. Letter to Filippov of 10 March 1887 in *Filippov Letters*, 408. On Leontiev's life at Optina, see especially E. Poselyanin, *K. N. Leontiev v Optinoi Pustyni* in *Pamiati 1891 goda*, 385ff.

3. These tendencies can be seen clearly in the title of one of the articles in the series *Letters of an Anchorite* of 1887–89, titled "My Historical Fatalism."

4. "Who Is More in the Right? Letters to Vladimir Sergeyevich Solovyev," LCW, Vol. 8.2, 112.

5. *Letters on Eastern Affairs*, LCW, Vol. 8.1, 44.

6. Letter to Gubastov of 5 December 1876, LCW, Vol. 11.2, 53.

7. *The Fate of Bismarck and Katkov's Silence*, LCW, Vol. 7.1, 282.

8. "The Pessimist," LCW, Vol. 5, 572–73.

9. Leontiev discusses recent developments in Europe and elsewhere at length in "Nationalist Politics as a Weapon of World Revolution," LCW, Vol. 8.1.

10. *The Fruits of Nationalist Movements in the Orthodox East*, LCW, Vol. 8.1, 591.

11. *Our New Christians: On Universal Love*, LCW, Vol. 9, 222. Hatred of modern Europe, though not of individual Europeans, stayed with Leontiev until the end. See letter to Aleksandr Kireyev of 14 August 1891 in *Russkoe Obozrenie*, 1895, Vol. 5, 262.

12. *The Fruits of Nationalist Movements in the Orthodox East*, LCW, Vol. 8.1, 604, 584–85.

13. *Leading Articles of the Warsaw Diary*, LCW, Vol. 7.2, 81.

14. *More on Dikarka: Messrs. Soloviev and Ostrovsky*, LCW, Vol. 9, 121. *Dikarka* is a comedy in four acts by the playwright A. N. Ostrovsky,

15. *Unseasonable and Seasonable*, LCW, Vol. 8.1, 636. In *The Egyptian Dove* Leontiev describes European clothes as a "symbol of decline, the disfigurement of fashion, its death and mourning." LCW, Vol. 5, 229.

16. *Letters on Eastern Affairs*, LCW, Vol. 8.1, 90.

17. *The Fruits of Nationalist Movements in the Orthodox East*, LCW, Vol. 8.1, 619.

18. *Leading Articles of the Warsaw Diary*, LCW, Vol. 7.2, 43, 107.

19. On this see, e.g., *EdCom* in LCW, Vol. 8.2, 1201ff. Leontiev's defense against this accusation is his article "Who Is More in the Right? Letters to Vladimir Sergeyevich Solovyev," in LCW, Vol. 8.2.

20. *At the Grave of Pazukhin*, LCW, Vol. 8.1, 450.

21. *The Fruits of Nationalist Movements in the Orthodox East*, LCW, Vol. 8.1, 619.

22. "Nationalist Politics as a Weapon of World Revolution," LCW, Vol. 8.1, 507.

23. "Who is More in the Right? Letters to Vladimir Sergeyevich Solovyev," LCW, Vol. 8.2, 119.

24. Letter to Gubastov of 26 June 1868, LCW, Vol. 11.1, 264.

25. *Leading Articles of the Warsaw Diary*, LCW, 7.2, 78.

26. *The Fruits of Nationalist Movements in the Orthodox East*, LCW, Vol. 8.1, 619.

27. *Leading Articles of the Warsaw Diary*, LCW, 7.2, 11. In his diary entry for 20 January 1879 Leontiev goes so far as to advocate the death penalty for open rebellion. See *From the Diary of K. Leontiev* in LCW, Vol. 6.2, 13.

28. *How and Why Our Liberalism Is Harmful*, LCW, Vol. 7.2 120.

29. *Leading Articles of the Warsaw Diary*, LCW, 7.2, 92.

30. "Mr. Katkov and His Enemies at the Pushkin Festival," LCW, Vol. 7.2, 193. For Leontiev's in-depth assessment of Proudhon see "The Average European as the Ideal and Weapon of Universal Destruction," LCW, Vol. 8.1, 176ff.

31. *Two Chosen Women*, LCW, Vol. 5, 70.

32. Frank describes Leontiev's orientation as "arch-reactionary" in his *Dostoevsky: A Writer in His Time*, 841.

33. Letter of 13 June 1891 in *Rozanov Letters*, 75.

34. *The Fruits of Nationalist Movements in the Orthodox East*, LCW, Vol. 8.1, 552.

35. "The Average European as the Ideal and Weapon of Universal Destruction," LCW, Vol. 8.1, 206.

36. Letter to Aleksandrov of 23 October 1891, letter LXIV in *Aleksandrov Letters*.

37. "Slavophilism in Theory and Slavophilism in Practice," LCW, Vol. 8.1, 461ff.

38. LCW, Vol. 8.1, 466.

39. Leontiev's late "disciple" Lev Tikhomirov gives an excellent account of exactly why Leontiev could not be considered a reactionary even though he consciously proclaimed himself to be one. See his *Russkie idealy i K. N. Leontiev* in *Konstantin Leontiev: slavianofil'stvo i griadushchie sud'by Rossii*, Institute of Russian Civilization, Moscow, 2010, 1098ff.

40. *My Literary Destiny*, LCW, Vol. 6.1, 79. Adapting a phrase of Herzen, see *EdCom* in LCW, Vol. 6.2, 320.

41. Letter of 24–26 February 1882, LCW, Vol. 11.2, 451.

42. *Leading Articles of the Warsaw Diary*, LCW, 7.2, 73.

43. "Chrizó," LCW, Vol. 3, 43.

44. *Byzantinism and Slavdom*, LCW, Vol. 7.1, 429.

45. *Leading Articles of the Warsaw Diary*, LCW, 7.2, 58.

46. *More on Dikarka: Messrs. Solovyev and Ostrovsky*, LCW, Vol. 9, 124.

47. "Mr. Katkov and His Enemies at the Pushkin Festival," LCW, Vol. 7.2, 199.

48. *The East, Russia and Slavdom*, Moscow, 1886, Vol. 2, dedication. V. I. Ger'e (more commonly known by the French version of his name, Guerrier), 1837–1919, professor of history at Moscow University, author of *The Relationship of Leibniz to Russia*.

49. *Why and How Our Liberalism Is Harmful*, LCW, Vol. 7.2, 135.

50. *Letters on Eastern Affairs*, LCW, Vol. 8.1, 65.

51. "Who Is More in the Right? Letters to Vladimir Sergeyevich Solovyev," LCW, Vol. 8.2, 131.

52. *The Fruits of Nationalist Movements in the Orthodox East*, LCW, Vol. 8.1, 611.

53. Letter of 29 March 1891 in *Filippov Letters*, 620.

54. "The Average European as the Ideal and Weapon of Universal Destruction," LCW, Vol. 8.1, 230.

55. "Vladimir Solovyev versus Danilevsky," Vol. 8.1, 354–55.

56. LCW, Vol. 8.1, 467.

57. *Letters on Eastern Affairs*, LCW, Vol. 8.1, 56.

58. "Vladimir Solovyev versus Danilevsky," LCW, Vol. 8.1, 333–34.

59. *The Egyptian Dove*, LCW, Vol. 5, 330.

60. Adapting an idea originating in Tyutchev (with reference to the reconciliation of Poland and Russia). *The Fruits of Nationalist Movements in the Orthodox East*, LCW, Vol. 8.1, 579–80.

61. As noted by Rozanov in *Rozanov Letters*, 87n11.

62. *With the Mind of a Stranger*, LCW, Vol. 8.1, 493–94.

63. *Leading Articles of the Warsaw Diary*, LCW, 7.2, 41.

64. *At the Grave of Pazukhin*, LCW, Vol. 8.1, 445ff.

65. LCW, Vol. 8.1, 454.

66. "Slavophilism in Theory and Slavophilism in Practice," LCW, Vol. 8.1, 464.

67. "Nationalist Politics as a Weapon of World Revolution," LCW, Vol. 8.1, 524. Leontiev's acquaintance with the Pseudo-Dionysius is noted by Poselyan in *Pamiati 1891 goda*, 396.

68. *Notes of an Anchorite*, LCW, Vol. 8.1, 249. In his discussion of social hierarchies Leontiev may have been drawing on the work of A. D. Pazukhin (1841–91), especially the latter's *Contemporary Condition of Russia and the Question of the Estates*. See *The Fruits of Nationalist Movements in the Orthodox East*, LCW, Vol. 8.1, 583–84. Leontiev admired the conservative reformer Pazukhin and composed a eulogy on his death, *At the Grave of Pazukhin*, nine months before his own.

69. *Four Letters from Athos*, LCW, Vol. 7.1, 174–75.

70. In *Also sprach Zarathustra* Nietzsche makes eternal recurrence a key aspect of the prophet's teaching. See, e.g., the section "Der Genesende."

71. Sidney Monas, "Leontiev: A Meditation," *Journal of Modern History*, September 1971, 484.

72. "The Average European as the Ideal and Weapon of Universal Destruction," LCW, Vol. 8.1, 202.

73. LCW, Vol. 8.1, 212, 218.

74. LCW, Vol. 8.1, 209.

75. LCW, Vol. 8.1, 209.

76. Herzen, *SS*, Vol. 6, 110; also Vol. 10, 122–23.

77. "Vladimir Solovyev versus Danilevsky," LCW, Vol. 8.1, 333–34.

78. LCW, Vol. 8.1, 331.

79. Letter to G. I. Zamarayev of 12 April 1889 in *Russkaya Mysl'*, 1916, Vol. 3, 113. One wonders to what extent Leontiev had himself in mind here.

80. See, e.g., "The Average European as the Ideal and Weapon of Universal Destruction," LCW, Vol. 8.1, 207–8.

81. *With the Mind of a Stranger*, LCW, Vol. 8.1, 490; "Nationalist Politics as a Weapon of World Revolution," LCW, Vol. 8.1, 515.

82. "Vladimir Solovyev versus Danilevsky," LCW, Vol. 8.1, 337.

83. *Notes of an Anchorite*, LCW, Vol. 8.1, 242.

84. *The Fruits of Nationalist Movements in the Orthodox East*, LCW, Vol. 8.1, 598.

12. The Feudalism of the Future

1. *Letters on Eastern Affairs*, LCW, Vol. 8.1, 60. Leontiev first mentions a desire to meet Solovyev in a letter of 15 January 1877 to Vsevolod Solovyev, the philosopher's elder brother. (LCW, Vol. 11.2, 62.) On 11 February 1878 Leontiev wrote to his niece Marya Vladimirovna detailing their first meeting. (LCW, Vol. 11.2, 154–55.)

2. Letter of 13 June 1891in *Rozanov letters*, 81n15.

3. *Rozanov Letters*, 106.

4. See letters to Gubastov of 17 June and 9 August 1885 in *Russkoe Obozrenie*, 1896, Vol. 11, 438, 450.

5. See letters to Aleksandrov of 15 January and 5 February 1888, letters VI and VIII in *Aleksandrov Letters*.

6. Letter to Gubastov of 1 July 1888 in *Leontiev Letters*, 377.

7. "Vladimir Solovyev versus Danilevsky," LCW, Vol. 8.1, 324.

8. Letter to Gubastov of 1 July 1888 in *Leontiev Letters*, 377.

9. "Vladimir Solovyev versus Danilevsky," LCW, Vol. 8.1, 343.

10. Letter to Aleksandrov of 7 October 1888, letter XIX in *Aleksandrov Letters*.

11. In a letter of 5 June 1889 Leontiev asked Gubastov to obtain a copy of *La Russie* for him. (*Leontiev Letters*, 463.) As Ivask points out, this indicates that Leontiev was unacquainted with *La Russie* at this time. Following Fudel', Ivask suggests that Leontiev acquired an intimate knowledge of Solovyev's ideas chiefly from personal conversations. (Ivask, 322.)

12. See Vladimir Solovyev, *La Russie et l'Eglise universelle*, translated by Herbert Rees, London, Geoffrey Bles, The Centenary Press, 1948, 8–13.

13. Solovyev, *La Russie*, 12.

14. Solovyev, *La Russie*, 15.

15. Solovyev, *La Russie*, 25.

16. Solovyev, *La Russie*, 17, 18, 24.

17. Solovyev, *La Russie*, 25.

18. Solovyev, *La Russie*, 76. Leontiev was not opposed in principle to a greater degree of independence for the Orthodox Church in Russia. In a late article titled "'Moskovskie Vedomosti' on Co-Jurisdiction" we find him mocking the old Slavophile chestnut that Russia had been "saved" from the evils supposedly inherent in the Western separation of powers between Church and State and asserting: "We have no cause for celebration that we had *no separation of powers*, but rather cause for sorrow

that our Church is too dependent on the temporal power. We could do with *a bit of separation*" (LCW, Vol. 8.2, 15).

19. Solovyev, *La Russie*, 69–70. Ironically, at least one biographer of Solovyev believes that his own ecumenicalism may have been decisively influenced by Leontiev's assertion of the primacy of the community of faith over racial nationalism as the ideal principle of cultural unity. See Egbert Munzer, *Solovyev: Prophet of Russian-Western Unity*, New York, Philosophical Library, 1956, 42.

20. Solovyev, *La Russie*, 75.

21. Solovyev, *La Russie*, 31, 77, 79, 81. This patronizing dismissal is the closest Leontiev gets to a mention in Solovyev's book.

22. See remark in his letter to Filippov of 3 September 1889 in *Filippov Letters*, 559.

23. Letter to Gubastov of 17 August 1889 in *Leontiev Letters*, 469.

24. Letter to Gubastov of 5 June 1889 in *Leontiev Letters*, 463.

25. *At the Grave of Pazukhin*, LCW, Vol. 8.1, 445.

26. "'MoskovskieVedomosti' on Co-Jurisdiction," LCW, Vol. 8.2, 16.

27. Letter of 26 January 1891, LCW, Annex 1, 268.

28. LCW, Annex 1, 272.

29. LCW, Annex 1, 273.

30. Letter to Rozanov of 24 May 1891 in *Rozanov Letters*, 56.

31. Cited by Fudel' in *K. Leontiev and V. Solovyev in Their Mutual Relations*, LCW, Annex 1, 405.

32. Letter of 25 September 1890 in *Filippov Letters*, 600.

33. "On the Decline of the Medieval Worldview," in Solovyev, *Sobranie sochinenii*, Vol. 6, 381–93.

34. Letter to Aleksandrov of 23 October 1891, letter LXIV in *Aleksandrov Letters*.

35. Letter of 31 October 1891, letter LXV in *Aleksandrov Letters*.

36. Letters to Gubastov of 1 July 1888 and 5 June 1889 in *Leontiev Letters*, 376, 465.

37. Iosif Fudel', *My Acquaintance with Leontiev (Letter to S. N. Durylin)*, LCW, Annex 1, 462. This aspiration was also mentioned by Marya Vladimirovna in her conversation with Durylin in 1925. See *EdCom* in LCW, Annex 1, 702.

38. See Kologrivov, 226. On Solovyev's spiritual crisis, see S. L. Frank's introduction to *A Solovyev Anthology*, Charles Scribner's Sons, New York, 1950, 24–27.

39. Letter to Fudel' of 6 July 1888, LCW, Annex 1, 89.

40. *K. Leontiev and V. Solovyev in Their Mutual Relations*, LCW, Annex 1, 414.

41. *Father Kliment Zedergol'm*, LCW, Vol. 6.1, 330, 333.

42. Letter to Gubastov of 1 July 1888, *Leontiev Letters*, 377.

43. *Leontiev Letters*, 377.

44. Letter to Fudel' of 6 July 1888, LCW, Annex 1, 91.

45. Letter to Fudel' of 26 January 1891, LCW, Annex 1, 267–68.

46. LCW, Annex 1, 270.

47. Solovyev, *La Russie*, 31.

48. Cited by S. L. Frank in *A Solovyev Anthology*, 18.

49. "Vladimir Solovyev versus Danilevsky," LCW, Vol. 8.1, 336.

50. Letter to Fudel' of 26 January 1891, LCW, Annex 1, 269; *At the Grave of Pazukhin* (1891), LCW, Vol. 8.1, 452.

51. *Four Letters from Athos*, LCW, Vol. 7.1, 140.

52. Letter of 23 April 1878 to Ekaterina Sergeyevna Kartsova, LCW, Vol. 11.2, 217.

53. "Nationalist Politics as a Weapon of World Revolution," LCW, Vol. 8.1, 541.

54. Diary entry for 20 January 1879, LCW, Vol. 6.2, 12–13.

55. *Letters on Eastern Affairs*, LCW, Vol. 8.1, 47.

56. *The Fruits of Nationalist Movements in the Orthodox East*, LCW, Vol. 8.1, 578.

57. "The Average European as the Ideal and Weapon of Universal Destruction," Chapter 5, "Herbert Spencer," LCW, Vol. 8.1, 205–8. Leontiev worked on this essay almost until his death but the section on Spencer was almost certainly written in late 1885 after Anatoly Aleksandrov sent him a copy of Spencer's *Essays*. See *EdCom* in LCW, Vol. 8.2, 920.

58. Herbert Spencer, "Progress: Its Law and Cause," in *Essays, Scientific, Political and Speculative*, London, Williams & Norgate, 1868, Vol. 1, 3.

59. Spencer, "The Social Organism," in *Essays*, Vol. 1, 396–97.

60. Letter to Aleksandrov of 3 May 1890, letter XLV in *Aleksandrov Letters*.

61. *How and Why Our Liberalism Is Harmful*, LCW, Vol. 7.2, 133.

62. See *EdCom* in LCW, 8.2, 958.

63. The claim is from a fragment held in a private collection. The degree of convergence certainly appears to have forcibly struck the editors of Leontiev's Collected Works. See *EdCom* in LCW, Vol. 8.2, 920.

64. There is a footnote on page 123 dating to 1885, but otherwise no indication of any major revision post-1880.

65. Letter of 20 September 1882, LCW, Vol. 11.2, 489; *Proroki Vizantizma*, 233.

66. "The Average European as the Ideal and Weapon of Universal Destruction," LCW, Vol. 8.1, 201.

67. LCW, Vol. 8.1, 215.

68. By, among others, Bertrand Russell. For a discussion, see H. B. Acton, *The Alleged Fascism of Plato, Philosophy*, Vol. 13, No. 51 (July 1938): 302–12.

69. "The Average European as the Ideal and Weapon of Universal Destruction," LCW, Vol. 8.1, 176.

70. Repnikov, *Ot Leontieva do Stalina*.

71. *Note on the Need for a New Widely Read Newspaper in Saint Petersburg*, LCW, Vol. 8.1, 16.

72. Letter of 5 June 1889 in *Leontiev Letters*, 463.

73. *Letters on Eastern Affairs*, LCW, Vol. 8.1, 103.

74. *Leading Articles of the Warsaw Diary*, LCW, 7.2, 90. There is an echo here of Leontiev's *Pochvenniki* days.

75. Letter to Gubastov of 15 March 1889 in *Leontiev Letters*, 437.

76. *Leontiev Letters*, 437. Leontiev's reference to Constantine here predates by several months his first acquaintance with *La Russie*, suggesting that Ivask is right to regard his most fruitful interaction with Solovyev as a personal one.

77. Letter to Gubastov of 5 June 1889 in *Leontiev Letters*, 465.

78. Letter to Gubastov of 17 August 1889 in *Leontiev Letters*, 473. Leontiev concludes this extract by saying: "And then this pan-America of Renan can go to the devil!" Ernest Renan (1823–92), French scholar and historian of religion, held that nationhood depended on the free exercise of the will of the people involved to adhere to a collective identity, approximately the polar opposite of Leontiev's idealist determinism. As a Russian commentator has pointed out, in view of later developments in the Cold War this

juxtaposition on Leontiev's part of a "Socialist Czar" with antipathy to America as the standard bearer of bourgeois liberalism is a poignant one. See Yuri Pushchaev, *K N Leontiev i A F Losev: sravnitel'ny analiz otnosheniya dvukh mysliteley k sotsializmy i kommunizmy*, 2019, available online at https://cyberleninka.ru/article/n/k-n-leontiev-i-a-f-losev-sravnitelnyy-analiz-otnosheniya-dvuh-mysliteley-k-sotsializmu-i-kommunizmu.

79. Letter of 13 June 1891 in *Rozanov Letters*, 77.

13. The Red Czar

1. Mikhail Mikhailovich Prishvin, 1873–1954, Russian writer of nature and children's stories, friend and former pupil of Rozanov. Taken from Prishvin, *Diaries 1930–31*, Vol. 7, cited by Olga Volkogonova, *Konstantin Leontiev*, Moscow, Molodaya Gvardiya, 2013, 439.

2. Letter of 13 June 1891 in *Rozanov Letters*, 76.

3. See his letter to Filippov of 3 September 1889 in *Filippov Letters*, 561.

4. *Letters on Eastern Affairs*, LCW, Vol. 8.1, 106–7.

5. "What Do We Mean by Connecting with the People?" LCW, Vol. 7.2, 179.

6. Letter from Leontiev to Fudel' of 6 July 1888, LCW, Annex I, 92–93.

7. By David M. Glantz in his *Colossus Reborn: The Red Army at War, 1941–1943*, University Press of Kansas, Lawrence, KS, 2005, 549–50.

8. See the *Letter of an Anchorite* titled *The Fate of Bismarck and Katkov's Silence*, LCW, Vol. 8.1, 280ff.

9. *With the Mind of a Stranger*, LCW, Vol. 8.1, 492.

10. "Nationalist Politics as a Weapon of World Revolution," LCW, Vol. 8.1, 525.

11. Letter to Gubastov of 3 August 1890 published in *Russkoe Obozrenie*, 1897, Vol. 6, 909.

12. Letter to Gubastov of 22 October 1888, *Russkoe Obozrenie*, 1897, Vol. 3, 457.

13. *Notes of an Anchorite*, LCW, Vol. 8.1, 271n. For Leontiev's joyful reaction to Wilhelm's decision to "drop the pilot," Bismarck, thus as he believed paving Russia's way to the conquest of Czargrad, see the postscript to his letter to Filippov of 14 March 1890 in *Filippov Letters*, 585.

14. "The Pessimist," LCW, Vol. 5, 573.

15. *Byzantinism and Slavdom*, LCW, Vol. 7.1, 327; *At the Grave of Pazukhin*, LCW, Vol. 8.1, 447; "Nationalist Politics as a Weapon of World Revolution," LCW, Vol. 8.1, 534.

16. *Byzantinism and Slavdom*, LCW, Vol. 7.1, 410; *Four Letters from Athos*, LCW, Vol. 7.1, 173.

17. "The Average European as the Ideal and Weapon of Universal Destruction," LCW, Vol. 8.1, 201.

18. *Letters on Eastern Affairs*, LCW, Vol. 8.1, 50.

19. *At the Grave of Pazukhin*, LCW, Vol. 8.1, 458. On the potential violence of the masses and the hopeless position of liberalism in Russia, see also Herzen, *From the Other Shore*, SS, Vol. 6, 108f, 124f.

20. "Mr. Katkov and his Enemies at the Pushkin Festival," LCW, Vol. 7.2, 205–6.

21. *Note on the Need for a New Widely Read Newspaper in Saint Petersburg*, LCW, Vol. 8.1, 14.

22. K. M. Dolgov, *Voskhozhdenie na Afon: zhizn' i mirosozertsanie Konstantina Leontieva*, Moscow, Otchiy Dom, 1997, 321.

23. Letter to Aleksandrov of 3 May 1890, letter XLV in *Aleksandrov Letters*.

24. Leontiev's warm-hearted and caring nature comes across strongly in Olga Fetisenko's description of his relations with his young "disciples" in Moscow in the 1880s. See the chapter "Semistolbniki iz denezhnogo pereulka" in her article "Otche i druzhe moi" in LCW, Annex 1, 7–15.

25. "Vladimir Solovyev versus Danilevsky," LCW, Vol. 8.1, 360.

26. Leontiev mentions this event in his *List of Works by Leontiev with Descriptions*, LCW, Vol. 6.2, 23; also in letters to Filippov of 11 January 1886 and 27 April 1889 in *Filippov Letters*, 324, 535, and to Gubastov of 30 January 1886 in *Russkoe Obozrenie*, 1896, Vol. 12, 1015, cited in *EdCom* in LCW, Vol. 6.2, 638 and Vol. 8.2, 785, n23. See also a bibliographical note on his *Father Kliment Zedergol'm* in *V. V. Rozanov i K. N. Leontiev: Materialy neizdannoi knigi*, edited by A. P. Dmitriev, Rostok, SPB 2014, 440. The purchase is also confirmed by Konoplyantsev in *Pamiati 1891 goda*, 124.

27. See the description in Robert Service, *Stalin: A Biography*, London, Macmillan, 2004, 34.

28. Service, 13.

29. Geoffrey Roberts, *Overview of Stalin's Personal Library*, published in the Stalin Digital Archive, Yale University Press: https://www.stalindigitalarchive.com/frontend /guide-to-fond-558-opis%E2%80%99-3.

30. Service, 30, 36.

31. See the list of authors in, e.g., Roberts.

32. Sergo Beria, *Beria—My Father: Inside Stalin's Kremlin*, London, Gerald Duckworth, 2001, 143. Quoted in Service, 580.

33. Erik van Ree, "Stalin and the National Question," *Revolutionary Russia*, Vol. 7, No. 2 (1994): 228. Available in the University of Amsterdam Digital Academic Repository: https://dare.uva.nl/search?identifier=9dc0b01e-9251-4571-a01e-de6a70bce6d9.

34. J. Stalin, "Marxism and the National Question," 1913, Chapter 4: "Cultural-National Autonomy," Marxists Internet Archive: https://www.marxists.org/reference /archive/stalin/works/1913/03a.htm.

35. J. Stalin, "Marxism and the National Question," 1913, Chapter 1: "The Nation."

36. *Byzantinism and Slavdom*, LCW, Vol. 7.1, 379.

37. J. Stalin, *Anarchism or Socialism?*, 1906–7, Chapter 1: "The Dialectical Method," Marxists Internet Archive: https://www.marxists.org/reference/archive/stalin/works /1906/12/x01.htm.

38. Stalin, *Anarchism or Socialism?*, Chapter 1: "The Dialectical Method."

39. Danilevsky, *Russia and Europe*, 354.

40. Stalin, "Marxism and the National Question," Chapter 1: "The Nation."

41. Stalin, "Marxism and the National Question," Chapter 7: "The National Question in Russia."

42. Stalin, "Marxism and the National Question," Foreword.

43. *Who Is More in the Right? Letters to Vladimir Sergeyevich Solovyev*, LCW, Vol. 8.2, 119. Stalin again refers to a "nationalist epidemic" in Chapter 6 of *Marxism and the National Question*, "The Caucasians, The Conference of the Liquidators."

44. *Leading Articles of the Warsaw Diary*, LCW, 7.2, 43.

45. *Byzantinism and Slavdom*, LCW, Vol. 7.1, 333.

46. Stalin, "Marxism and the National Question," Chapter 6: "The Caucasians, The Conference of the Liquidators." Ethan Alexander-Davey notes Leontiev's

advocacy of regional diversity within states and his debt in this to the German ethnographer Wilhelm Heinrich Riehl (1823–97).

47. *Byzantinism and Slavdom*, LCW, Vol. 7.1, 326.

48. Service, 560.

49. Beria, 143.

50. Letter of 22 October 1948 to Alexei Kosygin, cited by Simon Sebag Montefiore, *Young Stalin*, London, Phoenix, Orion Books, 2008, 74.

51. "Vladimir Solovyev versus Danilevsky," LCW, Vol. 8.1, 316.

52. *At the Grave of Pazukhin*, LCW, Vol. 8.1, 456–57.

53. For an interesting discussion of Stalin's debt to Orthodoxy, see the review of Mikhail Vaiskopf's *Stalin the Writer* by Erik van Ree in his essay "Stalin as Writer and Thinker" in *Kritika*, Vol. 3, No. 4 (2002): 699–714, especially 702–4. Available in the University of Amsterdam Digital Academic Repository: https://dare.uva.nl/search?identifier=d202ba95-bac6-430f-98ab-5b367a6faa39.

54. Van Ree, *Stalin and the National Question*, 229.

55. See Mikhail Agursky, *Ideologiia natsional-bolshevizma*, Moscow, Algoritm, 2003, 81. Cited in Repnikov, *Ot Leontieva do Stalina*.

56. Repnikov, *Ot Leontieva do Stalina*. The theme is absent from most mainstream literature but has recently surfaced in an article published under the pseudonym varjag2007su titled *Sotsialisticheskaia monarchiia v rabotakh Konstantina Leontieva*, 2017, https://varjag2007su.livejournal.com/739659.html.

57. Attributed to Stalin by the *Washington Post* columnist Leonard Lyons in 1947. There are a number of alternative attributions.

58. Repnikov, in *Ot Leontieva do Stalina*, opines that: "By the end of the second world war, once Stalin had bestowed upon the previously persecuted Orthodox Church a definite place in his system of government, the USSR came somewhat to resemble to the sort of society predicted by Leontiev."

59. "Moskovskie Vedomosti on Co-Jurisdiction," LCW, Vol. 8.2, 15.

60. See Rozanov, *Neuznanniy fenomen*, 183. Rozanov was never shy of hyperbole.

61. *Our New Christians: On Universal Love*, LCW, Vol. 9, 201.

62. *With the Mind of a Stranger*, LCW, Vol. 8.1, 494.

63. *Notes of an Anchorite: "My Historical Fatalism,"* LCW, Vol. 8.1, 270.

64. Repnikov, *Slavianskii tsar': Leontiev, Tikhomirov i sotsializm* (*The Czar of the Slavs: Leontiev, Tikhomirov and Socialism*), first published in 2004 at pravaya.ru, available online: https://www.portal-slovo.ru/history/35496.php.

65. *Leading Articles of the Warsaw Diary*, LCW Vol. 7.2, 25–26. Stalin himself was a lifelong admirer of Ivan the Terrible. See, e.g., Service, 340–41.

Epilogue

1. *V. V. Rozanov i K. N. Leontiev: materialy neizdannoi knigi*, 58–59.

2. See, e.g., his comments in his letter to Filippov of 27 April 1889 in *Filippov Letters*, 538–39.

3. Correspondence between Leontiev and Fudel', Kristi, and Aleksandrov is the subject of three annexes to Leontiev's collected works; the first two have been published, the third, Aleksandrov, is in preparation.

4. Fudel', K. Leontiev and V. Solovyev in Their Mutual Relations, LCW, Annex 1, 401.

5. See Rozanov Letters, 26.

6. Rozanov, Opavshie list'ia, 203. In making this assessment, Rozanov may have been under the influence of Strakhov, who described Leontiev in similar terms in his letter to Rozanov of 21 May 1891, cited earlier: "Leontiev is very gifted and stylish, though his tastes are a bit perverse, but he has no ideas of his own, in the strict sense of the word idea, none." That there should be "nothing to ponder about" in Leontiev's works is a curious estimation, to say the least. It is clear though that Strakhov's judgment was distorted by his personal distaste for Leontiev's sexuality.

7. This was Leontiev's enthusiastic response to the first draft of Rozanov's *Esteticheskoe ponimanie istorii* (*The Aesthetic Understanding of History*), published in *Russkii Vestnik*, 1892, Vol. 1.

8. Rozanov, Opavshie list'ia, 203.

9. *Rozanov Letters*, 26.

10. Rozanov, *Pamiati dorogogo druga Konstantin Leontiev* (*To the Memory of a Dear Friend Konstantin Leontiev*), 1896, in *Polnoe sobranie sochinenii*, Vol.1, 413.

11. See Tikhomirov, *Russkie ideally i K. N. Leontiev*, available online: http://www .naslednick.ru/articles/culture/culture_11978.html.

12. Entry for 31 October 1889, cited by Repnikov in *Slavianskiy tsar'*. For a detailed account of the relationship between Leontiev and Tikhomirov, see also O. A. Milevsky, "L. Tikhomirov and K. Leontiev: k istorii vzaimootnoshenii," available online: https://cyberleninka.ru/article/n/l-tihomirov-i-k-leontiev-k-istorii-vzaimootnosheniy.

13. Letter of 7 August 1891, cited in Repnikov, *Slavianskiy tsar'*.

14. Letter of 21 November 1890, cited in Repnikov, *Slavianskiy tsar'*.

15. Letter of 20 September 1891, cited in Repnikov, *Ot Leontieva do Stalina*.

16. Tikhomirov's *Teni proshlogo. K N Leontiev*, 1905, contains his lengthy discourse on the project for setting up a propaganda cell along the lines of revolutionary organizations, which ends with his acknowledgment of failure. Available online: http://russianway.rhga.ru/upload/main/02_tihom.pdf (also reported in O. L. Fetisenko, "Otche i druzhe moi" Otets Iosif Fudel', LCW, Annex 1, 13–14).

17. *Against the Current*—the title of a selection of works by Leontiev translated by George Reavey and edited by George Ivask, New York, Weybright and Talley, 1969.

18. Letter to Filippov of 7 January 1886 in *Filippov Letters*, 314.

19. In a letter to Filippov of 4 October 1888 Leontiev emphasizes, in a curious about-face, that he would not agree to subordinate his religious or political convictions to his art (*Filippov letters*, 511–12).

20. Rozanov, "Neuznannyi fenomen" in *Pamiati 1891 goda*, 184.

21. Cited by Repnikov in *Slavianskiy tsar'*.

22. *Who is more in the right? Letters to Vladimir Sergeyevich Solovyev*, LCW, Vol. 8.2, 166.

BIBLIOGRAPHY

This list contains works I have found useful in the compilation of this book and ones I feel will enhance the reader's understanding of Leontiev. With the non-specialist in mind I have attempted to lay before the reader all the material available in the English language (some of which is out of print and hard to find). This list does not claim to be a comprehensive bibliography of works in Russian, especially those published since perestroika, and Russian speakers are advised to consult bibliographies in, for example, Fetisenko and Volkogonova.

Primary Sources

K. N. Leontiev: Polnoe sobranie sochinenii i pisem v dvenadsati tomakh, editor-in-chief V. A. Kotelnikov, deputy editor O. L. Fetisenko, published by Vladimir Dal', SPB, 2000 onwards. Already published are volumes 1 to 11 and two Annexes containing correspondence. Volume 12 and a further Annex are work in progress. This is the latest and definitive collection of Leontiev's works, superseding the original edition published in nine volumes in 1912–13 by V. M. Sablin. It contains a number of works absent from the earlier edition and a considerable amount of correspondence. The extensive Editorial Commentaries to each volume are an invaluable source with a wealth of previously unpublished archive material. The mining of the archives by Kotelnikov and Fetisenko and their colleagues is thorough and exhaustive and I have not felt it necessary to attempt to duplicate it the preparation of this book.

V. V. Rozanov i K. N.Leontiev: materialy neizdannoi knigi, edited by A. P. Dmitriev, SPB, Rostok, 2014. Contains correspondence, unpublished texts, articles about Leontiev, compilation and commentary by E. A. Ivanova. Contains two sets of (the same) correspondence between Rozanov and Leontiev, a large number of articles about Leontiev by his contemporaries found in archive notebooks, and all the articles Rozanov wrote about Leontiev.

Leontiev's Letters

As Leontiev's collected works are rolled out they should ultimately contain the bulk of his correspondence. At the time of writing Volume 11 (in two parts) covering the years 1853 to 1882 and separate annexes (1 and 2) dedicated to correspondence with Iosif Fudel' and Ivan Kristi are available. Volume 12 and a third annex containing correspondence with Aleksandrov are advertised but appear to be currently unobtainable.

Konstantin Nikolaevich Leontiev: izbrannye pis'ma (1854–1891), SPB, Pushkinskii Fond, 1993. Contains a large selection of letters covering Leontiev's whole active life. Some are abridged.

Pamiati Konstantina Nikolaevicha Leontieva 1891 goda, SPB, Sirius, 1911. Correspondence with Filippov, Gubastov, the family Kartsov.

Pamiati Konstantina Nikolaevicha Leontieva i pis'ma k Anatoliu Aleksandrovu, Sergiev Posad, 1915. Biographical details and letters to Aleksandrov. http://az.lib.ru/a/aleksandrow_a_a/text_1915_leontiev.shtml. http://az.lib.ru/l/leontxew_k_n/text_1891_pisma_aleksandrovu_oldorfo.shtml

Konstantin Leontiev: pis'ma k Vasiliiu Rozanovu, London, Nina Karsov, 1981. Correspondence with Rozanov. Also in *V. V. Rozanov i K. N. Leontiev: materialy neizdannoi knigi*.

Proroki Vizantizma, SPB, Pushkinskii Dom, 2012: correspondence with T. I. Filippov. Introduction and commentary by Olga Fetisenko.

Russkoe Obozrenie: contains correspondence with Gubastov, A. A. Fet, Archimandrite Leonid Kavelin, A. A. Kireyev, S. Vasilyev, and V. A. P-aya. See 1893, Vols. 1, 4, and 9; 1894, Vols. 9 and 11; 1895, Vols. 5, 11, and 12; 1896, Vols. 1, 2, 3, 11, and 12; 1897, Vols. 1, 3, 5, 6, and 7; 1898, Vol. 1.

Russkaia Mysl': Letters to G. I. Zamarayev. See 1916, Vol. 3.

Leontiev in English Translation

"The Average European as an Ideal and Instrument of Universal Destruction," in *Russian Philosophy*, edited by J. M. Edie, Chicago, Quadrangle Books, 1965, Vol. 2.

Against the Current: Selections from the Novels, Essays, Notes and Letters of Konstantin Leontiev, edited by Yuri Ivask, translated by George Reavey, New York, Weybright and Talley, 1969.

Byzantinism and Slavdom, translated and introduced by K. Benois, Taxiarch Press, Zvolen, Slovakia, and London, 2020.

The Egyptian Dove—Child of the Heart, translated by George Reavey, introduction by Yuri Ivask, New York, Weybright and Talley, 1969.

"The Novels of Count L. N. Tolstoy: Analysis, Style and Atmosphere," in *Essays in Russian Literature. The Conservative View: Leontiev, Rozanov, Shestov*, edited by Spencer E. Roberts, Athens, OH, Ohio University Press, 1968.

Books and Essays on Leontiev in English

Avramenko, Richard, and Alexander-Davey, Ethan, eds., *Aristocratic Souls in Democratic Times*, Lexington Books, Lanham, Boulder, New York & London, 2018. The chapter by Alexander-Davey "Aristocracy and the Kallipolis: Konstantin Leontiev and the Politics of 'Flourishing Complexity'" is a useful potted introduction to Leontiev's "aristocratic" political outlook, although the author's basically hostile perspective does peep through at times.

Berdyaev, N. A., *Konstantin Leontiev: A Sketch from the History of Russian Religious Thought*, Paris, YMCA Press, 1926, English translation by George Reavey, London, Academic International Press, Russian series, Vol. 15, London, 1940.

A much more objective and less hostile assessment by Berdyaev, written after the Apocalypse; herein lies the pathos of this book, which is still one of the best introductions to Leontiev's thought.

Berdyaev, N. A., *Konstantin Leontiev, Philosopher of Reactionary Romanticism*, 1904, available in English as chapter 15 in his *Sub Specie Aeternitatis*, SPB, M. V. Pirozhkov, 1900–1906, English edition by Frsj Publications, 2019. A negative assessment of Leontiev as a forerunner of Nietzsche in a bad sense, his works superficial and under-researched, his religion "satanism in Christian clothing," his politics proceeding from supposedly sadomasochistic leanings. A superficial analysis that says more about the author than his subject matter.

Copleston F. C., *Philosophy in Russia: From Herzen to Lenin and Berdyaev*, University of Notre Dame Press, Bloomington, IN, 1986. Basic account, basically hostile.

Dowler, E. W. "Two Conservative Views of Nationalism and Personality: A. A. Grigoriev and K. N. Leontiev," *Studies in East European Thought*, 1991, Vol. 41, No. 1, 19–32.

Glatzer Rosenthal B., ed., *Nietzsche in Russia*, Princeton University Press, Princeton, 1986. A sparse treatment of Leontiev's affinity to Nietzsche.

Hare, R. G., *Pioneers in Russian Thought: Studies in Non-Marxian Formation in 19th Century Russia and its Partial Revival in the Soviet Union*, Oxford University Press, 1951. Hare's desire to establish the continuity of Leontiev's thought with the policies of the Soviet regime leads him to miss most of the salient features of Leontiev's outlook and to the fallacious conclusion that he sought to bolster Petrine Russia. Ignores Leontiev's aestheticism entirely, but good on Belinsky, Chernyshevsky, and so on.

Ivask, Yuri (George), "Konstantin Leontiev's Fiction," *Slavic Review*, December 1961. Thorough, if idiosyncratic, study, useful work of reference with exhaustive bibliography. Turned into a book in Russian-language only (see the Books in Russian section). Ivask sees Leontiev as "Narcissus," the superhero of his own novels. See also his introduction to the selection *Against the Current* in the Leontiev in English translation section.

Khatuntsev, S. V., "The Sociopolitical Views and Intellectual Evolution of K N Leont'ev in the 1860s and early 1870s," in *Russian Studies in Philosophy*, Spring 2008, Vol. 46, No. 4. Traces the development of Leontiev's mature thought back to his early influences in Russia and the Ottoman lands.

Kline, G. L., *Religious and Anti-Religious Thought in Russia*, University of Chicago Press, 1968. Basic account of Leontiev and Rozanov in chapter 2: "Religious Neo-Conservatives."

Lukashevich, S. *Konstantin Leontiev: A Study in Russian Heroic Vitalism*, New York, Pageant-Poseidon, 1967. Rather weak and superficial study, beset by excessive psychoanalysis.

Monas, S., "Leontiev: A Meditation," in *The Journal of Modern History*, September 1971. A review of Ivask's *Against the Current* and Lukashevich. In a perceptive essay Monas notes the dualistic basis of Leontiev's faith, his concern with ethicism, and the instrumentalism in his approach to literature. Sees Leontiev as comparable to, but less than, Nietzsche.

Mondry, Henrietta, and Thompson, Sally, *Konstantin Leont'ev: An Examination of His Major Fiction*, Moscow, Nauka, Oriental Literature Publishers, 1993. An unusual perspective in that it majors on Leontiev's often-neglected fiction. Mondry and Thompson's careful textual analysis places Leontiev in the context of his times in an original and insightful way.

Pipes, Richard, *Russian Conservatism and Its Critics*, Yale University Press, New Haven, 2005. A short, negative, and superficial assessment, though Pipes does recognize Leontiev's unique position in the history of Russian thought.

Robinson, Paul, *Russian Conservatism*, Ithaca, NY, Cornell University Press, 2019. Places Leontiev in the context of conservative thought in Russia.

Rzhevsky, N., *Russian Literature and Ideology*, Urbana, IL, University of Illinois Press, 1983 (chapter titled "Leontiev's Prickly Rose"), also in *Slavic Review*, No. 35, 1976. A discussion of Podlipki, *A Place of One's Own*, and *A Husband's Confession*. Rzhevsky sees "romantic nihilism" as the key to understanding Leontiev's life.

Thaden, E. C., *Conservative Nationalism in Nineteenth Century Russia*, University of Washington, Seattle, 1964. Intelligent and even handed, strong on Leontiev's relationships with Strakhov, Ivan Aksakov, Danilevsky, Pobedonostsev, and Filippov.

Walicki, Andrzej, *A History of Russian Thought*, translated by Hilda Andrews-Rusiecka, Clarendon, Oxford, 1980. A short outline of Leontiev's political views. Walicki sees Leontiev as linked to the Slavophiles via a common root in German conservative romanticism.

Books in German

Florovsky, G., *Die Sackgassen der Romantik* in *Orient und Occident*, 1930, Vol 4. See description in the Books in Russian section.

Frank, Simon, *Konstantin Leontiev: ein russischer Nietzsche*, Hochland, 1928–29. Leontiev as a Faust figure, precursor of Nietzsche and Spengler and prophet of Russian bolshevism.

von Kologrivov, Ivan, *Von Hellas zum Mönchtum*, Regensburg, Gregorius-Verlag, 1948. One of the best studies, thorough and readable, if at times excessively dependent on Berdyaev, Rozanov, and others. Kologrivov was born in Petersburg, emigrated after the revolution, and became a Jesuit. At his best considering the vexed questions of Leontiev's religious outlook and moral philosophy.

Books in Russian

Adrianov, B. and Malchevsky, N., eds., *K. Leontiev, Nash sovremennik*, SPB, Izdatel'stvo Chernysheva, 1993. As the title suggests, an attempt to stress Leontiev's contemporary relevance to Russia in the immediate aftermath of perestroika. Contains excerpts from Leontiev's journalistic work and appraisals by his contemporaries (Vladimir Solovyev, Korolyev, Astafyev, Frank, Tikhomirov) and by modern writers.

Aggeyev, K. M., *Khristianstvo i ego otnoshenie k blagoustroeniiu zemnoi zhizni*, Kiev, Petr Varskii, 1909. Perceptive study of Leontiev's religious outlook, includes numerous extracts from Leontiev's notebooks. Aggeyev sees a close relation between Leontiev and Nietzsche, and confirms that the former never knew of the latter. See also his "Konstantin Leontiev kak religioznyi myslitel'" in *BogoslovskyVestnik*, 1909, Vols. 4–8.

Aleksandrov, Anatoly, "Konstantin Nikolaevich Leontiev," in *Russkii Vestnik*, 1892, Vol. 4. Important biographical source from one of Leontiev's disciples. Contains the "Piotrovsky" incident. Also *Pamiati Konstantina Nikolaevicha Leontieva i pis'ma k Anatoliiu Aleksandrovu*, SergievPosad, 1915. Biographical details and letters. Available online, see "Letters" section. *Pamiati K. N. Leontieva* also in P&C.

Berdyaev, N. A., *Konstantin Leontiev, filosof reaktsionnoi romantiki*, 1904 (P&C); available online: http://az.lib.ru/b/berdjaew_n_a/text_1905_leontiev.shtml.

Berdyaev, N. A., *Konstantin Leontiev: ocherk iz istorii russkoi religioznoi mysli*, Paris, YMCA Press, 1926 (P&C). See descriptions in the Books in English section.

Bocharov, S. G., "Esteticheskoe okhranenie v literaturnoi kritike (Konstantin Leontiev v russkoi literature)," *Kontekst*, 1977. An excellent and ideology-free study of Leontiev's aesthetics, including the early critical essays. Along with Durylin's notes to Leontiev's *My Literary Destiny*, the best thing on Leontiev to have come out of the Soviet Union.

Bulgakov, S., *Pobeditel'-pobezhdennyi* in the collection *Tikhie dumy*, Moscow, Leman and Sakharov, 1918 (P&C). Bulgakov sees the concept of dread behind not only Leontiev's religion but his politics and sociology as well. Strong on the Islamic-utilitarian side of Leontiev's faith.

Dolgov, K. M., *Voskhozhdenie na Afon: zhizn' i mirosozertsanie Konstantina Leontieva*, Moscow, Otchiy Dom, 1997. Standard but detailed and broadly sympathetic treatment of Leontiev as impoverished aristocrat with mother complex whose thinking was informed primarily by an aesthetic outlook which never left him. Contains a useful chapter on the attitude of his contemporaries and near-contemporaries including Vladimir Solovyev, Trubetskoy, Struve, Rozanov, Bulgakov, Berdyaev, Frank, and Milyukov.

Durylin, S. N., *V rodnom uglu*, Moscow, Moskovskii Rabochii, 1991. Includes conversations with Leontiev's niece Marya Vladimirovna towards the end of her life; see also Durylin's introduction and notes to the edition of Leontiev's *My Literary Destiny* in the series *Literaturnoe nasledstvo*, 22–24, Moscow, Zhurnal'no-gazetnoe Ob'edinenie, 1935. This is some of the best background material to be found anywhere, with an intelligent and objective commentary.

Emelyanov-Lukyanchikov, M. A., *Ierarkhiia radugi*, Moscow, Russky Mir, 2008. A comparative examination of the history of culture with reference to Leontiev, Danilevsky, Spengler, and Toynbee.

Fetisenko, O. L., *"Geptastilisty": Konstantin Leont'ev, ego sobesedniki i ucheniki: idei russkogo konservatizma v literaturno-khudozhestvennykh i publitsisticheskikh praktikakh vtoroi poloviny XIX–pervoi chetverti XX veka*, SPB, Pushkinskii Dom, 2012. An exhaustive study by the indefatigable deputy chief editor of Leontiev's Collected Works, placing him in the tradition of Russian Conservative thought she styles "Heptastylist" (from the Greek for an edifice resting on seven columns, a phrase used by Leontiev himself to describe his cultural ideals—and by T. E. Lawrence in his autobiographical *Seven Pillars of Wisdom*). Contains a mass of detail concerning Leontiev's correspondents and his "disciples." Pages 14–15 list works about him Fetisenko considers worth reading.

Filippov, B. A., "Strastnoe pis'mo s nevernym adresom," in *Mosti*, 1962, Vol. 9, 1963, Vol. 10, also published as the introduction to the 1965 *Slavic Series* edition of Leontiev's *My Literary Destiny*. Good concise account of Leontiev's life and work. Also lucid and readable are his introductions to the 1954 edition (in Russian) of Leontiev's novels *The Egyptian Dove* and *Child of the Soul*, and to the Nina Karsov edition of his letters to Rozanov.

Florovsky, G., *Puti russkogo bogosloviia*, Paris, 1937, also *Die Sackgassen der Romantik* in *Orient und Occident*, 1930, Vol. 4. Florovsky is perceptive but basically hostile, he denies that Leontiev knew "true religion" but somewhat surprisingly takes his side against Dostoevsky.

Fudel', Iosif. Annex 1 to Leontiev's collected works is dedicated to Fudel'. Contains his *Kul'turnyi ideal K. N. Leontieva* (P&C), also *Konstantin Leontiev i Vl. Solovyev v ikh vzaimnykh otnosheniiakh* (P&C) and a number of other articles and reminiscences by one of Leontiev's warmest supporters, together with their voluminous correspondence. Invaluable source material on Leontiev's last years, especially his religious thought and his relations with Vladimir Solovyev.

Griftsov, B. A., "Sud'ba Konstantina Leontieva" in *RusskaiaMysl'*, 1913, Vols. 1, 2, and 4 (P&C). Lengthy study with an unusually intelligent discussion of Leontiev's early work. Griftsov sees Leontiev as a "decadent before his time." He later deteriorates into wordiness and conventionality.

Gusev, N. N., *Letopis' zhizni i tvorchestva L. N. Tolstogo*, Moscow, Gosudarstvennoe izdatel'stvo khudozhestvennoi literatury, 1958. Contains an account at pages 752–53 of Leontiev's meeting with Tolstoy on 28 February 1890.

Ivask, Yuri (George), *Konstantin Leontiev: zhizn' i tvorchestvo*, Bern, Herbert and Peter Lang, 1974 (P&C). Book based on Ivask's 1961 essay described in the Books in English section.

Khatuntsev, S. V., *Russkii Iupiter*. Short overview of Leontiev's historical significance. See also the Books in English section. Available online: https://politconser vatism.ru/thinking/russkiy-yupiter.

Konstantin Leontiev: Pro et Contra: Lichnost' i tvorchestvo Konstantina Leontieva v otsenke russkikh myslitelei i issledovatelei posle 1917 g, SPB, Russian Christian Humanities Institute, 1995. An anthology of essays, studies, and reminiscences about Leontiev. Many of the works listed below appear in this collection. Where so, they are marked (P&C).

Milevsky, O. A. L., *Tikhomirov i K. Leontiev: k istorii vzaimnootnoshenii*, 1997. Brief overview of their relationship. Available online: https://cyberleninka.ru /article/n/l-tihomirov-i-k-leontiev-k-istorii-vzaimootnosheniy.

Pamiati Konstantina Nikolaevicha Leontieva 1891 goda, SPB, Sirius, 1911. Important collection of articles by people who knew Leontiev personally, including Konoplyantsev, Aleksandrov, Rozanov, Gubastov, Poselyanin, and others. Konoplyantsev was Leontiev's first biographer and this work forms the starting point of most subsequent studies.

Preobrazhensky, P., *Gertsen i Konstantin Leontiev* in *Pechat' i revoliutsiia*, 1922, Vol. 2, No. 2. Draws an interesting parallel between Herzen and Leontiev, both seeking escape from the nineteenth century.

Pushchaev, Yu. V., *Otnoshenie K. N. Leontieva k kommunizmy*. Interesting discussion of how far Leontiev can be seen as a prophet of Soviet Communism. Available online: https://cyberleninka.ru/article/n/otnoshenie-k-n-leontieva-k-kommunizmu-sotsializmu-o-nesostoyavshemsya-soyuze-sotsializma-s-russkim-samoderzhaviem-i-plamennoy-mistikoy.

Pushchaev, Yu. V., *K. N.Leontiev i A. F.Losev: sravnitel'nyi analiz otnosheniia dvukh myslitelei k sotsializmy i kommunizmy*, 2019. Available online: https://cyberleninka.ru/article/n/k-n-leontiev-i-a-f-losev-sravnitelnyy-analiz-otnosheniya-dvuh-mysliteley-k-sotsializmu-i-kommunizmu.

Repnikov, Aleksandr, *Ot Leontieva do Stalina: konservatizm, sotsializm i liberalism*, in *Nash Sovremennik*, No. 10, 2005, available online: http://nash-sovremennik.ru/p.php?y=2005&n=10&id=10.

Repnikov, Aleksandr, *Slavyanskii tsar': Leontiev, Tikhomirov i sotsializm*, first published in 2004 at pravaya.ru, available online: https://www.portal-slovo.ru/history/35496.php. This is Leontiev from the conservative-nationalist viewpoint. Repnikov questions why there has been no in-depth study of Leontiev and Stalin.

Rozanov, V. V., *Konstantin Leontiev: pis'ma k Vasiliiu Rozanovu*, Nina Karsov, London, 1981. The introduction, postscript, and notes by Rozanov to these letters are beyond doubt the best thing ever written in connection with Leontiev. Concerns their correspondence during the last year of Leontiev's life. Believing his days to be numbered and that he had at last found someone who could appreciate him, Leontiev pours out his soul and his entire worldview in condensed form. The exchanges sparkle with a rare mix of intellectual depth and emotional intensity.

Rozanov, V. V., "Neuznannyi fenomen" in *Pamiati Konstantina Nikolaevicha Leontieva 1891 goda* (see above); *Opavshie list'ia*, 1913, Vol. 1, in V. V. Rozanov, *Izbrannoe*, Munich, A Neimanis, 1970; *Literaturnie izgnanniki*, SPB, Novoye Vremya, 1913; *Esteticheskoe ponimanie istorii*, in *Russkii Vestnik*, 1892, Vol. 1 (P&C); *O Konstantine Leontieve* (P&C). See also entries in his *Polnoe sobranie sochinenii v 35 tomakh*, SPB, Rostok, 2014. Rozanov understood Leontiev as few others and everything he wrote about him is well worth reading, the more so in that Rozanov is anything but sycophantic.

Solovyev, Vladimir, *Pamiati K. N. Leontieva*, in *Russkoe Obozrenie*, 1892 (P&C). An attempt to demolish Leontiev as a thinker while ostensibly paying respects to his personal good qualities. Also "Konstantin Leontiev," in *Entsiklopedicheskii slovar' Brokgauza i Efrona*, 1896, Vol. 34, *Novyi Entsiklopedicheski slovar'*, Vol. 24. Published by Brokgauz and Efron, SPB, 1889–1930. Faint praise from a man who owed Leontiev an enormous intellectual debt.

Tikhomirov, Lev, "Russkie idealy i K. N. Leontiev," a defence of Leontiev against his detractors, first published in *Russkoe Obozrenie*, 1894, Vol. 10; now in *Konstantin Leontiev: slavianofil'stvo i griadushchie sud'by Rossii*, Institute of Russian Civilisation, Moscow, 2010; available online: http://www.naslednick.ru/articles/culture/culture_11978.html.

Tikhomirov, Lev, *Teni proshlogo: K N Leontiev*, 1905 (P&C), available online: http://russianway.rhga.ru/upload/main/02_tihom.pdf.

Trubetskoy, S., *Razocharovannyi Slavianofil* in *Vestnik Evropy*, 1892, Vol. 10 (P&C). Negative appraisal of Leontiev as the "pessimist of Slavophilism."

Trubetskoy's assessment of Leontiev's religious outlook in his "Pamiati K. N. Leontieva" (published in *Russkoe Obozrenie*, 1892, Vol. 11) is much more generous.

Volkogonova, Olga, *Konstantin Leontiev*, Moscow, Molodaya Gvardiya, 2013. Exhaustive biography, contains probably every known fact about Leontiev's life. Its usefulness as a source is hampered by the lack of an index, but it does contain a considerable bibliography.

Volodikhin, A. M., *Vysokomernyi strannik: filosofiia i zhizn' Konstantina Leontieva*, Moscow, Manufaktura, 2000. Contains interesting background and biographical material. Sees Leontiev as forerunner of the twentieth-century existentialism. Has interesting slant on Leontiev's influence on the Eurasianist Lev Gumilev.

Zakrzhevsky, Aleksandr, "Odinokii myslitel'" in *Khristianskaia Mysl'*, Kiev, 1916. Leontiev as "vampire-inquisitor." Zakrzhevsky rates Leontiev more highly than Nietzsche but fails to notice his moral preoccupations, seeing in him only aesthetic-amoralism. Despite being carried away by his dislike of Leontiev's religious outlook, Zakrzhevsky still achieves some important insights into his philosophy. Available online: https://www.prlib.ru/item/433675.

Zen'kovsky, V. V., *Istoriia russkoi filosofii*, Vol. 2, chapter 12, "K. Leontiev. V.V. Rozanov," Paris, YMCA Press, 1948. Excessively intellectualised study but perceptive on the development of Leontiev's religious outlook.

General Works

Agursky, Mikhail, *Ideologiia natsional-bolshevizma*, Moscow, Algoritm, 2003.

Bassin, Mark, *The Gumilev Mystique: Biopolitics, Eurasianism, and the Construction of Community* in *Modern Russia (Culture and Society after Socialism)*, Cornell University Press, Ithaca, NY, 2016.

Beria, Sergo, *Beria—My Father: Inside Stalin's Kremlin*, London, Gerald Duckworth, 2001,

Berlin, Isaiah, *Historical Inevitability*, Oxford University Press, 1955.

Chizhevsky, Dmitro, *Hegel in Russia*, Paris, 1939.

Clogg, Richard, *A Short History of Modern Greece*, Oxford University Press, 1979.

Dawson, Christopher, *The Dynamics of World History*, New York, Sheed and Ward, 1957.

Eltchaninoff, Michel, *Inside the Mind of Vladimir Putin*, London, Hurst & Co, 2018.

Frank, Joseph, *Dostoevsky: A Writer in His Time*, Princeton University Press, 2010.

Frank, S. L., Introduction to *A Solovyev Anthology*, New York, Charles Scribner's Sons, 1950.

Gumilev, Lev, "Seek Out What Is True," interview, *Soviet Literature*, 1990, Vol. 1.

Jakowenko, Boris, *Geschichte des Hegelianismus in Rußland*, Prague, Buchdruckerei Josef Bartl, 1938.

Lehmann, Jürgen, *Der Einfluß der Philosophie des deutschen Idealismus in der russischen Literaturkritik des 19. Jahrhunderts*, Heidelberg, C Winter, 1975.

Montefiore, Simon Sebag, *Young Stalin*, London, Phoenix, Orion Books, 2007.

Munzer, Egbert, *Solovyev: Prophet of Russian-Western Unity*, London, Philosophical Library, 1956.

Nietzsche, Friedrich, *Also sprach Zarathustra*,1885. Available in English online as *Thus Spake Zarathustra* at: http://www.gutenberg.org/files/1998/1998-h/1998-h.htm#link2H_4_0002.

Petrovich, M. B., *The Emergence of Russian Panslavism, 1856–1870*, New York, Columbia University Press, 1956.

Popper, Karl,*The Open Society and its Enemies*, London, Routledge, 1945; *The Poverty of Historicism*, London, Routledge, 1957.

Rand, Ayn, *Atlas Shrugged*, New York, Random House, 1957.

Roberts, Geoffrey, *Overview of Stalin's Personal Library*, published in the Stalin Digital Archive, Yale University Press: https://www.stalindigitalarchive.com/frontend/guide-to-fond-558-opis%E2%80%99-3.

Schwegler, F. K. A., *Geschichte der Philosophie im Umriss: Ein Leitfaden Zur übersicht*, Stuttgart, Franck'sche Verlagshandlung, 1848.

Service, Robert, *Stalin: A Biography*, London, Macmillan, 2004.

Sorokin, Pitirim, *Social and Cultural Dynamics*, single volume edition, Boston, Porter Sargent, 1957; *Social Philosophies of an Age of Crisis*, Boston, The Beacon Press, 1951.

Stalin, J., *Anarchism or Socialism*, 1906–7, available online: https://www.marxists.org/reference/archive/stalin/works/1906/12/x01.htm.

Stalin, J., *Marxism and the National Question*, 1913, available online: https://www.marxists.org/reference/archive/stalin/works/1913/03a.htm.

Terras, Victor, *The Idiot: An Interpretation*, Boston, Twayne Publishers, 1990.

Van Ree, Erik, *Stalin and the National Question* in *Revolutionary Russia*, 1994, Vol. 7, No. 2, Available in the University of Amsterdam Digital Academic Repository: https://dare.uva.nl/search?identifier=9dc0b01e-9251-4571-a01e-de6a70bce6d9.

Van Ree, Erik, "Stalin as Writer and Thinker" in *Kritika*, 2002, Vol. 3, No. 4. Available at: https://dare.uva.nl/search?identifier=d202ba95-bac6-430f-98ab-5b367a6faa39.

Walicki, Andrzej, *The Slavophile Controversy*, Oxford University Press, 1975.

Ward, Lester F., *Glimpses of the Cosmos*, Vol. 6, New York & London, G. P. Putnam Sons 1918.

Woodcock, George, *Anarchism: A History of Libertarian Ideas and Movements*, Cleveland, Ohio, World Publishing Company, 1962.

Other Sources Cited in Text

Chernyshevsky, N. G., *Polnoe sobranie sochinenii v 15 tomakh*, Moscow, Goslitizdat, 1939–53.

Danilevsky, N.Ya., *Rossiia i Evropa*, SPB, Obshchestvennaia Pol'za, 1871.

Dobrolyubov, N. A., *Sobranie sochineniiv 9 tomakh*, Moscow, Gosudarstvennoe izdatel'stvo khudozhestvennoi literatury, 1963.

Dostoevsky, F. M., *Polnoe sobranie sochinenii v 30 tomakh*, Leningrad, Nauka, Leningradskoe Otdelenie, 1972–88.

Hegel, G. W. F., *Werke*, Berlin, Duncker und Humblot, 1833–37.

Herzen, A. I., *Sobranie sochinenii v 30 tomakh*, Moscow, Nauka, 1954–65.

Leibniz, G. W., "Monadology," in *Philosophical Papers and Letters*, edited by L. E. Loemker, Dordrecht, Reidel, 1972; *Theodicy*, edited by A. Farrer, translated by E. M. Huggard, London, Routledge & Kegan Paul, 1952.

Lenin, V. I., *Collected Works*, Progress Publishers, Moscow 1973.

Saltykov-Shchedrin, M. E., *Sobranie sochinenii v 20 tomakh*, Moscow, Gosudarstvennoe izdatel'stvo khudozhestvennoi literatury, 1965–77.

Schelling, F. W. J., *Werke*, edited by M Schröter, Munich, C H Beck, 1927.

Solovyev, Vladimir, *Sobranie sochinenii*, SPB, Prosveshchenie, 1911–14; *La Russie et l'Eglise Universelle*, translated by Herbert Rees, London, Geoffrey Bles, The Centenary Press, 1948.

Spencer, Herbert, *Essays, Scientific, Political and Speculative*, London, Williams & Norgate, 1868.

Strakhov, N. N., *Pis'ma k V. V. Rozanovu*, Moscow, Direkt-Media, 2010, available online: http://az.lib.ru/s/strahow_n_n/text_1896_pisma_k_rozanovy.shtml.

Turgenev, I. S., *Polnoe sobranie sochinenii i pisem v 30 tomakh*, Moscow, Nauka, 1987.

Index

CPSIA information can be obtained
at www.ICGtesting.com
Printed in the USA
LVHW091319121121
703166LV00010B/90/J